Forging America

THE STORY OF

Bethlehem Steel

THE MORNING CALL

A TRIBUNE PUBLISHING COMPANY

FORGING AMERICA
The Story of Bethlehem Steel

EDITORS: Ardith Hilliard, David Venditta

WRITERS: Matt Assad, Mike Frassinelli, David Venditta, Frank Whelan

COPY CHIEF: Terry Rang

PRODUCTION COORDINATOR: David Dawson

LIBRARY RESEARCH DIRECTOR: Lois Doncevic

LIBRARIANS: Laurel Bruce, Ruth Burns, Dianne Knauss

DESIGN DIRECTORS: Jeffery Lindenmuth, Craig Larimer

DESIGNERS: Barbara Curmaci Mathews, Jessica DeLorenzo

PHOTO EDITOR: Naomi Halperin

PROJECT PHOTOGRAPHER: Chuck Zovko

COPY EDITORS: Mary Mooney, Karen Phillips, Andromeda Weissman

CONTRIBUTING EDITORS: David Erdman, Chris Krewson, James Wilkerson

CONTRIBUTING REPORTER: Kurt Blumenau

THE MORNING CALL
101 North Sixth Street
P.O. Box 1260
Allentown, PA 18105

ISBN: 978-0-9829422-0-8
Library of Congress Control Number: 2010935612
Second edition, updated and revised
Originally distributed December, 2003, as a supplement to *The Morning Call*

CONTENTS

ACKNOWLEDGMENTS

We are indebted to the many people who helped us tell the story of Bethlehem Steel. Foremost among them are **Lance E. Metz**, historian for the National Canal Museum in Easton and an authority on the company, who shared his encyclopedic knowledge; **Bette Kovach**, Bethlehem Steel spokeswoman, who provided documents, photos and tours of the Bethlehem plant and the company's plants at Steelton, Sparrows Point, Md., and Burns Harbor, Ind.; **Donald Stuart Young**, a font of information after his four decades at the company, who identified photos and reviewed our manuscript for technical accuracy, offering insights and great detail; and **Craig L. Bartholomew**, a Steel employee for almost 34 years who guided us with his expertise in 19th century iron- and steelmaking, checked our work and suggested many improvements.

Books written about Bethlehem Steel and the Lehigh Valley proved invaluable in crafting a tale that takes place in three centuries. We spoke with and are deeply grateful to scholar **Robert Hessen**, author of a brilliant biography of Steel founder Charles M. Schwab; **John Strohmeyer**, the Pulitzer Prize-winning editor of the now defunct Bethlehem Globe-Times whose poignant "Crisis in Bethlehem" tracks the company's decline and illustrates the impact of lost jobs; former Lehigh University political science professor **W. Ross Yates**, a prolific chronicler of local history; and former Baltimore Sun reporter **Mark Reutter**, whose provocative book about Sparrows Point explores the factors that lifted Bethlehem Steel and tore it apart.

Dozens of people gave generously of their time to share their memories and knowledge. We could not have told this story without them.

Penny Porter graciously lent us a copy of her revealing, privately printed book about her grandfather, longtime Steel chief executive Eugene G. Grace. Catasauqua historian **Martha Capwell Fox** and south Bethlehem historian **Joan Campion** gave us glimpses of the way their communities once were. Writer **Susan Cunningham** shared her research into the life of entrepreneur and politician Asa Packer. **Ann E. Bartholomew**, Craig's wife and the National Canal Museum's publications manager, helped enhance the two chapters set in the 19th century. **Ray Holton**, a former editor of The Morning Call who once covered the steel industry, advised us.

Andrew M. Stanten, director of communications at Lehigh University, and communications manager **Linda Harbrecht** steered us toward history and economics experts on Lehigh's faculty. **Mary Gotzon**, administrative assistant to the Bethlehem mayor, and **Trudy Dougherty** of the former Bethlehem Steelworkers Memorial Committee provided information on work-related deaths at the Bethlehem plant.

For research assistance, we thank **Christopher Baer**, assistant curator for manuscripts and archives at the Hagley Museum and Library in Wilmington, Del., who sent us records of the Bethlehem Iron Co., forerunner of Bethlehem Steel; **Thomas A. Smith**, collections manager and director of public programs for the National Canal Museum; **Meg Sharp Walton**, curator of archives and exhibitions for the Historic Bethlehem Partnership; **Jane Gill**, public services coordinator for the Bethlehem Area Public Library; Lehigh County Historical Society librarian **Carol Herrity**, and **Ilhan Citak**, an assistant in the special collections room at Lehigh University's Linderman Library.

PROLOGUE

Once, the gargantuan Bethlehem Steel blast furnaces breathed fire that sweating steelworkers had to feed before they could feed their families.

Now, it is a silent shuttered place, an abandoned witness to an American way of life extinguished.

Unthinkable.

Once, in the days when steam meant progress, plumes from the blast furnace smokestacks touched the sky. Now they stand stark and empty, emitting nothing.

Unthinkable.

Once, in a time viewed now in sepia and black and white, Bethlehem Steel was the backbone of America. It forged the steel for ships and armaments that helped win two world wars, the beams for buildings that transformed the skyline of New York City and built the Golden Gate Bridge.

This mythical place, at its peak a virtual city of 31,000 with its own police force and fire department, its own hierarchy and its own societal rules, so dominated its landscape that it even gave the children of south Bethlehem, the working people's side of town, their lullaby each night.

Bang. Boom.

A steam hammer pounded an ingot.

Bang.

The hammer returned to its starting position. Boom.

Be happy for the sound, fathers would tell their little ones. "When you don't hear it no more, you're gonna cry."

The silence came on Nov. 18, 1995.

Now, even the name Bethlehem Steel has passed into history.

No bang, no boom, except in memory.

There are weeds where there were workers, graffiti where there was fresh paint and broken windows where buildings once were new.

When it was alive, it was a rough place, dirty and dangerous.

The coke works was the worst. It smelled like rotten eggs. Men there wore protective wooden shoes and wool clothing. They donned long johns even in the summer to buffer them from heat. It was hell.

The workers talked in coarse language befitting such a place.

"How's your wife and my kids?"

Hundreds died here. Others lost limbs or years off their lives.

But at its peak, "The Steel" lifted its rulers to the highest rung of American life. And for a few golden decades, it lifted its common workers into a safe, comfortable middle-class existence that they thought would never end.

Now, among the hulk of ghostly buildings, those people seem just out of view, as though they had left a few hours before, soon to return for another grueling shift.

They lived in a world of billets and beams, forging and fire, hot steel and fractious strikes.

But they won't be back.

It is a world that is gone forever.

ONE

A Welshman cracks the code

The fire that would help transform America was lit by a man born poor on a farm in South Wales at the close of the 18th century.

David Thomas spent his early years in the rolling green countryside of Glamorganshire helping his family raise sheep and grow barley, oats and potatoes. But the brilliant boy was destined to play a leading role in the revolution already under way in the British Isles and soon to sweep the quiet, gentle hills and valleys of eastern Pennsylvania.

Within a few decades, developments he pioneered would set the stage for the making of steel in the small town of Bethlehem. There, along the south bank of the Lehigh River, one of the most powerful companies the world has ever seen would arise and make an indelible mark on history.

The Bethlehem Steel Corp., descendant of a 19th century iron company, would contribute mightily to U.S. military strength, providing the steel that helped America and its allies win the two global wars of the 20th century. At home, Bethlehem's steel would go into appliances, autos, ships and planes. From sea to sea, it would permanently alter the landscape with buildings and bridges unmatched in their majesty.

Like other industrial giants early in the 1900s, Bethlehem Steel was ruthless in pursuit of profit, hostile to the common laborer's early struggles to improve his lot and arrogant in its unwillingness to change.

This relentless drive nevertheless forged the company into a massive enterprise that at the height of its power employed hundreds of thousands at plants, railroads, mines and shipyards across the country and beyond.

By 1979, when the corporation marked its 75th anniversary, the amount of steel it had shipped, rolled into the beam that made Bethlehem famous, would have circled the Earth 370 times.

David Thomas provided the spark.

Thomas' hardworking parents did not have much. But they had a son with a good mind. By the time he left their tiny stone house at 17 to become an apprentice at an ironworks, they had scrounged to give him advanced schooling, hoping he would have a bright future. They could not have imagined how bright, or to what heights their son would go in the decades to come.

Awaiting him was a vast infant nation more than 3,000 miles across the Atlantic Ocean, still languishing in an age of wood. Awaiting him too were adventure and fame.

But in 1823, despite years of hard work, his career was stalled, his extraordinary talent dormant. He was employed at the ailing Ynyscedwyn (pronounced innis-KED-win) Ironworks in South Wales' Swansea Valley, a company so shaky financially that it rarely fired up its furnaces.

Then one-time hardware merchant George Crane bought the company. He quickly spotted young Thomas' potential and encouraged him to experiment.

At that point in industrial history, the fuels of choice to make iron were charcoal or coke — almost pure carbon produced from bituminous coal that had been burned to eliminate other elements.

The problem was that coke was made miles away from the ironworks and had to be hauled there, driving up the cost of the whole process.

Right underfoot in South Wales lay another substance that would become a main ingredient of Thomas' place in history.

Anthracite. Hard coal, the only place in Britain that had it.

There it was in abundance. But to that time, no one had figured out how to use it to make iron. The problem was getting the hard coal to burn at the 2,800 degrees needed to extract iron from ore and make the iron flow.

Thomas took up the challenge, but at first had to fight what so many innovators face—the shortsightedness of conventional wisdom.

His initial experiment was to combine anthracite with coke. "This did very well," he said, according to a biographical sketch of him in an 1883 edition of the Welsh magazine Red Dragon. "But whenever anything went wrong with the furnaces, the fault was always laid on the coal; and the men became so prejudiced against it that I had to give it up."

Years went by without much progress, although Thomas continued to experiment.

Then he came across another inventor's work, and he was on the road to putting the pieces of a new technology together.

The other fellow was a gasworks operator, James Beaumont Neilson, who had come up with the notion of heating air, then blasting it into a furnace onto coke to make it burn more efficiently.

This idea, seemingly so simple and which remained the key process in making iron and steel into the late 20th century, was revolutionary at the time.

In fact, the conventional wisdom then was the opposite. Ironworkers used cold blasts in the furnaces, believing that since the devices worked better in winter, cold air must help. They were wrong. The variable was not air temperature; winter's lower humidity accounted for the higher efficiency of the furnaces.

Having discovered Neilson's work, Thomas merely had to bring the invention together with the local supply of anthracite.

He tested his thoughts one night while in the library of Crane's home. Thomas picked up a bellows and used it to blow air on anthracite burning in the fireplace.

"You had better not, David," Crane warned. "You will blow it out."

Thomas said, "If we only had Neilson's hot blast here, the anthracite would burn like pine."

"David, that is the idea precisely!"

Thomas got a license from Neilson to use

the hot-air blast. In early 1837, he built an oven and connected it to a furnace. Blowing engines blasted hot air onto the anthracite. It burned fiercely, smelting the iron ore. Out came good iron, and lots of it.

In all the world, it was the first commercially successful attempt to make iron with anthracite.

A little more than a year later, two Pennsylvania businessmen learned of Thomas' amazing new technology and saw what it might do for them and their enterprise.

Josiah White and Erskine Hazard were the owners of a company named Lehigh Coal & Navigation, and had been busy making money for years on a rapidly increasing demand for coal.

They had figured out that the rich anthracite deposit in northeastern Pennsylvania's Carbon County and the river system that connected the mountainous region with the growing communities to the south were an invitation to grow rich.

They already had overcome one big hurdle. They had built dams and a canal to control the unreliable natural flow of the Lehigh River and were doing a brisk business moving coal by mule-drawn barges to city folks through Easton to Philadelphia and New York. On the trips back, according to lore, they brought horse droppings from the city streets to sell to farmers for use as fertilizer.

Providing coal for heating was a lucrative and well-timed pursuit. Every 10 years in the early 1800s, the population of the region was doubling. At first, the substance that sustained this growth was wood. It was so plentiful in this big new land, and it was used for all sorts of everyday things like cooking utensils, agricultural tools, butter churns and furniture. It also was converted into charcoal for making iron. As early as 1775, eastern Pennsylvania already was the hub of ironmaking in the United States because of its ore deposits and seemingly endless forests. The Lehigh Valley had an added resource — limestone, used to remove impurities.

But the timber supply was not endless.

And besides, charcoal was inefficient and hard to transport. It took a collier 10 days to two weeks tending a smoldering stack of wood around the clock to produce the stuff. One acre of hardwood forest was consumed to make enough charcoal to keep one iron furnace going for 24 hours. Besides, furnaces had to be near the fuel supply, out in the woods and away from population centers, because moving charcoal more than a few miles turned it to dust.

Coal certainly made sense as an alternative. White and Hazard had the supply in Carbon County and the navigation system to move it.

Meanwhile, the Lehigh Valley was rapidly becoming an attractive center for commerce.

The Valley, mainly farmland where Pennsylvania Germans plowed fertile soil and grew corn, wheat, barley and oats, was linked by canals to America's two largest cities. Easton especially flourished in its strategic location at the fork of the Lehigh and Delaware rivers. It also was a stagecoach hub and magnet for lawyers, bankers, merchants and artisans. In 1830, about 3,500 people lived there, more than twice as many as in the borough of Allentown and the Moravian village of Bethlehem.

White and Hazard knew that wider use of coal could rapidly escalate industrial growth in the Lehigh Valley. But the piece they were missing was the same one Thomas spent years pursuing — how to make anthracite burn hot enough to smelt iron ore. They had tried but failed. They tried again after hearing about Thomas' new technique, actually starting up a furnace in the community of Mauch Chunk in Carbon County. But without the Welshman and his expertise, the furnace was not good enough to be commercially viable.

So Hazard sailed to Wales in late 1838 to negotiate with George Crane, who held both the British and U.S. patents for the hot blast of anthracite.

Hazard's hope was to return with the right to use the technology and with someone who could help his company build the furnaces. To his surprise and delight, Crane offered Thomas himself.

Why would Crane willingly give up the inventor to an American?

It appears that success had degraded the relationship between Crane and Thomas. The invention was in place and working fine, Crane had the rights to it and had even taken credit for the idea. His ironworks was turning a profit. He simply did not need Thomas anymore.

For Hazard, the prospect of getting the man who made anthracite burn was hitting the mother lode. He was impressed with Thomas, who looked more like a scholar than a ruddy ironmaster. He had a regal bearing and a clean-shaven face, with dark eyes behind spectacles perched on the bridge of a long, straight nose. His lips were thin. His full, black hair featured thick sideburns that reached down to the tips of his earlobes.

Hazard enticed him with a dazzling offer. Lehigh Coal & Navigation would supply Thomas with land, capital and resources to set up an ironmaking business "on or near the banks of the River Lehigh." He would have five years to build a blast furnace and start making iron for what would be the Lehigh Crane Iron Co. The family's moving expenses would be paid, and Thomas would get 200 pounds annually. He would get an additional 250 pounds if the furnace proved successful, and 50 pounds more for each blast furnace he built. If he failed, the company would pay the cost of moving his family back to Great Britain.

Still, Thomas almost didn't come to the Lehigh Valley. He was 44 years old, and most people of that era didn't live past 55. He was an ardent Welsh patriot who spoke and loved to hear his native language. And his mother was still alive. He knew if he left for America, he would never see her again.

His wife, Elizabeth, intervened. She was a woman of strong opinions in an age when a wife was considered little more than her husband's property. She implored David to take the family to America for the children's sake, believing that their three young sons would have better opportunities in the New World. She also felt that David would do well to move on from Crane's ironworks. Her arguments won him over, and on Dec. 31, 1838, he signed a contract.

Thomas, his wife and their sons and two daughters said goodbye to their family and friends in Wales and boarded a coastal steamer bound for Liverpool in the first week of the following May. At the great English port city, they booked passage on the sailing packet Roscius. The voyage was brief by the standards of the day, a near-record 23 days to cross the Atlantic. But it almost killed Thomas, who contracted a fever aboard the Roscius. The family spent a month on Staten Island, N.Y., where David recovered. When he was healthy again, he and his 13-year-old son, Samuel, trekked to Philadelphia to consult with Hazard, White and the other board members of the newly formed Lehigh Crane Iron Co. After the meeting, they returned to Staten Island.

On July 6, 1839, the Thomas family, in Samuel's words, "turned our faces to the Lehigh Valley, our future home." The first part of the four-day journey was from Jersey City to New Brunswick, N.J. They rode a train on poor-quality rails, which Thomas' innovations ultimately would improve. At New Brunswick, the Thomases boarded a stagecoach to Easton. The next day, July 9, they arrived by stage in Allentown, where wood-frame houses and small stores stood in rows on high ground between the Little Lehigh and Jordan creeks. After resting for a day at Haberacker's Hotel, David and Samuel Thomas walked the three miles north to the hamlet of Biery's Bridge, now Catasauqua, along the Lehigh River. As their journey ended, they found themselves atop a high ridge. In the distance to the north rose the majestic Blue Mountain. As an old man, Samuel would recall the view and his wonder at a country where possibilities seemed as limitless as the far horizon.

After taking in the scenery, they climbed down the hill. As they approached Biery's Bridge, a loud noise startled them. They crossed the Lehigh at the chain bridge, called that because it was held up by two large iron chains. Biery's Bridge had a tavern, a half-dozen houses and a building that served as a gristmill, sawmill and fullingmill for beating and cleaning cloth. Several farms dotted the area, and woods lay beyond the hamlet to the east and south.

Samuel wished he had brought the gun he had asked his father to buy him in England. The boy had heard that savages and wild animals roamed the forests of America and could attack at any time. But the gun was still packed in the trunk, making the slow canal boat trip across New Jersey.

Father and son were directed to a large man on the tavern steps, Frederick Biery, the "village nabob," or most important resident. Biery owned the land on which the furnace would stand and was selling it to Lehigh Coal & Navigation. As they spoke with Biery about the furnace, they again heard the loud noise. It was the rattling of a water-powered upright saw slicing a large log into boards — a sign of the era that David Thomas would be instrumental in ushering out.

The Welshman wasted no time. Urged on by Lehigh Coal & Navigation, he began building an ironworks along the eastern edge of the Lehigh Canal parallel to the river, mainly using machinery and equipment made for him in the British Isles.

A letter Thomas sent to a friend in Wales offers a glimpse of life in the Valley at the time. "We live in a very fertile country where every sort of grain, vegetable and fruit is very abundantly grown," he wrote on Dec. 11, 1839. "The climate is very healthy; and the weather has been hitherto very good. The people are hospitable and kind, chiefly from German origin. There is much of that language spoken here, which I am learning very fast. The children can talk it better than I can."

He was in a land where natural resources were plentiful, where most people had adequate food, shelter and clothing, and where society watched out for the less fortunate. "Poverty is rarely known here except among the intemperate or idle. Old people, widows, and orphans are very well taken care of. The law of the land is very lenient to the actual poor, but very much otherwise to imposters. I have only seen three people begging, two of them Irish and one a German."

The cost of living was modest because "provisions are very cheap, in fact, everything for the use of man is very moderate except woolen cloths, which are about double of those bought in England. Calico and cotton prints are as cheap here as you can get them there, and cotton goods of every sort are very cheap." American horses were good, "if not better generally," than those in Wales. "Pigs are very cheap and abundant" and well fed on Indian corn. There was flour "which makes bread pretty nearly as white as this sheet of paper I am writing upon."

People had breakfast at 6 in the morning, dinner at noon, and supper or tea at 6 in the evening. "They have plenty of meat on the table for each meal whatever house you go into. All classes eat very much alike about the same times."

Then as now, the government supported education but not religion, and the young had opportunities to advance. "Places of worship and schools are numerous. Many denominations are supported by voluntary contributions; the schools by a tax, every State appropriating so many thousand dollars for the use of schools. There is one built in my neighborhood where every one can educate his children for almost nothing, to any branch of science or literature."

The Valley's nearness to major cities was as much a plus for Thomas as it is for today's residents. "Philadelphia is 54 miles and New York is 93 miles, to either of which places we can go from here in one day. Traveling here is very expeditious, as there are canals and railroads in every direction. The town nearest to us is Allentown which is three miles from our works."

Thomas was also pleased with his benefactors at Lehigh Coal & Navigation. "We have been treated here with much kindness. My employers have done everything in their power for my comfort; they have built me a very good house, with garden and every convenience that one could wish, and I have reason to believe they are satisfied with me. I have under my care about 100 men with proper foremen to look after every department; I give the orders and pay them."

Almost seven months after Thomas wrote his letter, his creation was ready to be "blown in," or fired up.

No. 1 Furnace was an imposing presence along the canal and river. Its cluster of buildings included a stock house for storage, a weigh house for measuring ingredients, the tall stack where ore became melted iron, and a casting house where molten iron took shape. There also were contraptions such as pipe stoves and blowing cylinders.

At five-and-a-half stories, the stack was the tallest structure in the Lehigh Valley. Built of limestone and lined with firebrick, it reached 45 feet and had a chimney that rose out the top an additional dozen feet. It was 30 feet square at the base and tapered to 23 feet square at the top. At its core was the chamber where iron ore was converted to metallic iron. Like an oil lamp, the chamber swelled outward halfway up, then curved in toward the peak.

At 5 p.m. July 3, 1840, the furnace was blown in for the first time. A sluiceway, dug on the slope between the canal and the river, diverted water from the canal. Dropping down the sluiceway, the water hit and turned a breast wheel that powered a blowing engine. The engine's two cylinders sent compressed cold air through a pipe under the canal. The air went into a brick chamber, where it was heated to more than 600 degrees in four coal-fired, cast-iron pipe stoves.

Anthracite and wood were piled in the stack's bottom, called the hearth. From outside, a worker set fire to the wood to get the coal burning. Limestone, iron ore and anthracite were hoisted to a platform at the top of the stack with a "water balance," a chain elevator that used water to weigh down one box enough to raise another box filled with the materials.

Once the fire was going hot, workers on the platform dropped the "charge" — the limestone, iron ore and anthracite — down the stack in layers. The blowing engine sent the hot air or "blast" from the pipe stoves into the stack through nozzles called tuyeres (pronounced TWEE-ers). The hot air hit the burning anthracite, which smelted the ore. A clay plug filled a notch at the bottom of the hearth, where the molten iron settled. The next day, when it was time to tap the furnace, a worker broke the plug with a long iron bar resembling a shepherd's crook, and the iron flowed into the casting house. Workers raked off the slag, the impurities that floated to the top.

The iron sloshed down an incline called a "runner," where men in thick water-soaked wooden clogs and woolen clothing used paddles to channel it into troughs carved into the sand floor and to dam the runner. The liquid metal flowed into molds called sows, and from those into smaller ones called pigs. The names come from the picture they made in the sand: pigs feeding from their mothers. After the iron cooled and hardened, workers broke the necks connecting the sows and pigs, and removed the bar-shaped casts from both types of molds.

The people at Lehigh Crane Iron Co. had more to celebrate than the 64th anniversary of American independence. Out of their furnace had come 4 tons of quality iron. It was the first furnace in the United States to use a fuel other than charcoal to make iron profitably. It stayed "in blast" 24 hours a day for six months, producing as much as 52 tons of "pig iron" a week, until a flood doused the fire.

The pig iron bars were sold to foundries, where they were remelted and cast into everything from pots and pans to industrial machinery. They were also sold to rolling mills with puddling furnaces, where they were first converted into wrought iron, then rolled into rails, plates, bars and other shapes. In puddling furnaces, pig iron was melted and stirred, or puddled, to oxidize out the unwanted carbon.

High-grade magnetic ore from New Jersey was brought to Catasauqua on the canal. Local ores, mainly mined by farmers, arrived in wagons. In the night, multicolored flames and sulfur fumes shooting from the chimney did a hellish, curling dance above the Lehigh. Skeptics had to swallow their taunts. In a variation of "I'll eat my hat," a charcoal-burning ironmaker had blustered, "I will eat all the iron you make with anthracite." Thomas invited him to a dinner cooked in the Catasauqua furnace.

And so with a menu of iron ore, limestone, anthracite and hot air, the immigrant from Wales established himself as a pioneer of America's Industrial Revolution. The age of smoke and iron had arrived. Thomas had introduced it to an area that had been unaffected by machines and technology, a place where most people made their living off the soil. He and the ironmasters who followed him drew their employees from the surrounding farms for work that was unlike anything the field hands had known.

On farms, people toiled at their own pace, on their own schedule, to reach goals they set for themselves. But men employed at the Valley's early ironworks had to adapt to an entirely different reality. They had to learn the rhythms that Thomas brought with him from already industrialized Wales. That meant working 12 hours a day, seven days a week while the furnace was in blast, with maybe a Sunday off every two weeks. They had to work in shifts, charging and tapping the furnace throughout the day and night. Noise and awful odors bombarded them.

Some jobs required skilled men who were handsomely paid. Besides Thomas, the ironmaster who supervised production, there were engineers to run the machines, teamsters to drive the wagons, clerks to keep the books, and the auto mechanics of the 19th century: millwrights and blacksmiths to make repairs.

At the start, Lehigh Crane had a few hundred men on the payroll, some of them Welshmen familiar with ironmaking who had come to America at Thomas' urging. That number would grow to as many as 700. But most of the workers were unskilled, mainly Pennsylvania Germans who would be on a farm if they weren't at the plant. Compared with what they earned for laboring in fields, the pay was good, but conditions were tough for the inexperienced, and the work was hazardous. Dust, dirt and gas damaged lungs. Machinery maimed and killed. More common, though, were strangulated hernias from the constant lifting and lugging of heavy loads.

Charging the furnace was a horrible task. Standing on a wooden platform at the top of the stack, with nothing but leather aprons to protect them, the men who fed the beast were assaulted by smoke, cinders, carbon monoxide and searing heat from the fire below.

In this harsh setting, Thomas proved to be an honorable master, a model of sobriety and thrift. By observing him, his workers could learn how to become successful and lift themselves up to a higher station, as Thomas himself had done. Following the Protestant ethic, he encouraged church-going and temperance. A sober, God-fearing worker is a good worker, he believed.

Thomas added four furnaces before leaving Lehigh Crane in 1854 to start his own ironworks, the Thomas Iron Co., with his sons in nearby Hokendauqua. He had cleared the path. Others followed, turning the Lehigh Valley into the iron center of America. Investors and capitalists from the big cities arrived. Pig iron furnaces began transforming rural landscapes into industrial work sites. Farm fields and hillsides swarmed with iron ore seekers almost as fanatical in spirit as the miners who were turning California upside down looking for gold. Ironton and Orefield emerged as major ore fields.

By 1850, anthracite was making half of America's iron, and about a quarter of all the iron produced in this country was made in Lehigh and Northampton counties and the adjacent areas of Carbon and Bucks counties and Warren County, N.J. Over the next two decades, the Lehigh Valley's population exploded from 72,700 to 118,300, a 63 percent increase.

Thomas became so well known that the Republicans asked him to run for Congress in 1866. He agreed, even though he wasn't interested in politics. After a half-hearted campaign, during which he never bothered to make a speech, he lost. But he had the popular vote of fellow ironmasters, who nicknamed him "Papa" because he was their hero — the father of the American anthracite iron industry. He was 88, rich and famous when he died in Catasauqua in 1882.

For 81 years, iron poured from Lehigh Crane, which at the turn of the century came under a holding company, Empire Steel & Iron. The furnaces stopped roaring in 1921, and five years later, the Fuller Co. took over the property to make equipment for moving cement. At the Catasauqua plant, now owned by F.L. Smidth of Denmark, a historical marker on Front Street notes the location of Papa Thomas' triumph. But all that remains of the Lehigh Crane Iron Co. is some concrete trestle supports.

A few blocks east, Thomas' grand house still stands on the hill at Second and Pine streets, and in Alburtis, home of another furnace he founded, the Lock Ridge Museum stands as a reminder of the momentous work he did in the Lehigh Valley. It was work that opened the way for a steel company destined to become a colossus.

By burning anthracite in an iron furnace, Thomas had sparked a revolution in American industry that established the Valley as the ironmaking capital of the nation. That encouraged a fledgling railroad to build an ironworks in south Bethlehem along the Lehigh River, several miles downstream from Lehigh Crane, to make iron rails for tracks. And that, in turn, led to a vast improvement on the same site: construction of a steel plant to make better rails.

At the start of the 1860s, the millionaire owner of the Lehigh Valley Railroad, the civil engineer who built and ran it, and an ironmaster recruited from the western part of the state began creating the framework for Bethlehem Steel.

Birth of a giant

A sa Packer, Robert Sayre and John Fritz had no blueprint to follow. Like everyone else who chose to lead the Industrial Revolution, they found their own way into the new age of iron and steel, of machines and mass production. But the blending of their minds and talents in one place, at key points in time during the 1800s, was unique and critical to the business that eventually became the Bethlehem Steel Corp. With the confluence of these geniuses, the men and the hour had met.

Packer was a tall, taciturn New Englander, not well educated but shrewd and daring in business, an orchestrator with panoramic vision who seized opportunities, accurately sized up the abilities of other men, and insisted on the best.

His protege, Sayre, was introspective, visionary, deeply religious, organized, detail-oriented and interested in all things, from his asparagus patch to the writings of the ancient Romans. He was gifted at knowing how to connect technologies.

Fritz was a self-taught mechanic, a highly skilled engineer who knew machinery instinctively, a ceaseless tinkerer who was absolutely sure of himself and showed an independent streak that annoyed his superiors.

The enterprise they nurtured at a railroad junction along the south bank of the Lehigh River, the Bethlehem Iron Co., would have its ups and downs through the end of the century. Each time it appeared that failure threatened, the company redefined itself and rose to new heights of success. That wouldn't always be the case with Bethlehem Steel in the next century, especially toward the end. But it was a hallmark of its predecessor, Bethlehem Iron, which converted to steelmaking when steel rails proved far better than iron ones and made the leap to armor plate and gun forgings for warships when it could no longer sell steel rails competitively.

Always in the forefront at Bethlehem Iron was Robert Sayre. He might have grown up to be an Episcopal clergyman or a prosperous Philadelphia merchant, except that the depression after the War of 1812 knocked his father down a few notches.

William Sayre made handsome profits in the shipping trade as a member of Philadelphia's mercantile elite. But then the war with Britain sank his firm and drained away almost all his money. He and his wife retreated to the only holding they had left, a small farm she owned in Columbia County near the Susquehanna River. Robert Heysham Sayre was born there in 1824. He and four siblings would grow to adulthood; six other Sayre children would not.

When Robert was 4, the family moved east to Mauch Chunk, a Carbon County mining settlement that got its name from the Indian term for Bear Mountain, which faced the town from across the Lehigh River. It had about 1,300 people and was the home of the Lehigh Coal & Navigation Co. The elder Sayre got a good job running the Mauch Chunk weigh lock, where he determined tolls by a boat's weight and collected the money.

A devout Episcopalian, William became friends with a young carpenter and canal-boat captain from Mystic, Conn. Asa Packer, who had helped build an Episcopal church and was married by an Episcopal minister in Susquehanna County, was 27 when he came to Mauch Chunk in 1833. He and William Sayre became friends, their families socialized together, and Sayre was instrumental in founding St. Mark's Church, where Packer had a leadership role.

For a couple of years, Packer built and piloted boats that hauled coal to Philadelphia. He opened a boatyard with his younger brother and bought a general store on the riverbank. The brothers got major contracts to build dams and locks on the Upper Division of the Lehigh Canal, finishing in 1836, and to build coal boats in Pottsville the following year.

Returning to Mauch Chunk, Packer leased and mined anthracite fields, shipping the coal on his own boats. He made real estate deals in the newly bustling coal towns of Carbon and Schuylkill counties.

As he grew richer, he took note of the bright schoolboy Robert Sayre, who was showing an interest in civil engineering. Sayre joined his father at Lehigh Coal & Navigation, which lent the 16-year-old to the Morris Canal & Banking Co. in New Jersey to help upgrade its canal, the conduit for iron ore coming into Pennsylvania. That same year, 1840, David Thomas was in Catasauqua helping to ignite America's Industrial Revolution with anthracite iron.

Two years later, Sayre returned to Mauch Chunk and Lehigh Coal & Navigation, the company whose owners had brought Thomas to America. Sayre spent a winter in Bradford County, 85 miles to the north, tending to mules that towed the boats on the canal. The mules were idle in winter because ice always shut down the waterway. After that, Sayre focused on the company's rail lines, on which cars rode downhill by gravity and were pulled up the tracks by mules and later by steam-driven inclined planes. He showed so much skill as a surveyor and builder, he became supervisor of all the company's rail operations.

Meanwhile, Packer began ascending to power. He became a state assemblyman, a Carbon County judge and a two-term Democratic congressman. A contemporary described him as "a man of excellent presence, with a finely chiseled face that was almost a stranger to visible emotion, and he was severely quiet and unassuming in conversation."

While a lawmaker in Washington, Packer spoke little for the record, making no speeches from the House floor in all four years. But oddly for a man who would later distinguish himself as a humanitarian, he supported a pro-slavery measure. He was among four of the state's 25 House members to back a bill that would let Kansas and Nebraska residents decide whether they could own slaves. Pennsylvania's Democrats liked him anyway. He was their favorite son candidate for president in 1868 and almost won a race for governor the following year.

Public service didn't keep him from aspiring to wealth. At midcentury, while his mining operations expanded, he wanted to ship more coal, and faster, than the Lehigh Canal allowed. He wanted a carrier that would run regardless of ice and not depend on mules for power. He wanted a steam-locomotive-powered railroad. But railroads were costly to build and maintain.

Though Packer was among investors in a proposed Delaware, Lehigh, Schuylkill & Susquehanna Railroad, squabbles among them prevented any work from being done on it for five years. He got fed up with waiting. In the fall of 1851, he bought control of the railroad. The following year, he tapped 27-year-old Robert Sayre to be its chief engineer and made a deal with the stockholders to build the line himself in exchange for stocks and bonds. On Jan. 7, 1853, he changed the name to the Lehigh Valley Railroad.

He had what he wanted, including Sayre.

Part of Packer's confidence in his new right-hand man had to do with attitude. Like other professionals of the era, Sayre saw himself as an agent of progress whose purpose was to serve civilization by spreading the wonders of technology.

He was handsome and powerfully built, but had lost the sight in his left eye when, at the age of 8, he poked himself with a knife while whittling a stick. Like his father, he was religious. The faith he practiced extended to his work, which he approached with missionary fervor, as if God had called on him to excel as a civil engineer.

He collected and read books on history, literature and travel, always striving to improve himself. He could see the big picture and yet pay attention to details. For decades, he carried a diary in his pocket, every day penciling in at least an entry on the weather. "When I got up this morning," he wrote on Dec. 27, 1894, "there was 5 inches or more of snow on the ground … Sleighing quite good."

But he wasn't always strait-laced, as he noted during a business trip to Wilkes-Barre in 1867: "Evening at Hotel and made a fool of myself … I drank too much wine in the eve, which caused many great mortifications and grief" when he was hung over the next day.

Building the Lehigh Valley Railroad tested Sayre's ability to organize a project and see it

through. Years later, he recounted the obstacles he and his men faced:

"A single track from Easton to Mauch Chunk; iron of an inferior quality — the best of which we could at that time avail ourselves; track laid without ballast; not a single coal, freight, or passenger car of our own; no shops, no depots worthy of the name — in fact, nothing but the track and four locomotives."

Throughout construction, financing problems dogged Packer, who went up and down the line urging the men to work faster. In 1854, a cholera epidemic in the Lehigh Valley halted progress for several months.

But after three years of labor, the Lehigh Valley Railroad began regular passenger service in the summer of 1855. On Sept. 15, it hauled coal for the first time, a trainload from Mauch Chunk to Easton on a 46-mile route along the southern and western banks of the Lehigh.

From the start, the line was a moneymaker. Its rolling stock — the locomotives and cars — were rented at first. But within a year, the railroad bought 15 locomotives, six passenger cars, two baggage cars and 800 coal cars.

Packer, who preferred to hobnob with investors in Philadelphia and New York, made Sayre the railroad's superintendent as well as its chief engineer and let him run the business.

In 1856, Sayre made a decision that would have enormous consequences for the Lehigh Valley and the growing nation. He chose a site across the Lehigh River from Bethlehem for the railroad's operational headquarters.

At first glance, the location would seem to be an odd choice. Bethlehem, incorporated as a borough in 1845, had only 2,800 residents by the late 1850s and had fallen behind Easton and Allentown in the pace of development.

Bethlehem had long been a manufacturing center for the Lehigh Valley's farmers. Its primary residents for more than 100 years belonged to the pacifist Moravian Church, a Protestant denomination with roots in Bohemia and Moravia in what is now the Czech Republic. After fleeing religious persecution in Europe, Moravians founded Bethlehem in 1741 by staking out an enclave at the confluence of the Lehigh River and Monocacy Creek. Their descendants were now farming, working in mills and making agricultural tools.

But unlike the burgeoning boroughs of Easton and Allentown, sleepy Bethlehem had not become transformed by industry. It couldn't shake the reputation of John Rice.

Rice was a Bethlehem Moravian who in the 1840s swindled investors of an Allentown bank that subsequently failed. Known as the "Slippery Moravian" and the "Oily Herrnhuter," the German word for Moravian, Rice drained from Bethlehem almost all the capital that could have been used for large-scale investments and improvements. He duped many potential investors with his keg-of-nails ruse, which he pulled while trying to convince them that his Northampton Bank was flush with cash. He got a keg of nails and covered the top with a thin layer of gold coins, making it seem as if the entire keg were filled with gold.

Though the scandal blackened Bethlehem's eye, Sayre and other entrepreneurs ignored it. They looked beyond the borough's lagging growth and saw a place of great promise.

The advantages of making south Bethlehem the railroad's headquarters were clear. It was ideally situated between the New York and Philadelphia markets. It would become a key rail junction when the North Pennsylvania Railroad met the Lehigh Valley Railroad there in 1857. And nearby, ironmaking plants were multiplying so that by 1860 the Lehigh Valley would have 23 furnaces.

Using railroads and furnaces in tandem was a natural. The Lehigh Valley Railroad could bring in coal to fire up the furnaces, then haul finished materials north. The North Penn Railroad could take them south to Philadelphia. It could also carry passengers from Bethlehem to the port city in three hours — a trip that until now had taken eight hours by stagecoach or several days by canal boat. The Central Railroad of New Jersey, which reached Easton in 1852, gave access to New York City. And the East Pennsylvania Railroad, completed in 1859 between Allentown and Reading, opened a route west to Harrisburg and Chicago.

Railroads needed iron for locomotives and cars, and in the form of rails to repair and extend their lines. But local furnaces didn't make rails; they made pig iron, which was sent elsewhere to be cast into products or turned into wrought iron for rails and other shapes.

That put the Lehigh Valley Railroad in a bind. Unwilling to pay a high tariff on superior British rails, Sayre and Packer bought their supply from one of the few railmakers in this country — the Lackawanna Iron & Coal Co. in Scranton. Lackawanna's owners set up a railroad of their own, the Delaware, Lackawanna & Western, to compete with the Lehigh Valley Railroad as a coal carrier.

Sayre and Packer were not only subsidizing their competition but getting an inferior product. Lackawanna couldn't make decent rails. Nor could any other American company. Rather than pay for quality stock from Britain, most railroads bought rails that often broke.

Rails with hidden fissures and weaknesses would crack on the track and curl up into what were called snakeheads. Snakeheads would rip out the bottom of the wooden rail cars, causing wrecks and disemboweling passengers.

Just before he became president of the United States in 1852, Franklin Pierce, riding with his wife and 11-year-old son, saw his boy die when a snakehead gouged the train. The grief that overcame Pierce turned him into an alcoholic.

Commodore Cornelius Vanderbilt, who later emerged as the biggest rail baron in America, was involved in a snakehead wreck and swore in the 1840s that he never would have anything to do with railroads. He changed his mind 20 years later.

The problem with American mills such as Lackawanna's was that they didn't have the technology to roll rails efficiently. They had trouble finishing the rolling before the rails turned cold — they couldn't "strike while the iron is hot" — and that led to damaged machinery.

Packer and Sayre knew the answer: They needed their own mill and the technology to make good rails.

An opportunity arose when Bethlehem merchant Augustus Wolle formed the Saucona Iron Co. on April 8, 1857. Wolle wanted to open an anthracite-fueled ironworks that would feed on an ore bed he leased in the Saucon Valley. Packer was among investors who subscribed to the stock, and he got Sayre involved as well. But the venture, whose ironworks was to be built near the junction of the Lehigh Valley and North Penn railroads, existed only on paper.

Using Packer's money, Sayre and others with the railroad ensured that Wolle's company would succeed. Two years later, it was reorganized as the Bethlehem Rolling Mill & Iron Co. to more accurately reflect its purpose, but it still did not have a plant. Before building one, Sayre wanted to be sure the railroad would have an ironworks that could properly make rails. He turned to a discontented genius who had failed in the Lehigh Valley's iron industry when it had just started to boom.

John Fritz was born in 1822 on a farm in Londonderry Township in western Chester County. As a boy, he carried rye whiskey and spring water to the men harvesting hay and gathered sheaves of wheat. His German father, who was also a skillful millwright and machinist, gave him a taste for mechanics. His Scotch-Irish mother passed on to him her devout faith, which made him a dutiful Methodist.

He attended school until he was 16, when he was apprenticed to a blacksmith in nearby Parkesburg and learned to repair threshers and other farm machinery.

The first time he saw a shotgun, with its percussion cap lock, the teen immediately recognized it was superior to the standard flintlock gun. With no gunsmiths in the area, he converted his own flintlock into a cap lock. After word about his handiwork got around, he moonlighted as a gunsmith, refashioning his neighbors' weapons.

He also benefited from an exposure to machines outside the smithy. Parkesburg had the repair shops for the Philadelphia & Columbia Railroad, which ran through town and would become part of the great Pennsylvania Railroad. Fritz befriended the shop superintendent and learned all he could about the "iron horse."

In 1844, he helped build an iron mill in the Montgomery County borough of Norristown, gaining experience in blast furnace technology. "Never shirking a responsibility and never

missing an opportunity to acquire knowledge was at all times my guiding star," he wrote in his autobiography.

He moved on to a rail mill and blast furnace at Safe Harbor on the Susquehanna River, about 10 miles from Lancaster, despite a warning from an acquaintance that it was the worst place in Pennsylvania for a deadly "fever and ague."

Sure enough, Fritz became seriously ill, alternately chilled and feverish, with bouts of uncontrollable shaking. He had such "indescribable suffering," he didn't care whether he lived or died. No doctor he went to could help him.

Thinking a change in climate might help, he visited Michigan with a friend who owned iron ore fields near Lake Superior. After Fritz returned to Pennsylvania, the attacks persisted, but a colleague steered him to a Philadelphia doctor who cured him.

Fritz, now married, came to the Lehigh Valley in the early 1850s because it was the most productive ironmaking region in the nation. He built a machine shop and foundry in Catasauqua to make parts for the industry and got to know David Thomas. But for reasons that remain unclear, the business failed after a year.

Better luck awaited him in western Pennsylvania at the Cambria Iron Works in Johnstown, where he moved in 1854. But the town depressed him. It was "the most unattractive place I had ever been in," with streets of clay, planks for sidewalks, and cows, hogs and dogs roaming freely. "I should have been amused if I had not been there to stay."

In 1857, while Robert Sayre was maneuvering Saucona Iron and moving his railroad headquarters to south Bethlehem, Fritz developed a machine that solved the problem of inferior rails. He called it the "three-high" rail mill. Its magic was in rolling square bars of iron into inverted T-shaped rails while the bars were still hot. The "three-high" referred to three sets of rolls stacked one on top of the other. The iron passed between the bottom and middle rollers, then in the reverse direction between the middle and top rollers.

The industry standard at the time was the two-high mill, the culprit that produced faulty rails. At two-high mills, the iron bars or blooms passed through the rolls once and workers had to haul them back to the front for another pass-through. That delay allowed blooms to cool by the time the workers fitted them between the rolls for the second time. When the blooms cooled, they cracked or broke and fouled the machinery.

Fritz's machine kept the hot blooms moving through the rolls from both sides of the mill until they were finished rails. They didn't have time to cool.

The three-high mill wasn't Fritz's idea; it had been invented in Wales. But his triumph was in modifying it to match American technology. The result was uniformly high-quality rails made quickly and economically.

Sayre visited Fritz, and Fritz's work intrigued him. Here was a mechanical engineer who could visualize how a machine, any machine, would work. He could simplify ideas and technologies to make them mechanically efficient on a large scale.

He wasn't a metallurgist, but he understood metallurgy. He wasn't a civil engineer, but he had a sharp sense of design. He wasn't an architect, but he had architectural skills. The Lehigh Valley Railroad needed Fritz, and Sayre was eager to give the genius his playing field.

After six years in Johnstown, Fritz was eager to move on. He felt boxed in by the directors of the Cambria Iron Works, who had always battled him over his costly innovations. More important, he wanted a nicer place to raise his family, and a good education for his daughter, Gertrude. From his time in the Lehigh Valley, he knew about the fine Moravian girls schools in Bethlehem. Sadly, Gertrude would not have an opportunity to benefit from them. She died at age 7.

On May 1, 1860, Sayre wrote to Fritz, saying he could enhance his reputation as an ironmaster by coming to Bethlehem, which was ripe for the "establishment of a good mill" and "destined to be in my opinion the most populous and wealthy [area] in this or any other state."

"When I see the rapid strides that business has taken in this Valley for the past 10 years and think of the impetus that the improvements now in contemplation will give to it in the next 10, I predict a future for it that will surprise its most sanguine citizens."

Sayre emphasized that Fritz could run the mill as he saw fit.

"In regard to your having entire control of the establishment, I tell [the other investors] that a rolling mill is like a man of war, it must have one Captain. I do not apprehend any difficulty in the way of everything moving along pleasantly."

Fritz liked the idea that he'd have a free hand, that his family would live in a well-established community and that the company was in the core of a great ironmaking region.

The Bethlehem area was prosperous. It had factories that made pianos, carriages, barrels and farm implements. There were flour mills, a sawmill, a woolen mill, a brass foundry, a tannery, a distillery and a brewery. The biggest business was the Lehigh Zinc Co., which mined zinc in the Saucon Valley and converted it into oxides for paint pigments and into metallic zinc for galvanizing iron.

Fritz also liked the financial incentives. His contract, signed July 7, 1860, made him general manager and superintendent at $5,000 a year, or $107,580 in today's coinage, plus a bonus of 40 shares of company stock the following year and 20 additional shares in each of the next three years. In exchange, Fritz gave the company the use of his patent for the three-high mill.

Now Packer, Sayre and the others who controlled Bethlehem Rolling Mill & Iron had the ideal man to build and run the ironworks. For location, they had 11 acres south of the Lehigh Valley Railroad tracks and 6 acres north. Formerly Moravian farmland, the site was a narrow flood plain that stretched south for a quarter-mile before reaching the lower slopes of South Mountain.

It took more than two years to build the plant. The work suffered because of severe flooding in 1862 and shortages brought on by the Civil War. But even as the war slowed construction, it offered the infant company tremendous opportunity: It created a fresh demand for railroad equipment. Both sides relied heavily on trains for the rapid transfer of troops, weapons and supplies over long distances. To keep the trains running, new tracks had to be laid and old or damaged ones had to be replaced. Orders for rails would infuse the new ironmaker with profits.

As work on the plant progressed, it became clear that nothing about the machinery and the buildings Fritz designed was revolutionary. What distinguished them was their size and perfection. His theory was: Make it bigger, make it stronger, make it cheaper.

The buildings housed a blast furnace and a rolling mill with six heating furnaces and eight double puddling furnaces where pig iron was melted and stirred to become wrought iron for rails.

Fritz had seen the wooden Johnstown mill burn down, almost ruining his three-high rail machinery the day after it went into operation, and was determined not to let fire pose a hazard in south Bethlehem. He built the plant to last, not with wood but with hard rock from a South Mountain quarry, Lehigh Valley slate for the roofs and iron for the trusses. One of the buildings, a stock house, still stands.

Sayre was keenly interested in the project. He visited Fritz at the construction site almost daily, stood by Fritz's decisions and put the resources of the Lehigh Valley Railroad at his disposal. Sometimes they traveled together to see the operations of other ironmakers in the region.

Early in the project, in 1861, Bethlehem Rolling Mill & Iron was reorganized as the Bethlehem Iron Co. Most of its directors worked for the Lehigh Valley Railroad or owned stock in it, and Packer watched over them.

Finally, in January 1863, Fritz put the first furnace in blast, and in September the mill rolled its first iron rails.

Bethlehem Iron made good rails first for the Lehigh Valley Railroad and later for other customers in a hungry market. A fast-spreading reputation for quality had profits chugging in like a locomotive with a full head of steam.

In 1864, the company helped Gen. William Tecumseh Sherman conquer Atlanta. Sherman was stalled in Chattanooga, Tenn., unable to get badly needed supplies from the north because rebel guerrillas were wrecking the tracks. They'd tear up the rails, dump them on a bonfire and tie them around trees.

The Union turned to John Fritz and Bethlehem Iron. Fritz's brother, William, supervised construction of a mill in Chattanooga to reroll the rails. Northern troops cut the rails off the trees and took them to the mill, where others heated and rerolled them. Fitted onto the tracks, the repaired rails kept the trains running until Sherman reached the Georgia capital.

Meanwhile, the British — always in the vanguard of the Industrial Revolution — began mass-producing and shipping a new product that soon would lift Bethlehem yet again, and at just the right moment.

It was iron made harder than iron. It was steel.

The British were using it to make rails. During the early 1860s, they sold more than 140,000 tons of steel rails first to the Pennsylvania Railroad, then to others that also were willing to pay twice as much as the price of iron rails.

Sayre arranged to get a shipment in 1865 so he could see what the excitement was about. The company experimented with the British rails and determined that they would last 16 times longer than Fritz's wrought-iron rails, good only for about four years. The future, Sayre could see, was framed in steel.

Until an Englishman's invention in the mid-19th century, steel was made in painstaking fashion through a number of methods, the most effective of which was the crucible process. That involved taking wrought iron, putting it in a clay-and-graphite pot or crucible, mixing it with charcoal and heating and melting it. A controlled, small amount of carbon from the charcoal dissolved into the iron, giving it great hardness, making it steel.

For the workers, the process was the nearest thing to hell on Earth. They labored on top of a furnace, putting crucibles inside by using tongs to lift up refractory bricks. For protection from the heat, they wrapped themselves in wet leather and wore 4-inch wooden clogs and heavy leather gloves. As they lifted a 150-pound crucible of steel, smoke and flames surrounded them.

Crucible steel made razors, surgical instruments, Wilkinson swords and the springs and gears of high-quality watches and clocks. But the process was too expensive and too cumbersome to produce the blooms needed for the rolling of steel rails.

In the 1850s, English inventor Henry Bessemer opened the way for the mass production of steel that would satisfy the railroads' appetite. Bessemer's process took place in a pear-shaped vat, a "Bessemer converter," that was lined with refractory material and set on pivots so it could be tilted.

Pig iron was melted in a cupola furnace, which was smaller than a blast furnace and used cold air, and poured into a narrow opening at the top of the Bessemer converter. A powerful blast of cold air was forced through tuyeres, or holes, in the bottom. The air passed through the liquid metal, producing a tremendous heat reaction that shot a fierce flame and a fountain of sparks out of the mouth. Oxygen in the air, reacting with the metal, burned out carbon, silicon and other elements. After about 20 minutes, the reaction simmered down, meaning the "blow" had ended.

The iron was now liquid steel. To give it the desired properties, an iron-carbon-manganese alloy called spiegeleisen was added as workers tilted the converter and poured the steel into a ladle. The ladle then poured the steel into molds, where it solidified as ingots. Reheating the ingots softened them enough to be shaped into a bloom, which was then rolled into a smaller, longer section called a billet. The billet was reheated and passed through rolls to form a steel rail.

Of the myriad iron companies in the Lehigh Valley, Bethlehem Iron was the only one big enough and rich enough to get into steel production.

The other ironworks were small pig-iron producers that didn't have enough capital, while Bethlehem Iron could tap the financial resources of the Lehigh Valley Railroad. Packer, Sayre and others such as Elisha P. Wilbur, Packer's nephew and personal secretary, and Garrett Linderman, Packer's son-in-law, controlled both companies and the major banks, forming an Episcopal elite that could get whatever it wanted.

Still, Sayre almost had to pull his plant superintendent kicking and screaming into the Steel Age. Fritz didn't share Sayre's enthusiasm for the Bessemer process. He worried that Bethlehem Iron wouldn't be able to make good steel because it wouldn't have suitable ores. Ores that fed Bessemer converters couldn't contain large amounts of phosphorus, which made the product brittle and useless. Lehigh Valley and New Jersey ores had exactly that — too much phosphorus.

But Packer, Sayre, Quaker industrialist Joseph Wharton and others on the Bethlehem Iron board were determined that the Lehigh Valley Railroad have its own source of steel rails. They acknowledged that getting proper ores would be a problem, but still believed their ironworks could make steel rails as good as the British imports and at less cost. And they were confident that Fritz could overcome the obstacles.

Analysis of a steel rail made by another company eased Fritz's mind a little. The rail contained more phosphorus than specifications allowed, and yet it was adequate to lay in track. He was still reluctant, but that didn't stop the directors.

In 1868, in a move guaranteeing that Bethlehem Iron would survive and grow, they voted on a motion from Wharton "That this Company should proceed immediately to the production of Bessemer Steel, and that the Manager of this Company be and hereby is instructed to prepare without delay for the said manufacture at these works."

The directors had chosen to move ahead even though they hadn't arranged for long-term supplies of iron ore low enough in phosphorus to make quality steel rails. That bothered Fritz, who warned them: If the new plant fails, don't blame me.

Nevertheless, he got to work planning the best steel works his skill and imagination could muster. He visited the nation's first commercially successful steel mill at the Pennsylvania Steel Co. plant in Steelton, along the Susquehanna River just south of Harrisburg. He also went to Europe to study the Bessemer process. When he returned, he began erecting a steel mill across the Lehigh Valley Railroad tracks from the iron plant.

The mill, completed in five years, was a technological gem that combined rolling mills and Bessemer converters into one production unit and drew raves from other engineers. It wasn't America's first steel mill — nine others had come before — but it revealed Fritz's mastery of mechanics and design.

The structure survives today — a single, massive stone building in the shape of a double cross. The main stem is 931 feet long and 111 feet wide. Each of the two sections that cross the stem is 111 feet wide and 386 feet long.

Inside were hydraulic lifts, four Bessemer converters and their blowing engines, ladles, a plant to rebuild the converters' used-up bottoms, cast-iron molds for ingots, soaking furnaces where solidified ingots were heated to bring them up to rolling temperature, a blooming mill to make blooms, the three-high rail mill and cooling beds for the rails. All were in separate sections and under one slate roof 30 feet high at the eaves.

The lifts raised the molten iron and poured it into the converters. Each converter could produce 8 tons of steel in a blast, which was provided by an engine Fritz designed. The rolling mill, the largest part of the plant, could produce 20,000 tons of rails a year.

Everything was built to last. When a collaborator suggested that Fritz might have designed machinery to be more durable than necessary, he laughed: "Well, if I have, it will never be found out."

In the fall of 1873, the plant rolled its first steel rails and began filling orders for the Lehigh Valley and Jersey Central railroads. It used low-phosphorus ores from a mine near Port Oram (now Wharton) N.J., and from across the Atlantic and later, Cuba.

About 700 employees labored in noise and heat that Fritz had tried to lessen by keeping operations separate.

Like the plant's layout, the jobs were highly compartmentalized, with no sense of overall worker unity. Men worked 12 hours a day in departments under foremen who goaded them to keep moving. In serving the god of production, the men — mainly of German and Irish heritage — had to be skillful and strong to work with machinery and hot iron.

With the first steel rails came the year of The Panic, when a ruinous recession swept the country. The area's iron furnaces began to melt away in bankruptcies. However, buttressed by the Lehigh Valley Railroad, Bethlehem Iron survived. In a year, the company was recognized across the country for its high productivity and good steel rails.

But the rails weren't fine enough for Fritz, and his harping got him into a dispute with the directors. He wanted long-term contracts for low-phosphorus ore. The directors were content to buy ore as it was needed, and proper ores weren't always available on short notice. The result was mediocre quality.

"The condition of affairs as to the quality of steel we were making was sickening to me," Fritz said. He noted that the directors said Bethlehem Iron's rails were as good as those made by other companies and "they could see no reason why we should make them any better."

That's because they were making a lot of money. The Lehigh Valley Railroad was an empire by 1890, with 1,800 miles of track that stretched from New York City through Pennsylvania and up through western New York to the Great Lakes. Three-quarters of its income came from the transportation of coal, and it also owned mines.

With the combined success of the railroad and Bethlehem Iron, the Sayre, Linderman and Wilbur families piled up their riches and formed the core of the elite in South Bethlehem, a borough since 1865. Living in mansions in the exclusive Fountain Hill neighborhood, they had two main things in common: membership in the Episcopal Church and connections by blood or marriage to Asa Packer.

Sayre, in particular, had ties throughout the upper crust. He was married four times. One of the three daughters by his first wife married Robert P. Linderman, son of Garrett Linderman and one of Packer's daughters. Another married an official of Elisha P. Wilbur's bank. Sayre's second wife, a widow, was Garrett Linderman's aunt by marriage. His third wife was one of Packer's daughters.

Sayre and his associates heeded the admonition from their Episcopal priests that God had blessed them and they had done well, but now it was time to "do good." The elite followed their sense of noblesse oblige, the idea that responsibility came with power.

Packer used $500,000 to found Lehigh University in South Bethlehem in 1865 as a private, Episcopal school to teach engineering. He, Sayre and others started St. Luke's Hospital in Fountain Hill in 1873 to care for workers injured on the railroad and at the plant. They provided a company store for the workers and their families, though not housing. They set up soccer clubs to encourage young men to take part in athletics. For girls, there was an Episcopal school, Bishopthorpe Manor.

The oligarchs' active role stemmed partly from semi-feudal ideals and concepts in pre-industrial America and the Episcopal Church.

In the 18th century and early in the 19th century, employers felt personally responsible for their apprentices or clerks. When the head of a business spoke of "family," he meant his employees as well as his wife and children. He believed it was his duty to see that workers had a decent wage and a place to live and stayed warm in the winter. He took it on himself to care for their families.

That attitude was rooted in the medieval concept that a lord had to offer peasants protection in his castle in return for their willingness to farm his land and provide food.

When England began to industrialize, the system came under stress. The same thing happened when industry emerged in America.

As a devout member of the Episcopal Church, which was the American branch of the Church of England, Sayre was familiar with the spirit of obligation toward workers and abided by it. He and others in power sought a conservative ideal: Preserve the social contract between workers and owners as a means to promote a stable society.

Paternal leadership made sense in economic terms as well. Sayre believed that by providing a hospital, schools and athletics, the masters of industry were making their workers happy and more productive. They were also making the community a better place to live.

But noblesse oblige had its limits. The overriding one was that Bethlehem Iron's owners did not consult the workers about what was good for them. The owners said: This is what we're giving you. Defer to us, because we're your betters. We're educated and successful, and you're not, so we know what's best for you. Just follow our model and lead good Christian lives, and you'll be fine.

Bethlehem Iron's workers couldn't stomach that. They could see how well Sayre and his colleagues lived, while their own lot was to work long hours in savage heat and often deplorable conditions. The early iron- and steelmaking processes did not have electric power, so all machinery movement was steam-driven and hydraulic, which made for tedious and dangerous work. The men would go home dog-tired and pray that their aches and pains wouldn't keep them from the sleep they needed to work another day.

They weren't desperate, but they were poor. Because many were skilled tradesmen, they earned enough to provide the basics for their families but couldn't afford the finer things. They paid rent to entrepreneurs and real estate speculators to live in houses within walking distance of the plant or close enough to row a boat there.

With all that, they didn't want management shoving values down their throats.

Particularly troublesome for Sayre, judging from entries in his diaries, were the Irish, who had first come to South Bethlehem as laborers helping to build the railroad and made up a third of the borough's population. They would work intensively for a while, then walk off the job whenever they wanted. They didn't take well to paternalism, especially when it came from Episcopalians, whose attitudes seemed close to that of the English landlords they had fled Ireland to escape. And as Catholics, the Irish resented the view widely shared by Protestant Americans that they were a dangerous foreign influence.

Though someone like Sayre would never think of demanding that his workers join the Episcopal Church, the overwhelming impression left by Lehigh University, St. Luke's Hospital and other church-related institutions of the time was that the Episcopal Church was clearly superior to others.

Sayre might have contributed to that image through his visible commitment to the faith. When there was no church to attend, he invited fellow worshippers into his home for services, then founded the Church of the Nativity in the mid-1860s, as his father had founded St. Mark's in Mauch Chunk. And he taught Sunday school to workers every week, using two chapels, one at either end of the Bethlehem Iron plant.

Still, he would note in his diary at the end of a year that even though he had done well financially, his spiritual worth had fallen short.

"All going well with me except in a religious point of view," Sayre wrote on the last day of 1858. "Have progressed backwards this year, I fear. Hope with God's help to do better next."

Beyond matters of faith, Sayre and the other Bethlehem Iron directors did not limit workers' activities or behavior outside the plant. But inside, when it came to labor relations and unions, Sayre had little patience. In 1877, when Lehigh Valley Railroad workers joined a nationwide rail strike, Sayre "went fishing" until they returned to work on his terms, according to his diary.

He also adhered to a class system. For example, he protected Lehigh University boys who had gotten local girls pregnant. If they were working-class girls, they got nothing. If they were from middle-class families, as most were, Sayre arranged for them to have their babies in remote Bradford County, where he had tended mules many years earlier. The babies would be adopted, and the girls would return. They always got a cash settlement.

In 1879, Sayre lost his mentor. Asa Packer died in Philadelphia, leaving control of the railroad to his two sons, who squeezed Sayre out. "The boys have come to scalp me and have brought the hatchet," he scrawled in his diary.

Dismissed three years later, Sayre wrote bitterly: "I commenced work on the Lehigh Valley Railroad on May 11, 1852, and after serving it faithfully for 30 years I was finally given evidence of the desires of Judge Packer's family to get rid of me. So I have arrived at the conclu-

sion that honesty and faithfulness do not count for much in this world."

He went to work for the newly formed South Pennsylvania Railroad, which never laid a track but did plot the route that would become the Pennsylvania Turnpike.

Sayre outlived Packer's sons, however, and returned to the Lehigh Valley Railroad. But with much of America's rail network in place, he now focused on running Bethlehem Iron. The company had come to yet another critical crossroads. It had to deal with the threat from the west.

Until the 1870s, eastern Pennsylvania was the center of the iron industry partly because it had plenty of anthracite. But a different fuel was toppling hard coal's reign. Soft, better-burning bituminous coal emerged as the new king, as western Pennsylvania followed the east in running out of timber for charcoal. Bituminous coal's derivative, coke, is more efficient than anthracite.

The rise of coke-fired furnaces in the western part of the state, where Pittsburgh and the Monongahela Valley sat atop the world's greatest source of coal for coke, helped doom the Lehigh Valley's dominance of the iron industry. The Panic of 1873 and soaring costs of hauling anthracite also played a role.

Though Bethlehem Iron held on while many smaller operators went bankrupt, Andrew Carnegie and other Pittsburgh area steel producers now held the advantage. Their plants, which stretched for miles along the Monongahela River, came out on top even when Fritz thought he'd developed a way to one-up them.

In the two years after Fritz built the Bessemer plant, Bethlehem Iron had increased its capacity to make pig iron by adding two blast furnaces that were among the largest in the country, with blowing engines that delivered high-pressure blasts. Bethlehem was still using anthracite to smelt iron ore, so Fritz counted on the big furnaces to burn the hard coal well enough to keep Bethlehem competitive with the west. But he didn't figure that powerful blasts would also work effectively on coke.

"Some of my Western friends came to Bethlehem to see our new furnaces and learn how they were working," Fritz wrote in his autobiography. "They were so well satisfied with the result we had attained by high-pressure blast that they increased their blast pressure … and we were again beaten about as badly as we had been before."

In the late 1870s, Sayre and the company's other directors realized they could no longer make steel rails at a price competitive with the coke-rich companies. They began talking about making armor plate.

In June 1878, Wharton was among the dignitaries who attended the ceremonial launch of two Russian cruisers built at the Cramp & Sons shipyard in Philadelphia. It gave him an idea, according to W. Ross Yates' book, "Joseph Wharton: Quaker Industrial Pioneer."

European navies were equipping their ships with armor plate to shield them from the power of big guns. In Washington, there was talk of building a better navy to protect American shores. With a market for armor plate, and national security tied into it, Wharton suggested Bethlehem Iron consider making armor plate and other heavy forgings.

Fritz embraced the idea. In fact, in his autobiography, he contends he was the one who pressed the directors about the need for building large steel plates for ships, arguing that the nation desperately needed "a good forge and armor-plate plant." Iron was practically useless, he said, as a defense against steel shot and shell.

Earlier, Fritz had badgered the board to diversify the company beyond railmaking. He had recommended making structural shapes, but the directors weren't interested. They maintained that even though Bethlehem rails weren't selling as well, the company was still prosperous and didn't need to take a different path.

Fritz became as exasperated with the Bethlehem board as he had been with Johnstown's directors when they resisted building his experimental three-high rail mill.

But the idea to make heavy forgings, whether it came from Fritz or Wharton, caught on at Bethlehem because, as Wharton observed, the time was right. The United States was waking up and realizing it had perhaps the world's most inferior navy.

After the Civil War, all of the iron-clad ships were left to rust and rot or were sold to other nations. America turned its attention to shooting buffalo so the Indians could be herded onto reservations, building a transcontinental railroad, absorbing immigrants and reconstructing the South. Keeping coal-hogging steamer vessels was expensive and no longer a priority.

By the 1880s, the U.S. Navy was ranked 12th, not in the world — in the Western Hemisphere. Worldwide, it was ranked at 65, below Chile. America was a huge economic power with a fifth-rate Navy.

After American sailors were killed during a brawl in Valparaiso, Chile, the United States issued a stern warning to the Chilean government. The Chileans, who had just bought new cruisers from Great Britain, dared America, which had junky wooden boats with muzzleloading cannons that were obsolete by the end of the Civil War, to start a war. Both sides agreed to negotiate and settle the dispute.

Still, a 19th century aphorism held that "trade follows the flag." That meant a country pulled up with a big ship, put its guns out, raised its flag and negotiated an unequal treaty with a lesser power to force the weaker country to buy goods. Countries that didn't have ships with big guns didn't get respect.

And America didn't have ships with big guns. Bethlehem Iron would change that.

The Navy would soon begin awarding contracts for construction of steel warships. Bethlehem had an opportunity to provide these ships with guns, armor and machinery. But to do the work, the company needed a place to make heavy steel forgings.

"We will build the plant," Director Elisha P. Wilbur told Fritz, who then sailed to Europe to study the technology and secure the patent rights. Fritz also got the go-ahead to build an open-hearth plant, another component Bethlehem needed to accommodate the Navy.

An open-hearth furnace looked like a huge oven, with refractory brick making up the roof and side walls. While fires raged first on one end of the hearth and then on the other, hot air was forced from beneath the furnace, up and through ports at either end, spreading flames across the hearth and above the metal in the "bath." The process burned out the metal's impurities.

The new technology was better than Bessemer for several reasons. Unlike a Bessemer converter, which fed only on molten iron, open hearths could make steel from cold pig iron and scrap as well, and even from a combination of all three.

Open hearths gave steelmakers the power of precision and the ability to make steel with a wider range of qualities. After charging the furnace, workers could pull out samples at intervals and add ingredients to get the exact chemical properties required for the kind of steel they were making. When they tapped the furnace, the steel flowed out through a brick-lined chute into a ladle, into which they added spiegeleisen. Then, as in the Bessemer process, it was poured into iron molds and became solidified as ingots. The ingots were removed from the molds and reheated so they were malleable enough to be shaped.

The process took much longer than Bessemer — eight to 10 hours instead of 20 minutes — but closer control meant higher-quality steel with greater strength, which was what the Navy demanded. Another advantage was that an open hearth could produce 20 tons of liquid steel in a "heat," compared to 8 tons in a Bessemer blast.

Armed with the knowledge Fritz gleaned in Steelton and Europe, Bethlehem Iron was ready when the government sought proposals and won a $4 million defense contract in 1887. It spent the next four years building up operations to make gun forgings and armor for the Navy. Designed by Fritz, the heavy-forging plant became America's first.

Meanwhile, South Bethlehem was booming. Its residents numbered about 2,000 when it was incorporated as a borough separate from its neighbor across the river, the borough of Bethlehem. Twenty-five years later, in 1890, South Bethlehem's population had rocketed to 10,300.

Real estate speculators, who first came to town when they heard the railroads would go through it, continued to buy property and start businesses in hopes of making lots of money fast, and would do so for decades. Local contractors, employing hundreds of carpenters, were busy building houses for the iron and steel workers, who in the mid-1880s numbered more than 3,000. Including their families, about 7,000 people depended on the company.

Bethlehem Iron thrived, becoming the steelmaker the U.S. government turned to for propeller shafts, steam engine parts, armor plate, guns and shells.

Though Carnegie Steel Co. began making armor plate after Bethlehem Iron fell behind in its output, Carnegie didn't make guns. On the advice of his top executive, Charles M. Schwab, Carnegie chose not to sink $2 million into a new plant because Schwab didn't think gunmaking would be profitable. Besides, Carnegie was a pacifist.

Bethlehem Iron grew into a leader in the heavy forgings market partly because Sayre, Fritz and Fritz's assistant, metallurgist Russell W. Davenport, practiced a sensible business philosophy. They would pay steep prices to import cutting-edge methods and machinery from Europe, then make them better and more cost-effective than what the Europeans had. For example, Bethlehem Iron had a 14,000-ton press, the biggest forging press in the world.

Even the buildings were gigantic. Fritz built the No. 2 Machine Shop, which housed lathes and other machine tools, 1,779 feet long, almost a third of a mile. At 300,000 square feet, it was the world's largest machine shop. It would turn out battleship guns 60 to 70 feet long, and on some days, 20 to 30 naval guns. The cavernous shop was still standing in 2004. But its future was in doubt because a developer seeking to build on the site was considering tearing it down.

In 1891, Bethlehem Iron scored with the Army, getting a $4 million contract to make big guns. It made the armor and cannons for the Navy's first two steel battleships, one of which suffered a fate that propelled America into war with Spain.

"Heard this morning of the blowing up of the U.S. battleship Maine in the harbor of Havana," Sayre wrote in his diary for Feb. 16, 1898. "Great excitement all over the country. Reports that it was done by the Spaniards, but generally thought to be accidental."

The ships that won the Spanish-American War's battles at Santiago, Cuba, and Manila Bay in the Philippines had Bethlehem armor, Bethlehem engines and propulsion parts, and fired Bethlehem guns and Bethlehem shells.

The company's critical role in the war effort has passed into the realm of myth. According to an often-told tale, when the triumphant American fleet steamed up the Hudson River in August 1898, Sayre stood with President William McKinley on the reviewing platform in New York.

But the truth is that McKinley did not attend the ceremony, and though Sayre did, he was in the crowd, not among the officials on the stand.

Though Bethlehem's forging plant was best known for powering the Navy, it also served other purposes. It developed parts for electric power plants, especially heavy steel rotors to generate electricity, and built the center shaft of the first Ferris wheel, introduced in 1893 at the Columbian Exposition in Chicago.

The workers responsible for this prodigious output were generally treated better than those at plants that were larger and not as specialized, such as Andrew Carnegie's mammoth Homestead Works in Allegheny County.

Bethlehem employees made high-value products. One mistake on the factory floor could turn a thousand-dollar piece of steel into scrap.

Also, Sayre and the others in the Episcopal elite lived close to the plant, unlike Carnegie, whose Pittsburgh home was 10 miles from his Homestead Works. It made a difference. Each day when Sayre got up and looked out his window, he saw the buildings of Bethlehem Iron. Its smoke and grit were part of him.

At Homestead, the 3,800 workers saw nothing in their daily experience to uplift them, only tedium and a dreary mill. Their strike in 1892 over wage cuts and the company's bid to bust their union, the Amalgamated Association of Iron and Steel Workers, erupted into a confrontation with security agents that left 10 men dead.

Nevertheless, Bethlehem Iron was a hot, grimy, noisy and perilous place where men labored in difficult conditions day after day. But it had no union and saw no violence.

Beginning in the 1880s, the face of its work force changed. Germans and Irishmen were joined by immigrants from eastern and southern Europe eager to share in America's abundance. In the unforgiving heat of a blast furnace, they could prove their worth and provide a little more for their families than the old country allowed.

The new workers, coming mainly from the Austro-Hungarian and Russian empires, made South Bethlehem one of the most ethnically diverse communities in the country. Poles, Czechs, Slovaks, Turks, Slovenes, Ukrainians, Greeks, Italians and others built social clubs and churches that provided support as well as fellowship in a time when companies didn't offer health insurance or pensions. Like the Germans and Irish before them, they were overwhelmingly white Christians, reflecting the population of the Lehigh Valley, which had few if any racial or religious minorities.

Blacks, in particular, were not welcome at the plant. Bethlehem Iron discouraged them from applying for jobs, which might explain why South Bethlehem had so few — 115 of 13,000 residents at the end of the 19th century. Even in the 1920s, when Southern blacks came north for industrial jobs made available because of restricted foreign immigration, Bethlehem Steel didn't hire them. Instead, the company recruited Mexicans.

As Bethlehem Iron's work force was diversifying, the men who had managed the company for three decades were getting old. Fritz retired as general superintendent in 1892. Revered in the industry, he died in 1913. But his reputation lives. The Fritz Engineering Laboratory, which he designed, built and donated to Lehigh University, is a center for studies in structural engineering. The John Fritz Medal, presented annually for scientific or industrial achievement, is the highest award in the engineering profession.

Sayre's long ride with the Lehigh Valley Railroad ended in 1898. Laid low by the depression of 1893-97, the railroad slipped into the hands of investment banker J. Pierpont Morgan. Sayre once again was forced out — "a cold return after 45 years of service," he scribbled in his diary on Jan. 4, 1898.

A week later, he was still bitter.

"All right, my boy, I will get even with you if I live long enough," he wrote, referring to the railroad president who banished him.

But Sayre stayed on the board of Bethlehem Iron, and in the spring of 1899, he and the other major stockholders — directors Wharton, Wilbur and Robert Linderman, Garrett's son — reorganized and expanded the company. Even though Bethlehem Iron had grown over the years, it still had only $5 million in capital, far less than what it was worth.

"They had for years kept the company grossly undercapitalized, with the result that dividends were exceptionally high and very little of the stock changed hands on the open market," Yates says in his biography of Wharton, Bethlehem Iron's largest stockholder and the donor who launched the University of Pennsylvania's Wharton School.

First the directors boosted the company's capital 50 percent, to $7.5 million. Then they came up with a new name, one that matched the product they had been making for a quarter-century. It rang with power when spoken, but at first had no substance.

The company whose guns and ships would continue to play a key role in smashing the nation's enemies in wartime, whose beams and columns in the decades ahead would hold up buildings and bridges that could not be attempted before, whose name would resonate around the world as a symbol of corporate strength, was born as a mere shell.

The new Bethlehem Steel Co. was a holding company. It was set up on April 17, 1899, with a planned $15 million to hold the Bethlehem Iron Co. The idea was to use the sale of new Bethlehem Steel stock to enlarge the plant and buy additional machinery and properties. Bethlehem Iron would co-exist with Bethlehem Steel under a 999-year lease. As part of the deal, the holding company would spend at least $3 million to improve Bethlehem Iron over the next 10 years.

Sayre and the other old stockholders arranged a nifty stock purchase that allowed them to make large, unearned profits. It was a gift from the company, Yates says in his book, that "was obscure to all but an inner circle."

While these changes were taking place, the South Bethlehem plant hosted the world's first efficiency expert. Frederick W. Taylor had dabbled with scientific management while a foreman in the machine shop at the Midvale Steel Co. in Philadelphia. He believed that companies would be more efficient if they rewarded workers according to their performance. That way, good workers would have an incentive to do better. He also believed in the importance of improving machinery to save time and money.

In the spring of 1898, Bethlehem Iron's directors hired him to make their plant more efficient, in particular to streamline operations in No. 2 Machine Shop. But Taylor got off on the wrong foot by trying to reshuffle top management.

Arrogant and pushy, he spent a good deal of time annoying people, including the company's directors, with his time and motion studies. He did, however, add to Bethlehem Iron's prestige by overseeing the development of high-speed cutting tools. The tools, according to the company, made it possible "to double or triple the best previous speeds of machining." A pleased Sayre noted in his diary that the new high-speed tool steel, by cutting more steel faster, boosted output. The process revolutionized machine shop practices around the world.

Nevertheless, Bethlehem's directors frowned at Taylor's finding that only 140 men were needed to handle raw materials in the yards, not the more than 400 who were now doing the work.

"They did not wish me, as they said, to depopulate South Bethlehem," Taylor recalled, complaining that "when they saw we were cutting the labor force down to about one-fourth, they did not want it."

Nor did they like other suggestions he made for cutting costs and raising production levels. In April 1901, they fired him.

As for Sayre, his role in Bethlehem steel-making came to a halt four months later, when the Bethlehem Iron Co. ceased to exist. He ended an eight-year stint as president of Lehigh

University's board of trustees in 1905. Two years later, he died at age 81. He had outlived three of his four wives and had 12 children. One of them said of his father, "In fact, with one eye he saw more than anyone else that I know."

The railroad Robert Sayre built with Asa Packer would run for decades, until April 1, 1976, when, neglected and bankrupt after 129 years, it was absorbed by the government-sponsored Consolidated Rail Corp.

Sayre's other business interest would live long after him as well. In less than half a century, the Bethlehem Iron Co. had advanced from making rails to forging big guns and armor plate for great warships. It had turned farmland and a railroad junction into the home of a sprawling, spark-spitting plant teeming with workers.

Now, on the eve of the 20th century, the new Bethlehem Steel Co. was a successful but small enterprise with hopes of becoming larger. That would happen, and in dramatic fashion,

but not in the way its managers intended. Instead, control would soon pass to an outsider. The craftsman-like atmosphere at the plant would dissolve into employment of the masses, ultimately involving tens of thousands of people. And a new, hard-nosed drive to produce more steel at less cost would shatter the Episcopal elite's compact with the workers.

Benevolent leadership like Sayre's, it turned out, wasn't suited to Bethlehem Steel's emerging role as an industrial giant. In the years ahead, a rift between labor and management would widen and bring fateful consequences.

Several weeks after Bethlehem Steel's directors dismissed Taylor, they sold the company to steel titan Charles M. Schwab.

Schwab buried the old Bethlehem Iron Co. in the departed century and initially mired its descendant in a scandalous merger. But he ultimately expanded and diversified Bethlehem Steel beyond anyone's imagination but his own.

Asa Packer

John Fritz

Robert Sayre

CHAPTER
THREE

The king of steel

Cherry trees brought to Washington as a gift from Japan were in wondrous bloom that spring of 1918. But they gave a false sign of hope, as the carnage of World War I continued and a terrible flu spread through U.S. military camps on the way to becoming an epidemic that would kill 20 million people around the world.

Charlie Schwab hadn't come to the nation's capital to see the blossoms or any other tourist sights. He was there on business as head of the second largest steelmaker in America, waiting in the Oval Office of the White House for President Woodrow Wilson to appear.

Schwab had just finished a tense lunch with his No. 2 man from the Bethlehem Steel Corp., Eugene G. Grace, and Bainbridge Colby, a member of the U.S. Shipping Board, the agency in charge of providing cargo and troop ships for the war against Germany.

The Shipping Board desperately needed Schwab's help.

With the Germans on the offensive in the First World War, disaster loomed in Europe. Unless many more U.S. troops and supplies could reach France quickly, the Allies might collapse on the Western Front. But America didn't have enough ships and couldn't build good ones fast enough. Dock workers wallowed in construction delays, unable to get all the materials they needed, and bosses let poor workmanship pass.

The Shipping Board wanted a prominent businessman on deck to run the shipbuilding program and fire up the builders. Its first choice, automaker Henry Ford, gave a flat-out no.

Next was Charles Michael Schwab, the 56-year-old chairman of Bethlehem Steel, the largest shipbuilder in the world. Summoned to Washington in April, he met with three men from the Shipping Board who told him that he'd been drafted.

Oh no, I haven't, Schwab replied. I'm already building ships for the war, it's a full-time job, and I've put up millions of dollars of my own money so my plants can do the work. Besides, how can I give out government contracts to my own company?

We'll work something out, the board members said.

But a full day of bending Schwab's ear yielded only his promise to think it over, according to Robert Hessen's book, "Steel Titan: The Life of Charles M. Schwab," the only biography of Schwab and the source for most of the information in this chapter.

Schwab went home. Called again to Washington soon afterward, on April 16, he still was not persuaded as Colby, at the lunch, tried earnestly to enlist him. Grace urged his boss not to give in.

Time was running out for a 2 p.m. appointment with the president and Colby had exhausted his arguments, so he escorted the visitors to the Oval Office. As Schwab waited, he probably thought about how he would say no to the president, not because he hadn't supported him in the election, but because his company was busy producing ships and armaments. Bethlehem Steel needed him. He couldn't afford to turn away.

Wilson came into the office from an inner room and immediately strode to the portly Schwab, who was dressed in a modest suit and tie, stood about 5 feet 10 inches tall and had graying brown hair swept to the right over the top of his forehead.

Putting both hands out, the slim, bespectacled president greeted Schwab warmly, looked deep into his eyes, thanked him for agreeing to help the government and called him a patriot.

Schwab was stunned. He hadn't agreed to anything. Wilson's aides must have misinformed him or he had heard them wrong.

Still, Schwab must have known why the president of the United States would assume he was willing to take on the challenge.

From his boyhood in the Allegheny Mountains of western Pennsylvania to the present, he had succeeded wherever he turned. Leading by instinct, with relentless energy and optimism, a magnetic grin and eyes that flashed with good humor, he had reached the pinnacle of the American steel industry.

He had been president of the Carnegie Steel Co. in the 1890s. Then at the turn of the century he helped organize the largest industrial company in history, the U.S. Steel Corp., and was its first chief executive. Then he took over a small enterprise, Bethlehem Steel, and in a decade made it U.S. Steel's main competitor.

The decision he made as he stood toe to toe with Wilson would catapult him to even greater heights.

Ahead lay the towering achievements of the 1920s and '30s, when Schwab's Bethlehem Steel Corp. would transform the American landscape with new beauty and utility, girding many of the nation's skyscrapers and long-span bridges. Among them are the Metropolitan Opera House and Woolworth building in New York, the George Washington Bridge in New York and the Golden Gate Bridge in San Francisco.

Partly through his unique knowledge of steel, partly through the cult of personality that he helped promote, Schwab became synonymous with Bethlehem Steel's rise to greatness.

His friend, the inventor Thomas Alva Edison, called him "The Master Hustler." He was a gambler who wore a lucky horseshoe stick pin and "broke the bank" at Monte Carlo. A publicity hound, he had an agent and used a clipping service so he'd know what the newspapers were saying about him. He loved many women, one of them happening to be his wife. He spent millions on a pair of fabulous mansions and traveled in a $100,000 private rail car. He professed to love the working man, but forced him to labor long hours for low pay while he and his executives got rich. In pursuit of profits, he used cunning and brazen salesmanship. If he thought he could get away with cutting corners, he cheated rather than knuckle under to people he considered less knowledgeable about the making of steel.

His nurturing of the Bethlehem company would fortify it for the bloodiest conflict in history. With 283,765 people on the payroll during World War II, it turned out more than a thousand ships and a vast store of armaments, cementing America's role as the arsenal of democracy.

Schwab didn't live to see his creation covered in glory. He died a few weeks after the Second World War began. And though he had been wealthy and famous for much of his long life, he was penniless in the end.

"As I sit and look back," he said in 1932 while still wealthy, "I cannot for the life of me understand the whole thing. All I can do is wonder how it all happened. Here I am, a not over-good business man, a second-rate engineer. I can make poor mechanical drawings. I play the piano after a fashion. In fact, I am one of those proverbial jack-of-all-trades who are usually failures. Why I am not, I can't tell you."

He might not have been anything if his mother hadn't won an argument with his father, snubbing Abraham Lincoln's call to arms in April 1861. Pauline Farabaugh and John Schwab, both of whose parents were German-born Catholics, were married in western Pennsylvania a week after the president appealed for volunteers to put down the rebellious Southern states. John wanted to join the Union Army with his friends. Pauline talked him out of it.

Charles M. Schwab (no relation to the stockbroker of the same name) was born 10 months later, on Feb. 18, 1862, in Williamsburg near the Juniata River. Seven other children would follow. His father and grandfather ran a mill that made blankets and coats for the Union Army.

When he was 12, his family moved about 30 miles west to Loretto, a small center of Roman Catholic piety where his father bought a livery stable and got a contract to carry mail.

Charlie's job was to drive a wagon five miles to the railroad stop at Cresson, get the mail and deliver it to the people in the surrounding villages. Sometimes he took passengers.

The Schwabs' modest living allowed little Charlie few playthings. One Christmas, all he got in his stocking was a marble.

His family loved music, and Charlie had talent and self-confidence. He took singing lessons from a priest who had studied under composer Franz Liszt. His parents bought him an organ and paid his teacher with free meals. He jumped at opportunities to perform in front of an audience, often having major roles in school plays. When he had passengers in his mail wagon, he entertained them and got the nickname "The Singing Cabbie."

Once, when relatives visited on a Sunday afternoon, he amused them with handsprings, magic tricks, jokes and songs, then told them when they got up to go, "I can do something else yet!"

Doing "something else yet, something plus," as Eugene Grace put it many years later, "was a No. 1 Schwab principle."

After grade school, Charlie's intelligence, determination and an almost photographic memory put him at the top of his class at local St. Francis College, which provided high school courses. But he didn't graduate. A torpedoed romance with a pretty, 16-year-old actress from Pittsburgh ended his formal education and led him toward a life in steel.

The girl, Mary Russell, was visiting her sister in Loretto, and Charlie started hanging around their house at all hours to see her. They got googly-eyed over each other, and Mary suggested that with his fine voice and acting ability, he could make the stage his career. He had visions of stardom.

When the pair got engaged, Charlie's parents yelped. They didn't want their bright son marrying an actress or making a living as a lowly entertainer. Charlie threatened to run away with her, but they held him back. And Mary's sister, believing Mary was too young to wed, sent her back to Pittsburgh.

The dashed affair left Charlie moping, and his father thought he needed a taste of the real world. So in 1879, with a year left to go at St. Francis, young Schwab went west to Allegheny County and worked at a grocery and dry goods store in Braddock, home of Andrew Carnegie's Edgar Thomson Steel Works. One customer who regularly came in for cigars was William R. Jones, the plant's general superintendent.

Jones, who was born in Catasauqua and apprenticed at the Lehigh Crane Iron Co. when he was 10, liked Charlie's spunk and hired him as a stake driver on a surveying crew for $1 a day. Charlie pretended to know more than he did and was so convincing and so quick to learn that he soon rose to draftsman and then chief engineer.

For fun in his spare time, he studied Egyptology and the pyramids and read about his idol, Napoleon Bonaparte. For extra cash, he gave piano and organ lessons.

In 1883, when he was 21, he married Emma Eurania Dinkey despite his mother's disapproval. "Rana," whose family had moved to Braddock from Weatherly in Carbon County, was Presbyterian, not Catholic like the Schwabs.

At the steelworks, Jones grew tired of delivering his daily report to Carnegie, who lived 10 miles away in Pittsburgh, and started sending Schwab instead.

On one trip, Carnegie was late getting to his parlor, and Schwab played the piano while waiting for him. When Carnegie came into the room, Schwab stopped, but Carnegie told him to continue. He liked songs from his native Scotland and asked Schwab if he could play some at a party. Schwab spent the next three days learning Carnegie's favorites. With his smooth baritone voice and playing, Schwab was a hit with the boss and his guests.

Carnegie liked Schwab because he was fun to be around. When the boss checked on his mills, he saw dour managers with worried looks on their faces. But Schwab was different. He was easygoing, vibrant and uproarious. His jokes had Carnegie hooting and doubling over with laughter.

Schwab had a serious side as well, and always tried to improve himself. To learn about metallurgy, he set up a chemistry lab in his house and experimented at night.

When Carnegie needed a new general superintendent at his Homestead Works, Schwab got the job. He was only 24. Three years later, after Jones was killed in a furnace explosion, Schwab succeeded him as head of the Edgar Thomson Works, the largest steel plant in the country.

Schwab proved himself a keen motivator. Instead of needling and punishing his employees when they didn't perform well, he encouraged them with incentives, bonuses and promotions. He believed that men respond to challenges, that it's their nature to be competitive.

His theory served him well. The workers, who considered him fair and honest, met his expectations, and Carnegie was delighted with the Edgar Thomson plant's productivity. Schwab, he saw, was a superb manager with an excellent grasp of the business.

After the bloody Homestead strike of 1892 had fizzled, but while relations between workers and management were still raw, Carnegie transferred Schwab to Homestead to patch the wounds. He succeeded. And when 200 diehard strikers gave up and returned to the plant, Schwab boosted his standing among the employees by welcoming back each holdout.

"My feeling is that the average working man is a better man than the rest of us," he told Wall Street Journal owner Clarence Barron many years later during one of his annual steamship rides to Europe. "He is a good, loyal citizen and family man."

But for all of Schwab's skill at running a plant and managing people, he wasn't above cheating. One case was so serious, it came to the attention of President Grover Cleveland.

In 1893, the government accused Schwab of heading a conspiracy to defraud the Navy. While running the Homestead plant, according to the charges, he had knowingly sold substandard armor plate for ships, which some officials said could have put American sailors in peril.

Cleveland agreed with a Navy board of

inquiry that the armor plate should have been of better quality. He endorsed a fine against Carnegie Steel, but the amount was less than the Navy wanted. His decision, in effect, was a compromise.

Critics weren't satisfied. In Congress, a House subcommittee was formed to investigate whether Schwab authorized or allowed fraudulent practices. The most serious charges were that he failed to follow the Navy's specifications for armor plate, that he falsified test results and covered up defects, and that he had secretly re-treated plates so that they would pass a ballistics test.

Schwab, in his testimony, said that because the Navy wasn't knowledgeable about steel-making, it shouldn't be prescribing the armor-making process, but should only be concerned with results.

He admitted tampering with preliminary test results and hiding surface defects, but said that was to please Navy inspectors, who didn't know enough to see that the steel was actually of high quality. He said the plates for the ballistics test were re-treated as an experiment, and Navy officials weren't told because they "were not practical men and they would not have understood this thing."

The subcommittee found Schwab's arguments fell short and concluded that the results of his actions "would be the sacrifice of the lives of our seamen in time of war, and with them, perhaps, the dearest interests of our nation." It upheld the Navy's original findings and the reduced fine set by the president.

Carnegie, who was lashed in the press, stood by Schwab and in 1897 made him president of the Carnegie Steel Co., which had Homestead, Edgar Thomson and two other plants in the Pittsburgh area. He chose Schwab mainly because the two shared a belief in the importance of producing a high volume of steel at the lowest cost. Schwab swung the ax and drove up Carnegie Steel's profits.

Early in 1901, Schwab arranged a merger of Carnegie's interests and the steel interests of investment banker J. Pierpont Morgan to create U.S. Steel Corp., which combined 190 companies into the largest steelmaker in America and the world's first billion-dollar corporation.

Schwab had become rich working for Carnegie, who retired after selling out to Morgan, but the U.S. Steel deal made him even richer. Having owned 6 percent of Carnegie Steel, he got $25 million in the new corporation's bonds.

In April 1901, the 39-year-old Schwab became the company's first president and moved to corporate headquarters in New York, which became his playground. He dived into the social scene and began building a block-long mansion modeled after a French chateau.

He called his new home Riverside. Situated on Riverside Drive between 74th and 75th streets in Manhattan, it was the biggest private residence in the city — four stories high, made of steel and granite, with 90 bedrooms, a swimming pool, a bowling alley, a gymnasium, a wine cellar, an art gallery stocked with masterpieces, and its own power plant. It would take four years and $8 million to build, furnish and decorate.

Among the contents was a $100,000 organ on which Schwab had his personal organist play classics. As a finishing touch, Schwab had 100 Flemish women brought to America to weave tapestries to cover the pipes.

Schwab kept masseurs and three French chefs on call 24 hours a day. Not having the patience to sit through an entire opera, he hired Metropolitan Opera players to come and perform highlights from arias he liked.

"I suppose I am too much of a realist," he said, "to appreciate a man or a woman taking 20 minutes to die, warbling all the time."

Among the entertainers was famed tenor Enrico Caruso, who performed for Schwab and his guests for $10,000 a night.

For other pleasures, Schwab bedded Broadway showgirls. He also had a long affair with Boston businesswoman Myrtle Hayes that ended when he learned she had forged his name to $24,000 in promissory notes. In 1924, she admitted her guilt in court.

Unfortunately for Schwab, his days at the U.S. Steel office weren't as lighthearted as his night life. Hoping to run the company the way

THREE

he saw fit, he instead had to butt heads with a Morgan associate who was above him in the chain of command — Elbert Gary, the chairman of U.S. Steel's Executive Committee.

Opposites in manner and business philosophy, Schwab and Gary scraped against each other like tectonic plates. Schwab was a boisterous libertine who gambled, craved publicity and had mistresses. Gary was a preachy, teetotaling Methodist, reserved and respectable.

Schwab, who had worked in steel plants since he was a boy, slashed costs and prices, offered bonuses to workers and managers for jobs well done and liberally spent money for expansion.

Gary had been a lawyer and a judge with a reputation for honesty. As a businessman, he was a consolidator who wanted to make U.S. Steel's holdings more efficient, not add to them. He sought stable prices and harmony among competitors and didn't believe in bonuses for individual performance.

As Schwab had demonstrated with the Navy in the armor-plate scandal, he hated having to deal with people he believed didn't know the practical side of steelmaking. He tried to sidestep Gary's authority, and Gary responded by reining him in.

"Judge Gary, who had no real knowledge of the steel business, forever opposed me on some of the methods and principles that I had seen worked out with Carnegie — methods that had made the Carnegie company the most successful in the world," Schwab said later.

In May 1901, about eight weeks after joining U.S. Steel, Schwab bought the Bethlehem Steel Co. for himself. Bethlehem was a small, specialized company that made heavy steel forgings for guns and marine engines and was the only company other than U.S. Steel that produced armor plate. It had 4,000 workers, a plant that stretched for a mile and a half along the Lehigh River and substantial earnings that would total $1.4 million that year.

Bethlehem Steel's directors had taken steps to expand when they reorganized the company in 1899. But then came the U.S. Steel merger, which left Bethlehem out. Schwab later said Bethlehem wasn't included because it offered nothing but duplication.

Facing a giant with a lock on the nation's steel market, Bethlehem's directors decided to sell. Schwab got the company for $7.2 million.

He hadn't been the only party knocking on Bethlehem's door. Joseph Wharton, the company's largest stockholder, had been negotiating with Vickers' Sons & Maxim Ltd., the British maker of guns, armor plate and warships, which had teamed with the Cramp Shipbuilding Co. of Philadelphia. But Vickers-Cramp was rejected after offering $22.50 for each of Steel's 300,000 shares.

Robert Sayre, another large stockholder along with Robert Linderman and Elisha P. Wilbur, wrote in his diary that Bethlehem Steel rejected the offer because Vickers-Cramp "wanted the time given for examination of the works extended. Damn foolishness."

Meanwhile, Linderman was negotiating with Schwab. On May 30, 1901, two days after the Vickers-Cramp bid failed, Linderman sealed a deal with Schwab, who had made a counteroffer of $24 per share.

"It's such a strange thing," says Lehigh University technology historian John Kenly Smith Jr. "Schwab makes an offer to Bethlehem which is slightly higher than Vickers' and they take it. Why don't they then go back to Vickers and say: We got a better offer. You want to come back with another offer? But no, they sell to Schwab."

Several factors probably came into play. Bethlehem Steel's stockholders might have preferred Schwab as a way of keeping their company out of foreign hands. And Schwab, even though he bought Bethlehem Steel as a personal investment, was the president of U.S. Steel, which controlled 60 percent of the nation's steelmaking business and had an interest in seeing the Vickers syndicate thwarted.

If Vickers grabbed Bethlehem, the British conglomerate would have an opportunity to make deep inroads into the American steel and shipbuilding industries, cutting into U.S. Steel's dominance. The idea that Vickers was about to buy Bethlehem Steel "was unpalatable to U.S. Steel," Smith says.

But America's largest steelmaker was helpless to prevent Vickers from taking over Bethlehem. As a mammoth corporate entity, U.S. Steel could not have bought the little company for itself, given the antitrust climate in Washington. President Theodore Roosevelt would not have allowed U.S. Steel to absorb its only competitor in the armaments trade, because that would have reinforced U.S. Steel's position as a monopoly.

"Here's Bethlehem Steel, a firm that's a major supplier of the government," Smith says, "and all of a sudden it's going to be part of a monopoly? Politically, it couldn't have flown. Teddy Roosevelt and Congress were very suspicious of large new firms like U.S. Steel. They thought they were just going to use their power to jack up prices and profits."

Another factor was national pride. Officials in Washington would not have accepted the idea of Bethlehem Steel's being owned by British interests, Smith says. "Is Congress going to be happy with the fact that we're buying all our battleship armor and guns from a British firm?"

So it was the offer from Vickers, according to Smith, that led Schwab, the U.S. Steel president, to buy Bethlehem Steel. The sale was completed smoothly during the summer of 1901. On Aug. 15, Bethlehem Iron's stockholders accepted Schwab's offer, and the lease between the iron company and its holding company, Bethlehem Steel, was canceled.

Bethlehem Iron, formed by Asa Packer, Robert Sayre and their associates four decades earlier to make rails for the Lehigh Valley Railroad, vanished from the ledger books. Schwab took over the Bethlehem Steel Co., which now had operational control of the iron company's properties.

But he didn't keep it.

J.P. Morgan, who owned the syndicate that underwrote the U.S. Steel merger, apparently frowned on Schwab's ownership of the Bethlehem company. Morgan might have thought Schwab couldn't run it and effectively carry out his duties as president of U.S. Steel.

Schwab turned Bethlehem over to J.P. Morgan & Co. for the price he paid for it, $7.2 million. It stayed in Morgan's hands for almost a year.

In that time, Schwab's grip on U.S. Steel loosened. The beginning of the end came with a public relations nightmare he tumbled into while vacationing in Europe early in 1902.

On Jan. 8, he tooled into Monte Carlo in a roadster and hustled to the roulette tables. A reporter spied him, and wild stories about Schwab's luck at gambling burned up the cables to newspapers on both sides of the Atlantic. "Schwab Breaks the Bank," the New York Sun screamed on Page 1. His play at the tables, the stories said, whipped his audience into a frenzy.

His mentor, Carnegie, frothed in anger. He had always insisted on upright moral and social behavior by his lieutenants, and now Schwab — his favorite — had betrayed him.

Actually, Schwab had always brushed off Carnegie's rules of conduct but had never gotten caught. He even had fathered a daughter by a nurse working in his home. The beautiful redhead was tending to his wife Rana's younger sister, who was recovering from typhoid fever.

But none of his escapades had publicly embarrassed Carnegie.

This time, though, Schwab was nailed in the press for all to see. Carnegie sent him cables laden with sharp rebukes that hurt him deeply. And though Schwab denied the reports of "great winnings and losses," he couldn't calm down the old Scotsman. Back home in February, Schwab suffered an acute anxiety attack over Carnegie's badgering.

"I have been so depressed since my return," he wrote to his ex-boss, "that I only forget your condemnation when plunged in work. It is a nightmare from which I never seem to wake. I don't care for the newspaper criticism — I only mind yours."

Not only had he alienated Carnegie, who had lifted him up as a steelmaker for years, but he was in trouble with U.S. Steel managers who felt that publicity over his naughtiness in Monaco was smearing the company's name.

Only Morgan didn't seem to mind. He dismissed the fuss and told Schwab, "Forget it, my boy, forget it."

But Schwab couldn't. His doctors, concerned about the stress on his heart, told him that he had to get away and rest. So in August 1902, he and Rana and his youngest sister sailed for France, where they would remain for six months.

Before he left, Schwab set the stage for another scandal, one that was far worse than the debacle over his gambling. It would call into question whether he could do business honestly and leave him cleaning out his desk at U.S. Steel. At the center of the controversy was the Bethlehem Steel Co.

Schwab had gotten involved with some investors who were eager to build a construction empire. The investors picked seven shipyards on both coasts and a manufacturing company for a merger into one unit that would be called the U.S. Shipbuilding Co. Schwab offered to sell them Bethlehem Steel, even though he didn't own it at the time.

Dollar signs floated before their eyes. With Bethlehem as an anchor, the new company could build battleships complete with all their armor, guns and equipment.

But the investors couldn't afford Schwab's $9 million price tag or any amount near it, so he hatched another idea: They could have Bethlehem Steel for $10 million in bonds and $20 million in stock, instead of cash. On top of that, Schwab would protect his investment. He wanted a second mortgage on all the shipbuilding properties, full voting power on his bonds and enough orders to guarantee a 6 percent dividend on Bethlehem Steel stock.

It's a deal, the investors said.

Schwab bought Bethlehem Steel back from J.P. Morgan for $7.2 million, then sold Bethlehem's stock to U.S. Shipbuilding. The new business, incorporated in June 1902, included the manufacturing company, the seven shipyards and Bethlehem Steel.

But U.S. Shipbuilding foundered the next year. The only bright spot in the merger was the Bethlehem subsidiary, which did better than expected.

More trouble stirred when Bethlehem's directors and Schwab's representatives on the U.S. Shipbuilding board wouldn't let Bethlehem Steel throw a lifeline to the flailing parent company. Instead, Bethlehem's earnings stayed in South Bethlehem, where they were used to build up the plant and buy iron ore mines in Cuba.

In the spring of 1903, U.S. Shipbuilding was close to sinking. It was short $2 million to run the shipyards and make interest payments on Schwab's bonds.

Schwab came to the rescue, sort of. He agreed to put up the money, but only if his second-mortgage bonds were replaced with first-mortgage bonds, giving him the primary lien on all the company's properties.

That was fine with U.S. Shipbuilding's chief executive and some investors who wanted the company reorganized. But first-mortgage bondholders fought the plan, not wanting Schwab's claims to have priority over their own. In a suit filed in federal court, they charged that U.S. Shipbuilding was insolvent, had been mismanaged and was fraudulently promoted and organized.

The newspapers vilified Schwab, giving front-page coverage to the scandal for a year. His critics saw him as a pirate who had engineered the company's failure so he could pick up the pieces.

Schwab countered it wasn't his fault that the shipyards were failing. He was determined to protect Bethlehem Steel, he said, and didn't feel obligated to risk his assets to salvage the merger.

Still, his actions were questionable.

"There's a shady deal here," says Smith, the Lehigh University historian. "Why does the firm go under? Because Schwab demands that they pay him the interest on his bonds. But Schwab didn't have to foreclose on the company for not paying. He could have just said OK. Instead, he used a legal technicality to screw the firm. Why? There can only be one explanation: He wanted control of it."

But it's unclear why Schwab would want to own poorly performing shipyards.

"Charlie Schwab was not a person whose motives were always rational," Smith says. "He was not a cold, calculating capitalist. He was a romantic and a visionary and something of a speculator and a gambler, so his motives are rather hard to fathom sometimes."

On June 30, 1903, a federal judge accused Schwab of "ruinous extortion," ruled U.S. Shipbuilding insolvent and named a receiver to take over the company until its finances were put in order. That same day, U.S. Steel named an assistant to the president, citing Schwab's poor health.

The move was a first step toward Schwab's resignation, and Schwab had planned it himself. He knew the shipbuilding scandal had hurt his leadership at U.S. Steel and didn't want to be fired or asked to quit. Nor did he want to resign immediately because that would look as though he were admitting guilt. Instead, he would drop out in stages, blaming illness.

A month later, on Aug. 4, Schwab resigned as president of U.S. Steel, saying he was too sick to go on.

In the fall of 1903, the receiver issued a report supporting the allegation that Schwab caused U.S. Shipbuilding to fail. He accused Schwab of cheating the public and pocketing the profits. Schwab denied any wrongdoing, saying the charges were "false and malicious."

A trial examiner heard Schwab's testimony in the suit by the first-mortgage bondholders in January 1904. After that, the receiver suggested settling the dispute by dividing the stock between Schwab and the first-mortgage bondholders. Everyone agreed to the terms.

Schwab lost $996,000 but held on to his little gem, Bethlehem Steel. And little it was, with an ingot capacity that was less than 1 percent of the national total.

Yet Schwab, who had been savaged over Monte Carlo, hounded out of his top-of-the-world job at U.S. Steel and humiliated by the U.S. Shipbuilding fiasco, wasn't about to slink off into the shadows.

"I shall make the Bethlehem plant the greatest armor-plate and gun factory in the world," he said in August while touring the property.

Later, he expanded on that.

"I intend to make Bethlehem the prize steelworks of its class, not only in the United States, but in the entire world. In some respects, the Bethlehem Steel Co. already holds first place. Its armor-plate and ordnance shops are unsurpassed, its forging plant is nowhere excelled, and its machine shop is equal to anything of its kind. Additions will be made to the plant rather than changes in the present process of methods of manufacture."

On Dec. 10, 1904, the Bethlehem Steel Co. took on a new form, becoming the Bethlehem Steel Corp. With $30 million in capital, it was incorporated in New Jersey as a holding company operating the Bethlehem Steel Co. and the wreckage of the U.S. Shipbuilding merger — seven shipyards and the manufacturer.

As president of the corporation, Schwab sold off the unprofitable businesses, saving only three of the shipyards. He moved his office from New York to South Bethlehem.

"I was convinced that no great steel corporation can be managed from New York," he said a decade later, believing that U.S. Steel's directors tied his hands in New York when he should have been at the plants. "I [was] determined to reorganize the Bethlehem Steel Co. and have it managed entirely on the grounds."

He put together a team of 16 managers who were loyal to him, "The Boys of Bethlehem." They created their own corporate community, centered on the boardroom and later the golf course at the Saucon Valley Country Club.

Schwab believed that Bethlehem's future would be in jeopardy if the company relied exclusively on U.S. government contracts for armor plate and ordnance. He pressed for and won a larger share of the European arms market, putting Bethlehem on a level with the big armament makers such as Vickers in Britain and Krupp in Germany.

To take advantage of commercial opportunities, he spent a few million dollars adding facilities U.S. Steel didn't have — a crucible steel plant to make high-quality alloy steels and an open-hearth rail mill, which produced better steel rails than U.S. Steel's Bessemer converters.

He also wanted a product that would give

Bethlehem an advantage in the increasingly competitive structural steel market. To get it, the gambler did what he did best — he rolled the dice, betting that the nation was on the verge of a building binge and that the new structures would reach for the sky.

With real estate prices going through the ceiling in Chicago and New York, 19th century builders couldn't figure out the best way to build upward. They tried using stone, but the mass of the stone needed to support the walls left little interior space. They turned to iron and steel framing, which was used in 1885 to build the first skyscraper, the 10-story Home Insurance Building in Chicago.

Builders soon found that steel was stronger, more malleable and less brittle than iron. But architects were still limited in designing tall buildings. They needed stronger frames.

Engineers knew that beams with wide flanges were the answer. Plates and angles could be riveted together to form sturdy columns. But the process was time-consuming and expensive, and the beams weren't reliable for framing because they weren't uniformly shaped.

Then in 1897, an Englishman named Henry Grey developed a process for rolling wide-flange beams and columns in a single section directly from an ingot. These were beams that didn't need overlapping sections of steel that had to be riveted together. They were stronger, lighter, more adaptable and less expensive to make.

Still, no American steel producer dared to risk millions on a mill with an unproven product. Except Bethlehem.

Schwab realized Grey's beam was as innovative as John Fritz's "three-high" rail mill had been in the previous century. He had wanted to buy the rights to it when he was president of U.S. Steel, but couldn't get the company's Executive Committee under Elbert Gary to go along. Gary didn't believe the beams could be mass-produced.

Now as head of Bethlehem Steel in 1905, Schwab went to Luxembourg to see the first Grey mill in operation and decided that Bethlehem would build the beams and columns. As

a courtesy, he informed Gary, whose response was: Go ahead, we're not interested.

An economic crisis known as the Panic of 1907 put a crimp in Schwab's plans. With the patent rights in hand, Bethlehem needed about $5 million to build the Grey mill. Schwab wanted to float a bond issue, but the stock market collapsed and the money wasn't there. Bethlehem's "Boys" suggested dropping the idea.

Disheartened, Schwab rode a train to New York to think about it. Early the next morning, he phoned his secretary, James H. Ward, and said, "Get up, Wardie, we are going back to Bethlehem and talk to the boys. I've thought the whole thing over, and if we are going bust, we will go bust big."

He talked his suppliers and contractors into providing their services without payment until after the mill was running and showing profits.

The Grey mill and related operations were built on land purchased along the Lehigh River in the Saucon Valley, about a mile east of the main blast furnaces. The mill would form the nucleus of the Saucon Division of the Bethlehem plant, which also included open-hearth furnaces that made the steel, ingot molds, soaking pit furnaces to heat the ingots, and blooming mills. At the blooming mills, ingots were reduced to blooms, semi-finished steel forms with a rectangular cross-section, and to dog bone-shaped sections for further processing in the Grey mill.

Bethlehem began making Grey beams in January 1908, but within six months faced another crisis: It needed $1.5 million to keep operating the mill. Wherever Schwab held out his hand, no money plunked into it.

Enter Andrew Carnegie, who after four years had gotten over Schwab's Monte Carlo foibles and written him a nice letter that made them friends again. Carnegie lent Schwab U.S. Steel bonds as collateral for bank loans.

The new Grey beams, known as "Bethlehem beams," became Bethlehem Steel's corporate symbol. The first building they supported was the new headquarters for the Gimbel Brothers department store in New York City.

They also went into the Chicago Merchandise Mart and the Chicago Opera House.

When architects and builders saw that the beams were effective, orders started pouring in. By the end of the decade, Bethlehem Steel was giving U.S. Steel stiff competition.

But then came a shock — the company's first labor problem.

Both skilled and unskilled workers felt their pay was too low and their hours too long. Machinists worked 10 hours and 25 minutes a day for six days, including Sundays, and five hours and 20 minutes on Saturdays. They made up to 27 cents an hour. Unskilled laborers made 12.5 cents an hour and worked longer hours.

Long hours and dangerous work threatened safety. In the previous year, 10 percent of the 9,200 employees were involved in an accident, and 21 men were killed. When deaths happened, they were horrible. In 1903, Anton Reinfeld, a 43-year-old Austrian immigrant, got caught between two rail cars while working at the company's yards. "The unfortunate man's body was crushed about the hips almost into a jelly," The Morning Call reported. "Both legs were almost severed, and he was hurt about the head. He died soon after being taken to St. Luke's Hospital."

On Feb. 3, 1910, machinists held a work stoppage. They were joined the next day by unskilled laborers. The day after that, the workers voted to strike, with the machinists and laborers supporting one another and vowing not to give in until both groups had gotten more pay.

But the strikers amounted to a minority of the plant's work force and didn't have much pull, even though they got help in organizing from two unions, the International Association of Machinists and the American Federation of Labor.

Schwab offered the machinists one cent more per hour, but they wouldn't take it. The machinists stood by the unskilled laborers.

The strike intensified and spread to other work groups. Two hundred riggers walked out after Schwab refused to raise their hourly pay from 12.5 cents to 20 cents. A picket carried a sign that jabbed at Schwab: "May God Protect Our Homes — Charlie Won't."

Many strikers left Bethlehem for jobs that union organizers found for them. But some learned that Bethlehem Steel's tentacles extended far beyond Pennsylvania.

John Ofchus, a Polish immigrant who helped organize the strike, was no longer welcome at Bethlehem Steel. He tried to find work at a steel plant in Cleveland. He wrote down his name and, when asked where he worked previously, said "Bethlehem Steel." Managers at the Cleveland plant found out that Ofchus helped lead the Bethlehem strike and sent him away. He tried to find work in Chicago, but again was rejected.

At the U.S. Steel plant in Gary, Ind. — the town was named for Elbert Gary — Ofchus told managers that his last name was Wadolny, the surname of his half-brother, Ferdinand Wadolny. He got the job.

His half-brother's son, John Wadolny, who started work in a Bethlehem Steel forge shop in 1934, would go on to become one of the company's most respected union leaders.

The Bethlehem Steel strikers hoped to shut down the plant. Their anger turned away from Schwab to the men who were still working. Fearing violence, the governor sent in the state police.

One person died during the labor strife. A trooper chasing a rowdy striker guided his horse onto the sidewalk in front of the Majestic Hotel, headquarters of the union organizers. He fired into the hotel barroom, where the bullet killed Hungarian immigrant Joseph Szambo, a striker who had gone inside to buy wine to settle his wife's stomach after she had given birth. Trooper John Moughan was charged with manslaughter and acquitted in a trial after witnesses could not identify him.

Schwab, who had always asked workers to call him "Charlie," went up and down the streets, telling the strikers that he could outlast them. "If you can stand it, I can," he taunted.

He loathed unions, believing they got in the way of managers' efforts to cut costs and keep the company competitive. "I won't be in the position of having management dictated to by labor," he declared.

By the end of March, about 500 men were still on strike and 1,000 strikers had left town for jobs in other cities, but the plant was still running at nearly full steam. To replace men who had left, the company had recruited workers from other cities. It's not known how successful that effort was, but strikers had identified 121 "scabs."

At Schwab's urging, Bethlehem's businessmen lashed out at the strike's leaders, accusing them of trying to wreck the local economy.

A federal Bureau of Labor investigation authorized by Congress confirmed that the strikers were right about low wages and long hours at Bethlehem Steel. That came as no surprise to Schwab, but he took issue with the report because it didn't note that these were conditions common throughout the U.S. steel industry.

The strike ended with a whimper on May 18, 1910. The workers — no more than 600 still on strike — had been unable to shut down the plant or hurt the company's business. After 108 days, they had little to cheer about. They accepted Schwab's offer of optional overtime and Sunday work, but got no wage increases.

Despite the agreement, more than a year later workers who refused overtime were still being fired.

The strike was evidence that Bethlehem Steel had entered a new era. Its Grey mill had doubled the size of the plant and altered its character. No longer a place inhabited mainly by craftsmen, the company now needed masses of workers to turn out steel. By 1910, Bethlehem had more than twice as many employees as there were when Schwab took over. Many of them were European immigrants who lived near the plant and frequented the growing number of shops on Third and Fourth streets.

The infusion of workers transformed South Bethlehem into a rollicking, noisy, crowded frontier-like boomtown. Biographer Catherine Drinker Bowen, who lived there and was the daughter of an early Lehigh University president, said the borough was "like another place and another planet, a Wild West of its own." Another resident declared, "There was a vitality here, a basic industrial thrust, a roaring go-ahead, get-ahead atmosphere of America on the move."

Inside the plant, ethnic groups worked in clusters. One department might have all Hungarians; another, all Slovenes. With foremen having the power to hire and fire, they could shape the character of their shops.

The company's leadership had changed as well. Schwab, a Catholic from the western part of the state, tutored in steel by hardened industrialists Carnegie and Morgan, didn't fit in with the old Episcopal elite. Unlike Sayre and his Bethlehem Iron associates, Schwab was an outsider with no strong fealty to the workers or the community.

Nor did he try hard to fit in. His goal was to grow Bethlehem Steel so it could make lots of steel as cheaply as possible and keep using the profits to modernize and expand. In 1912, Schwab arranged for Bethlehem to buy the Tofo Iron Mines in Chile, important because they had large deposits of iron-rich ore. A purchase in 1913 made Bethlehem a major shipbuilder. It got the Fore River Shipbuilding Co., which had a yard in Quincy, Mass., near Boston. Now Bethlehem could build warships completely armored and equipped.

At first, Schwab's aggressive, hands-on style rankled veteran managers, who preferred the old way of doing things. One manager complained that Schwab's production goals were impossibly high. Schwab told him: "If we can get our blast furnace operations to such and such a state of efficiency, I'll pay off the mortgage on your house." Within months, the man accomplished the feat and had a mortgage-free house. Other managers got the message.

The company's accountants were amazed at Schwab's grasp of details. He could memorize 100 pages of cost data in less than an hour and pluck one of the figures from his mind in an instant.

Around him, he created a meritocracy in which a man's position was defined not by religion or ethnic background, but by his place in the company pecking order.

"To us, Schwab was always a dirty name,"

says Robert Packer Linderman Frick, grandson of Robert Linderman, the last president of the Bethlehem Iron Co. "It was a nice, quiet little organization until he came along. Then they had the strike and called in the state police. We didn't have that kind of thing before. But this brash New Yorker had to come in and made us modern."

Schwab bought, renovated and moved into the South Bethlehem mansion of Bethlehem Iron director Garrett Linderman — the house where Garrett's son, Robert, was born. It became known as the Schwab House, but that didn't sit well with the Linderman family.

"My mother used to have a fit every time they talked about the Schwab House," says Frick, of Bethlehem. "'I don't know what you're talking about,' she'd say."

It was her father, Robert Linderman, who had negotiated with Schwab on Bethlehem Steel's sale. In January 1903, about two years after closing the deal, he died from blood poisoning. His death left many local residents grieving.

"They did not realize that as they mourned, the age which Linderman symbolized had also passed away," according to "Bethlehem of Pennsylvania: The Golden Years 1841-1920" by W. Ross Yates. "It succumbed to the era of organization which Schwab was bringing to the Bethlehems."

Schwab's mind was set on building up Bethlehem Steel to make it "the greatest steel plant in the world. By that I mean the largest, most modern, the best equipped, the most highly specialized, and I fear also the most expensive steel works anywhere."

To do that, he was determined to direct the company his own way, without interference from anyone, especially from a union. The strike had stiffened his resolve.

In the summer of 1918, the National War Labor Board found serious morale and pay problems at Bethlehem Steel and demanded the company start bargaining collectively with its workers. Bethlehem Steel ignored the order.

The government kept up the pressure and in the fall, Schwab and corporation President Eugene Grace sought to deflect it with their own scheme — a company union called the Employee Representation Plan. Hatched by Schwab's publicity agent, Ivy Ledbetter Lee, it allowed workers to choose fellow workers as delegates to present grievances to management. But it did not allow them to bargain as equals with the company or to call a strike.

The idea was to make Bethlehem Steel look as though it weren't anti-union, when it was. As a result of the new policy and other issues, the Amalgamated Association of Iron, Steel and Tin Workers couldn't interest Bethlehem Steel workers in unionizing. And when a major steel strike hit the nation in 1919, only about 2,000 of the Bethlehem plant's 13,500 workers walked out to demand union recognition.

Besides keeping out unions, Bethlehem Steel was off-limits to outsiders on its board of directors. Schwab and Grace refused to include influential people from other industries and professions as other big companies did, insisting that only key Bethlehem men with firsthand knowledge of steelmaking should hold positions of authority.

The company's closed system served it well — then.

In the five years after 1910, employment doubled and a war that supercharged the company broke out in Europe.

World War I made Bethlehem one of the biggest and most profitable companies in the world. Even during the buildup that preceded the fighting, Steel had played a major role in the world arms bazaar. One of its customers was a soon-to-be enemy of the Allies, the Imperial Ottoman Empire, which bought ammunition, gun mounts and big guns. The Turks might have used some of these Bethlehem munitions in 1915 to slaughter Australians and New Zealanders at Gallipoli.

Soon after the war broke out in August 1914, Bethlehem received more than $50 million in ordnance orders from Britain and France. It also got the largest order in its history — $135 million from the British navy for howitzers, naval landing guns, shrapnel, shells and most important, 20 submarines.

The submarine deal showed Schwab's

stature and guile.

In October 1914, the British Admiralty secretly asked Schwab to come to London. He met with Winston Churchill, who as the first lord of the admiralty was the civilian head of the Royal Navy. Churchill and other negotiators asked Schwab to build the subs. Schwab wasn't sure Bethlehem could do them all at once, so he cabled his vice president for shipbuilding, H.S. Snyder, who checked with the company's subcontractor, the Electric Boat Co. of New York. Snyder told Schwab that half the subs could be built at Fore River near Boston and half at the Union Iron Works in San Francisco, which Bethlehem got when the U.S. Shipbuilding merger collapsed.

It usually took Bethlehem 14 months to build a submarine; Schwab promised to start delivering them in six months. In addition, he gamely proposed that Britain pay a $10,000 bonus per sub for each week Bethlehem beat a delivery deadline. If the company missed a deadline, it would forfeit $5,000 a sub each week. Churchill agreed, and Schwab went home with a $15 million down payment.

The deal hit a snag when details were leaked to the press, possibly by a German spy in the Admiralty. Schwab was called to Washington, where Secretary of State William Jennings Bryan told him on Dec. 2 that Bethlehem would violate U.S. neutrality if it delivered the subs to Britain.

America would not enter the war until 1917. Vessels intended for belligerent countries could not be fitted out, armed and shipped from U.S. waters when the nation was at peace. However, private trade in weapons, explosives and other war materials was permitted.

Bryan asked Schwab to cancel the submarine order, and Schwab said he'd think about it.

Schwab wasn't willing to give in. He had an idea for how to skirt the neutrality law. He rode a train to Canada and found a shipyard in Montreal that he believed could assemble the subs from parts made by Bethlehem and Electric Boat. It was owned by Canadian Vickers, a subsidiary of the British munitions giant that

was Bethlehem's failed suitor 13 years earlier.

On Dec. 4, Schwab phoned Bryan and said he "would not build submarines for any belligerent country for delivery during the war." The next day, under a false name, he sailed for London to ask Vickers for permission to use the Montreal yard. But first he stopped in at the Admiralty.

Churchill had heard that the Wilson administration opposed the submarine contract. Puffing madly on a cigar and pacing, he scolded Schwab for making a deal Bethlehem couldn't fulfill and wasting Britain's precious time.

When Schwab got a chance to speak, he said there was no problem. Bethlehem would build the subs if it could use the Vickers shipyard.

Churchill and the professional head of the Royal Navy, First Sea Lord John Fisher, were astonished.

"If that's all you want," Fisher blurted, "start back at once and take the yard."

Under a revised agreement, 10 of the submarines would be built in Montreal and the rest at Fore River, which Schwab wanted to use so he could finish the work quickly. He gambled he wouldn't get caught. Bethlehem would collect $100,000 more, or $600,000, for each of the subs fabricated at the Vickers yard. That would allow for what Schwab said was the higher cost of doing business in Canada.

Back in New York on Dec. 23, Schwab explained to reporters that he had gone to London to cancel the submarine deal. He hid what he was doing because Canada was an ally of Britain and a belligerent in the war.

Bethlehem sent two of its shipyard presidents and 500 workers and supervisors to Montreal, where they were sworn to secrecy. Executives told the press that the steel they were sending across the border would help replace bridges destroyed in Europe and was being shipped via Canada.

But the German ambassador to the United States wasn't fooled. Johann von Bernstorff complained to Bryan that Bethlehem Steel was secretly sending submarine parts to Canada, a breach of neutrality. When Bryan asked for an explanation, Bethlehem maintained that the materials were strictly commercial. Technically, the company argued, the parts weren't prohibited because they had to be further fabricated in Montreal before the subs were completed.

Bernstorff protested. He didn't believe what the Wilson administration was telling him: that the subs being built at Fore River and Montreal were not for delivery to Britain. But Wilson had stopped listening.

All 20 submarines were launched by September 1915, and Bethlehem Steel got $4 million in profits and bonuses for speedy delivery.

That year, the Bethlehem plant had 24,500 employees and covered 600 acres stretching for three miles along the Lehigh River. Among its major features were seven blast furnaces, three open-hearth furnace departments, two steel forging departments, seven machine shops, an electric furnace for melting tool steels, and the Grey mill.

During this era, the plant had produced turbines for the Niagara Falls Power Co., a sewage disposal plant for Baltimore, a pumping station for Detroit, heavy-duty pumping engines for Pittsburgh, an armor-plate forging plant for the Carnegie Steel Co. and a 338-ton armor-plate vault for the National Park Bank in New York. In the 1904-05 Russo-Japanese War, it was Bethlehem steel against Bethlehem steel, with the company supplying guns and armor plate for warships to both Russia and Japan.

Among Bethlehem Steel's holdings were the Philadelphia, Bethlehem & New England Railroad, a shipbuilding plant in Wilmington, Del., as well as the yards in San Francisco and Quincy, Mass., and ore mining operations in Cuba and Chile.

With the world war on, the company might as well have had its own money-printing machine. The price of its common stock had risen from $8 a share in 1907, to $30 a share in 1913, to $600 a share in 1915 and to a peak of $700 a share in 1916. It was the third largest industrial company in America, after U.S. Steel and Standard Oil of New Jersey.

"The most remarkable year in Bethlehem's history was 1916," Hessen notes in his book. "Its earnings in that year — over $61 million — exceeded all the gross sales of the first eight, prewar years that the company had been under Schwab's direction."

Before U.S. entry into the war, Germany's Kaiser Wilhelm II was so concerned about Bethlehem's production prowess on behalf of the Allies, he offered $100 million for control of the company. Schwab turned him down. Britain's leaders, hoping to guarantee that Bethlehem Steel would help them until the end, made a counteroffer of $150 million. Schwab rejected that, too, but pledged to keep his commitment to the British.

Bethlehem workers labored day and night building ships and munitions, stepping up their efforts dramatically after America joined the fight in April 1917. They considered themselves in the vanguard of a crusade, as C.B. Meadway of the No. 4 Shop wrote in a poem published in the company newsletter, The Bethlehem Booster, in October 1918.

America, we're making guns for you,
America, they'll shoot both fast and true;
They'll kill a German every minute.
That is what they are made to do.
America, we'll help you win this war.
We'll work and save and fight.
For whenever you're in trouble,
We'll come marching on the double.
America, we're your might.

By the Armistice on Nov. 11, 1918, Bethlehem had produced 60 percent of the guns and 40 percent of the artillery shells ordered by the U.S. government. It had made more than 65 percent of the artillery pieces manufactured by all the allied nations. For Britain and France alone, it produced 20 million artillery rounds, 70 million pounds of armor plate and 1.1 billion pounds of steel for shells.

To handle the work, the company spent more than $102 million on new buildings at the plant and for the first time hired women in significant numbers.

In 1918, the Bethlehem plant employed 31,000 people, 1,000 of them at the company's

Redington shell-loading plant and proving ground along the Lehigh in Lower Saucon Township. Today the city of Bethlehem owns the Redington tract and leases it to the Steel City Gun Club.

Early in the war, Schwab had his company build row houses in South Bethlehem to ease what had been a decades-old housing shortage. The company offered loans to employees as well. In 1917, it provided $2.7 million to those who wanted to buy or build homes. To help accommodate immigrants, the company built a labor camp on the grounds of the coke works. It housed about 250 people in barracks and two-family frame dwellings.

Many of the immigrants came from countries that were America's wartime enemies — Germany and Austria-Hungary, which along with Bulgaria and Turkey formed the Central Powers that opposed the Allies.

By 1916, people representing more than 30 nationalities — half of them Germans and Austro-Hungarians — lived in South Bethlehem. Schwab received death threats, presumably from some of these new residents, and agreed to have bodyguards. Then he amused himself by trying to shake them.

All the while, his company took in a windfall of cash.

"It was the luck of history," historian Smith says. "Bethlehem Steel is in the armaments business, and World War I turns out to be this unbelievable bonanza."

The company didn't make its big money off the United States, because steelmakers agreed to stabilize their prices after America entered the war. As a result, they got more orders but their profit margins were lower.

Rather, Smith says, the huge profits came from the "desperate Europeans" — America's allies, the French, British, Italians and Russians — who were willing to pay whatever prices Bethlehem set.

In the last eight months of the war, no munitions and ordnance maker served the Allies more than Bethlehem Steel.

But there was a dark and damning side to the company's pot of gold. The First World War was butchery on a scale never before known. Over four years, it killed 10 million people, wiping out an entire generation of young men in Europe. Pennsylvania, settled in the 17th century by peace-loving Quakers, was the home of a company that had provided a means to kill on a mass scale.

In 1934, Bethlehem and other armsmakers were condemned as "merchants of death" after a congressional panel headed by Sen. Gerald P. Nye of North Dakota began investigating their role in World War I. The companies were accused of seeking a market for their munitions by urging countries to fight one another. The claim was widely believed.

Both Schwab and Grace repeatedly denied the accusation, which had surfaced even before the United States entered the First World War.

"It is the most absurd and poppycock thing I have ever heard of," Grace told a House committee in 1916, "to think that, as citizens of the United States, because we have investments made in ordnance plants, we would advocate this country going into war so we could get business."

Nonetheless, World War I became the singular event in Bethlehem Steel's history, according to Smith. "The massive amount of money that came into Bethlehem Steel allowed it to grow," he says. "Schwab and Grace in the '20s used that money to buy up a bunch of competitors that made them a secure No. 2."

As early as 1916, the company bought the Pennsylvania Steel Co. at Steelton, on the east bank of the Susquehanna River just south of Harrisburg, and its Maryland Steel Co. subsidiary in Sparrows Point, at the confluence of the Chesapeake Bay and Baltimore Harbor. It also bought a major nuts and bolts maker, the American Iron & Steel Manufacturing Co. in Lebanon, coal mines in West Virginia and an interest in the Cornwall iron mines in Lebanon County.

His company's wartime prominence made Schwab a personality in the news because people wanted to know more about the man the press dubbed the "King of Steel." He laid out his philosophy of life and work in 1915 for readers of the New York Herald.

THREE

"There is misery at every corner for the person who sets pleasure above work, and likewise for the person who attempts to live by his wits, minus the monotony and routine of relentless toil. ... If more persons became so engrossed in their work that they had to be reminded when it was meal time, there would be infinitely more happiness in the world, and probably much less indigestion."

And in 1917, he published a how-to book, "Succeeding With What You Have," which was mainly taken from his speeches because he hated to write.

With Bethlehem Steel's huge role in the Allied war effort and Schwab's increasing popularity, it was no wonder President Wilson wanted him to help the U.S. Shipping Board in the gloomy spring of 1918.

When the president put his hands out to Schwab in the Oval Office, earnestly acknowledging his sacrifices and calling him a patriot, Schwab was deeply moved. In that moment, he agreed to take charge of the moribund agency providing Uncle Sam with troop and cargo ships. But Schwab wanted the president's pledge that he could run the Shipping Board's shipbuilding subsidiary, the Emergency Fleet Corp., his own way and without interference.

"Will you stand back of me?" he asked.

Wilson placed both his hands on Schwab's shoulders and said, "To the last resources of the United States of America."

Schwab, serving for a token $1 a year, packed his staff with men of proven business ability and set up headquarters in the shipbuilding center of Philadelphia. He changed the way government contracts were awarded, putting the onus on shipyard owners to operate efficiently, and offered incentives to workers and managers. He tripled the number of agency inspectors and visited shipyards to weed out wasteful practices and cheer on the workers.

Monthly production of ships nearly doubled in 90 days.

When the First World War ended, a grateful nation hailed Schwab as a hero for providing, in Wilson's words, "a service of unusual value and distinction."

By the time he left government service in December 1918, Schwab had a reputation for having the Midas touch, but not everything he touched turned to gold. Sometimes he made bad decisions that cost him thousands, perhaps millions of dollars.

One involved technologically advanced cars called Stutzes. They were the closest cars America had to European-style sports cars like the Bugatti and Alfa Romeo. Schwab thought the Stutz was the kind of car every American would want, so in 1919 he bought control of the Stutz Motor Co. But most American consumers who could afford a Stutz didn't want a high-strung sports car. They wanted to chug to the opera or social clubs in beautiful, boatlike cars with engines that they could keep in one gear all day. Schwab's investment in Stutz went up in exhaust fumes.

He called himself a "damn fool" after a bad decision he made while still president of U.S. Steel. A Canadian machinist had developed a pneumatic hammer and an adding machine. Schwab chose to invest in the hammer and started Chicago Pneumatic Tool Co., which did all right. William S. Burroughs invested in the adding machine and made millions.

While Schwab was building up Bethlehem Steel, he was also engaging his workers' talents outside the plant. He gave the employees $25,000 to develop athletics among themselves, and the result was a championship soccer team. Between 1913 and 1930, the Bethlehem Steel Soccer Club won 11 national trophies.

Spalding's Soccer Guide saluted Schwab in 1916, saying he "realizes the vast importance of a spirit of amity between the head of a great corporation and the army of men it employs."

Bethlehem Steel also had a baseball league, but more than anything, it was a shelter for big-league players trying to stay out of the First World War. Schwab formed the league in 1917 with instructions that he wanted "some good wholesome games that will furnish amusement and entertainment for the Bethlehem Steel Co.'s employees, and don't bother me about details of expense."

At first, plant workers did get to play ball. But in 1918, pros covered the diamonds. The War Department had issued a work-or-fight order, saying men had to have essential jobs or else don a uniform. Pros looking for ways to avoid military service flocked to Bethlehem Steel and other companies happy to have them. These companies promised the players undemanding jobs and better pay than many of them made at their ballclubs.

Among players who joined the Bethlehem Steel league were two of the game's all-time greats — Shoeless Joe Jackson, who left the Chicago White Sox to work at Steel's Harlan Shipyard in Wilmington, and Babe Ruth, then a Boston Red Sox pitcher whose name got on the payroll at the company's Lebanon mill in mid-September. He apparently left town about eight weeks later, right after the Armistice.

Beyond encouraging sports, Schwab used his money and influence to help mold Bethlehem and its culture, mainly after the 1910 strike had stunned the community and left residents believing he was harsh and uncaring. He couldn't help but do something. After all, it was his company's explosive growth that quadrupled Bethlehem's population in one decade, from 12,800 in 1910 to 50,300 in 1920.

Schwab endeared himself to the upper class by enticing the Bach Choir's founder back to Bethlehem in 1911. J. Fred Wolle had started the choir in Bethlehem in 1900 to publicly perform the works of Johann Sebastian Bach. But five years later, he left for a job in California and the popular choir disintegrated. Now Schwab was not only its savior but its biggest financial supporter.

He also gave money to the Lehigh Valley Symphony Orchestra and in 1910 started the Bethlehem Steel Co. Band, which gave free public concerts.

His company donated money to St. Luke's Hospital and to create a baby health center after the daughter of Lehigh University's president was shocked to learn that the infant mortality rate in South Bethlehem was the highest in the state. The center opened in 1915

and had three branches by 1920.

Schwab provided a building for a free public library and promoted construction of the city's only public high school, Liberty High, in 1922 and the landmark Hill-to-Hill Bridge over the Lehigh River in 1924. He encouraged others to build the grand Hotel Bethlehem, completed in 1921, so he wouldn't have to send clients to the dowdy Sun Inn. He gave money to Lehigh University and served on its board of trustees.

He was the catalyst in getting the boroughs of Bethlehem and South Bethlehem to merge into a city in 1917. The first mayor of the united Bethlehem was Steel executive Archibald Johnston. In 1920, the city annexed Northampton Heights, east of south Bethlehem. Northampton Heights was one of the richest boroughs in the state because it contained valuable steel company and railroad properties.

In 1919, Schwab celebrated the completion of his estate in his boyhood home of Loretto — Immergrun, German for "Evergreen," a 44-room mansion on 1,000 elaborately maintained acres that included a private golf course.

He also mourned the passing of his mentor, Andrew Carnegie, at age 84 in his mansion in Lenox, Mass. On Aug. 11, 1919, Carnegie asked his secretary to hand him a picture of Schwab. When he gazed at it, his lips curled into a smile and he died. His affection for Schwab had run deep until the end.

Years earlier, he had given Schwab a painting he said held a lesson for life. It showed an old monk happily rubbing his belly after a meal of nothing but an apple and a glass of wine.

"Any time that you feel blue or inclined to be despondent," Carnegie told Schwab, "just look at this old monk's happy countenance and your depression will disappear. Always remember that good business is never done except in a happy and contented frame of mind."

Schwab hung the painting in his company's boardroom and embraced its message. Not even the stock market crash of 1929 deflated him.

"Be not afraid," he told the press. "The stock market cannot stop or stem the prosperity that extends throughout this great country of ours."

He was wrong about that, but years later he was still holding on to his sunny disposition.

"I am glad I have been optimistic," he said at a meeting of the American Iron and Steel Institute, a trade group with headquarters in New York, "because it has resulted in so much pleasure in business, and because it has been true, and because it is the frame of mind that will make us all advance in our business progress, our human relations and our happiness in life."

By the early 1920s, Schwab no longer had his hands on the daily management of Bethlehem Steel. He was getting $150,000 a year as chairman, holding many millions of dollars in stock and pleased to have his "boy" Grace in charge.

The company continued to expand in the Roaring '20s while loaded with cash. In 1922, it bought the nation's fourth largest steelmaker, Lackawanna Steel Co. on Lake Erie just south of Buffalo, N.Y., and iron ore mines in the Great Lakes region. The next year, it took over the No. 3 steelmaker, Midvale Steel Co. of Philadelphia, except for its armor and ordnance plant. Midvale's subsidiary, Cambria Steel Co., provided Bethlehem with steel operations and coal mines in the Johnstown area.

These acquisitions gave Bethlehem Steel an ingot-producing capacity of 7.6 million tons a year, or 14.5 tons a minute, about 15 percent of the nation's total. They encroached a little on U.S. Steel's turf, but with Bethlehem dominating the market east of Pittsburgh, Schwab didn't mean to do any more than nip at U.S. Steel. He and Elbert Gary generally avoided competing head-on.

But early in 1926, their policy of tolerance broke down. Under Gary, the No. 1 steelmaker had slipped from having two-thirds of the American steel market at the turn of the century to one-third and was planning to do something about it. Schwab found out that

U.S. Steel was building a mill at Homestead to make Bethlehem Steel's patented Grey beam without permission. He confronted Gary, who denied that U.S. Steel planned to make the wide-flange beam.

"Gary, you're the goddamndest liar and double-crosser I've ever known!" Schwab shouted in a rare flash of anger. "Your word is no good, and I shall never trust you or have anything to do with you again."

About a year later, Gary became ill and asked to see Schwab. Gary admitted that U.S. Steel had done wrong and apologized. The rift was repaired. Bethlehem Steel and U.S. Steel would work out the problem together.

But Gary died several months later and the peace ended. Bethlehem Steel sued, accusing U.S. Steel of infringing on its patent. The suit was dropped in 1929 after U.S. Steel agreed to pay royalties for the right to make the Bethlehem beam.

From then on, Schwab sought to make inroads on U.S. Steel territory. He tried but failed to get a merger with Youngstown Sheet & Tube Co. in Ohio, which had new mills in the Midwest that might have broken U.S. Steel's stranglehold on the Chicago market. A minority Youngstown stockholder sued to bar the merger, and a judge found that the proposed deal undervalued the smaller company and that Bethlehem hadn't provided Youngstown's directors with adequate information.

In 1930, Bethlehem expanded to the West Coast, acquiring small steel plants in Los Angeles, San Francisco and Seattle when it bought Pacific Coast Steel Co. and Southern California Iron & Steel Co. The next year, Bethlehem bought McClintic-Marshall Corp., the largest steel fabricator and bridge builder in the world. It built the locks for the Panama Canal, which opened in 1914.

McClintic-Marshall had plants that bent, cut, twisted and riveted steel on the West Coast and in the Pittsburgh and Chicago areas, giving Bethlehem Steel a strong base on U.S. Steel's home turf. It used Bethlehem beams to make buildings and bridges, among them the Golden Gate Bridge.

Schwab's involvement with Bethlehem Steel and the industry in general wound down in the mid-1930s as his health declined. Besides heart trouble, he had been diagnosed with diabetes in the early '20s. Though he continued as chairman of the company, it was an honorary post that got him $250,000 a year for doing nothing.

In 1934, at 72, he stepped down as president of the American Iron and Steel Institute, which he had headed since Elbert Gary's death. He bled his wealth until there wasn't any left, partly because of the Great Depression, which wiped out his investments, and partly because money simply ran through his fingers. He gambled or gave it away or lost it in speculative business ventures such as a chain of roadside hot dog stands. One of his brothers estimated that Schwab's fortune totaled $25 million at the height of his career in the mid-'20s — $274 million in today's dollars — but Hessen, in his book, suggests that figure is too low. Schwab told a stockholder that he once had $40 million.

One of the biggest drains on Schwab's resources was the upkeep of his palatial homes in Loretto and New York. In 1936, he offered to sell Riverside to the city for $4 million, half what it cost him to build and decorate it, but officials weren't interested.

After his wife, Rana, died in January 1939, he lost Riverside to Chase National Bank for back taxes and moved to a small apartment on Park Avenue. At 9:30 p.m. Sept. 19, 1939, he suffered a heart attack and died in his apartment. He was 77. He and Rana had no chil-dren, and his personal kingdom was gone — he was $338,349 in debt.

Bethlehem Steel Corp. could have lifted its creator's estate out of insolvency. World War II broke out two weeks before Schwab's death. His executors sold his stocks immediately. If they had waited a year or more, the stock value would have jumped as a result of steel orders for the war effort.

In the next several years, Schwab's holdings were sold off. Prudential Insurance Co. bought Riverside for $1.5 million in 1947. The mansion was torn down and replaced by a pair of apartment buildings. The beams that supported them were made in Bethlehem.

The Immergrun estate in Loretto was sold in 1942 to St. Francis College and became a residence for seminarians.

In accordance with one of his last wishes, Schwab was laid to rest beside his parents in an unadorned vault at St. Michael's Cemetery in Loretto.

But in a former Moravian commune along the Lehigh River in eastern Pennsylvania, the king of steel left behind a magnificent castle, a corporation whose empire included major steel plants not only in Bethlehem but in Johnstown, Steelton, Sparrows Point and Lackawanna, as well as shipyards on both coasts.

With these possessions during Schwab's rule, Bethlehem Steel left its mark across the land. Its beams formed the backbone of many of the nation's tallest buildings and long-span bridges.

"I love Bethlehem," Schwab once said. "It is the great achievement of my life."

CHAPTER
FOUR

Marvels of steel

 squadron of Navy biplanes pierces a lead-gray sky as 18-year-old Lynn Beedle, draped in a troubadour outfit, stands at the entrance of the Golden Gate Bridge greeting mayors and governors determined to become part of history.

Beneath Beedle's feet is 68,000 tons of Bethlehem steel that went into building the span, and all around him is jubilation that the bridge many said could not be built is about to open.

It is May 27, 1937, and millions of Americans had lost their jobs, their money and even their homes to a Great Depression that still had the nation in its grip. But on this day, on this bridge, there is only extravagance.

No expense is spared, from the costume that makes the University of California-Berkeley architecture student look like a strolling minstrel, to the girls in fiesta dresses dancing around him, to the 19 battleships and heavy cruisers plying the San Francisco Bay.

It was the type of extravagance that Bethlehem Steel Corp. had grown accustomed to as it evolved from a fledgling company at the turn of the 20th century to the nation's No. 2 steel producer.

It was the kind of extravagance the company believed it earned by using its revolutionary Bethlehem beam to become the world's leader — even greater than its rival, U.S. Steel — in building skyscrapers.

On this day, the Golden Gate was becoming the longest and highest of the long spans, and San Francisco area officials determined that the opening of the greatest engineering feat to date would get a fitting welcome.

With schools closed and most businesses on holiday for the event, thousands flocked to the bridge. They walked, ran, tap-danced and stilt-walked across it.

By day's end, about 200,000 people, including 11 governors and representatives from Mexico and Canada, had flipped their nickels into the toll box to cross the bridge.

Everyone wanted a piece of history.

Everyone, that is, except Beedle. For the rest of the Bay area the celebration would last a week, but shortly after his opening-day task was done, Beedle, his thick black hair disheveled from the wind on the bridge, went home to his books and drafting table. He was only on the bridge because his influential uncle organized the celebration.

"I was just a college kid on a lark," Beedle said. "I didn't fully understand then what I was part of. I didn't even know the Golden Gate was a Bethlehem Steel bridge."

Beedle didn't know then that he was not only standing on an engineering and architectural marvel, but in the middle of a heated battle for supremacy between Bethlehem Steel, the contender, and U.S. Steel, the champion. The growing Bethlehem and its charismatic leader, Charles M. Schwab, had never challenged U.S. Steel's overall title as No. 1, but it had used its revolutionary Bethlehem beam to become king of tall buildings and bridges.

By the time Beedle wrapped his 5-foot 10-inch frame into that ridiculous outfit on the Golden Gate, Bethlehem steel was in the longest bridges and tallest buildings in the world. It was helping to reshape the skyline of Manhattan and big cities across the country by allowing developers to push farther into the sky than ever before. And it was using this golden age of the skyscraper to help the company through the lean years of the Depression.

At that moment in 1937, the 18-year-old bookworm didn't foresee that he would go on to a world-renowned engineering career that would have him conducting innovative tests on the very steel that Bethlehem would produce for warships. Or that only 10 years later he would find himself at Lehigh University's Fritz Engineering Laboratory on the hill overlooking 17,760 workers bustling about Bethlehem Steel's flagship plant on the South Side. He didn't aspire to be a 50-year Lehigh professor or founder of the Council on Tall Buildings and Urban Habitat, or to become the measuring stick for tall buildings around the world.

Beedle never set out to be an international giant in the field of giant buildings. It just happened that way.

Lynn S. Beedle was born in Orland, Calif., the son of Granville and Mary Beedle. His father's job as secretary-manager of the Lithographers Association would take the family to Hollywood, where young Lynn would often walk along Market Street with his head tilted oddly upward.

"I was fascinated by the tall buildings," Beedle recalled. "They were maybe 10 or 12 stories. But to me, it seemed like they were touching the sky."

Beedle's career path — and his unlikely ties to a steel company 2,850 miles away — began to unfold in a tiny wood shop in the Ramona Grammar School in Hollywood. In that elementary school shop class, Beedle made a small wooden box suitable for Mom's jewelry or Dad's cigars. With its brass hinges, beveled edges and carefully stained finish, it was an impressive piece of work for a 12-year-old. More important, the satisfaction of creating something from nothing inspired him.

He would be a carpenter, he decided.

Beedle's parents had other ideas. They never considered themselves wealthy but were comfortable in their suburban Hollywood neighborhood, and Granville Beedle was proud to be among the first on his block to own a Packard.

Surely a boy with Lynn's intellect could shoot higher than carpentry, they thought. He would be an architect, Granville Beedle decided.

"I was never one to argue with my parents, and architecture seemed to make a lot of sense," Beedle said. "I just wanted to build things."

Unwavering in his pursuit of that goal, Beedle entered the University of California-Berkeley in 1936 and majored in architecture. The schedule was grueling, but the work required the type of precision, focus and patience that Beedle enjoyed. While his friends and classmates were finding other ways to cut through the pressure, Beedle spent hours at his drafting table, meticulously sketching ornate columns, buildings or new styles of architecture.

Occasionally, he'd escape the rigors of school by spending a weekend at his grandmother's house in Marin County. There he'd blow off steam by chopping wood, building trails or hiking Mount Tamalpais, better known to the locals as the Sleeping Maiden for its resemblance to the silhouette of a woman lying down.

It wasn't easy getting to Grandma's house, a little more than 15 miles away. Beedle would need two cable cars and two ferries to get there, but he didn't mind.

He especially enjoyed riding the Sausalito Ferry across the San Francisco Bay. As the ferry crept along, he stared to the west at the massive towers that seemed to reach into the clouds. He was mesmerized by the fearless workers stringing cable across the 6,400-foot span. The $35 million project to connect San Francisco and Marin counties was an astonishing sight from the water.

The Golden Gate was being bridged before his eyes.

"It was a massive production," Beedle said. "Bethlehem Steel had quite a building operation going on there back then."

It was an operation toward which the steel company had been building for nearly four decades. Much of its dominance in structural steel — tall buildings and bridges — rested on a foundation of Henry Grey's beam and Schwab's $5 million gamble to build a plant to make it.

The wide-flange beam, pioneered by Grey and manufactured in Bethlehem in 1908 after Schwab scraped together enough money to build the country's first mill, was unlike any other produced in the United States.

Only two decades earlier the I-beam was a revolutionary advancement that allowed builders to use a steel frame to strengthen and stabilize buildings far better than stone or wood. It allowed developers to go higher.

But even the steel I-beam couldn't be counted on to push buildings much taller than 20 stories. Going higher would require riveting beams and plates together and adding support angles. It was expensive and in most cases the cost didn't justify the height.

Grey's beam changed that. What the I-beam did for building, the Grey beam did for building higher.

For Beedle, it was the foundation of what would become his life's work.

"Why do people want to know which building is tallest? I don't know. Why do they want to know that Mount Everest is the tallest mountain?" Beedle said. "There's something intriguing about things that are the fastest or longest or tallest. And when it comes to height, that beam started it all."

The I-beam was essentially a column of steel with narrow lips on the top and bottom, giving it the shape of an "I." Grey's process widened those lips to as much as 16.5 inches, creating a beam that looked more like a sideways "H." The wider lips, or flanges as they were called, greatly increased the strength of the beam.

The so-called Bethlehem beam used that wider flange to provide strength so that architects and developers could build up. Builders could move columns farther apart, allowing them to use less steel and build higher without rivets or angles.

The process was cheaper, too. If the steel company wanted to change the size or shape of the standard I-beam, it had to change the rolls. But with Grey's process, Bethlehem's new mill could change the weight per foot, or thickness, of the beam simply by adjusting the same set of rolls.

"Columns which are now riveted together at an expense of $9 to $14 per ton will be rolled in one solid section," Schwab wrote to investors he hoped would help fund his Grey mill. "To one familiar with the trade, the enormous advantages of such sections are quickly appreciated."

Or in the case of rival U.S. Steel, quickly feared. After Schwab weathered a stock market collapse in 1907 by getting suppliers and contractors to delay billing him for work on the Grey mill, word of the new beam's cost advantages began to spread. About 8,000 tons were ordered for the State Education Building in Albany, N.Y., and 3,000 tons for a sugar refinery in Boston, but the coming-out party for

Bethlehem's new beam was the headquarters for the Gimbel Brothers department store in New York. The 12,000-ton order, valued at $384,000 or the equivalent of $7.6 million today, was by no means going to make Bethlehem Steel's year, but it gave Schwab a showcase for his promising new beam, kicking off decades of dominance in the New York market.

By 1909, demand for the beam was so high that Bethlehem Steel had to turn away some orders, Schwab would tell The Wall Street Journal that year. The boom prompted Bethlehem Steel to spend $5 million to improve its Saucon plant, which contained the Grey mill and lay east of the blast furnaces in Bethlehem. Improvements included a new mill that could produce channels, angles and small beams from 6 to 12 inches.

The upgraded mill started operating in 1911, making Bethlehem Steel the eastern region's largest producer of structural steel, the technical name for the steel that went into making buildings and bridges.

In the coming years, the Bethlehem beam would go into the Metropolitan Life Insurance Co. Tower, the Time-Life Building, both in New York, and the 40-story Cadillac Tower, with its combination of Chicago School and neo-gothic architecture glistening in the Detroit skyline. Bethlehem Steel's rival on the other side of the state was beginning to get nervous.

By 1910, U.S. Steel officials were telling their board that their 51 percent piece of the structural steel business was down to about 25 percent. U.S. Steel had just lost structural steel contracts for five jobs in New England, and four of them had gone to Bethlehem Steel.

"Bethlehem is cutting quite a swath in the East at present on their 'H' sections, and taking some business from us," Henry Bope, the head of U.S. Steel's sales department, told fellow directors, "but we have felt that this condition is temporary."

Within a few months, Bope was realizing U.S. Steel had reason to worry.

"There was a time when there was probably not a single user of structural material in the United States who was not on our books for more or less of his tonnage," Bope said. "But

today, we are not getting any of this business."

In 1911, U.S. Steel would build a mill in Homestead that could roll 27-inch I-beams it hoped could compete with the Bethlehem beam. But it couldn't escape the fact it was selling an improved product from old technology while Bethlehem was selling the latest innovation.

A second Grey mill was built in 1918, enabling Bethlehem to expand its line of beams by adding smaller and lighter wide-flange shapes.

By 1922, with a capacity of 650,000 tons a year, the Bethlehem plant was much larger than U.S. Steel's structural plants in Homestead and south Chicago.

Despite a 50 percent increase in the demand for structural steel in the early 1920s, U.S. Steel's piece of that pie was shrinking fast. In 1926, about 926,000 tons of heavy structural steel was produced for building projects in the East, and only 74,000 tons of that was made by U.S. Steel, sales executive J.A. Coakley told his board.

Worse yet for U.S. Steel, Bethlehem was using its superior beam to invade U.S. Steel's traditional territory west of Chicago.

Bethlehem began to use the Bethlehem beam proceeds, along with massive revenues from its sale of ships and armaments during World War I, to buy new mills, shipyards and mines. By the time young Lynn Beedle was staring skyward in downtown Hollywood in 1925, the company that had 9,500 employees in 1905 had 68,884 on the payroll.

In 1926, Bethlehem built two Grey mills at the Lackawanna, N.Y., plant it bought four years earlier, and the next year 81,000 tons of rolled Bethlehem beams were shipped into the heart of U.S. Steel's Chicago territory. Roughly 52,000 tons of that went into Chicago's massive Merchandise Mart.

But even as Bethlehem was building its new Grey mills, U.S. Steel was secretly building a Grey mill of its own, violating Bethlehem Steel's patent on the beam. Bethlehem sued to preserve its patent right and eventually settled the case out of court when U.S. Steel agreed to pay royalties for the right to make the beam.

With the settlement, Bethlehem's monopoly on skyscrapers was over and the race was on. It was a race that Bethlehem, with its two-decade head start using the Bethlehem beam, would win for many years to come.

For many New Yorkers, it became commonplace to look out the window to see another building go up with Bethlehem steel.

"Several operations are going on near where I work, and all day the constant noise of drilling grates on our ears," prominent Allentown community leader Joe Hart read from a letter sent from New York City by his niece in 1929. "We can't hear the telephone or each other. It certainly makes things confusing."

Between 1923 and 1930, the collection of buildings erected with Bethlehem steel included the 70-story neo-gothic Bank of Manhattan Tower (now 40 Wall Street) and the 66-story American International Building, both in New York City; the 47-story Randolph Tower and the 45-story beaux-arts Morrison Hotel, both in Chicago; the 37-story Bank of America and the First National Bank buildings in Baltimore, and the University of Pittsburgh's neo-gothic Cathedral of Learning.

"U.S. Steel eventually made its mark in Chicago by getting most of the work there, but Bethlehem Steel owned New York," says Carson F. Diefenderfer, Bethlehem Steel's chief engineer for buildings for 28 years. "Bethlehem was king in Manhattan."

It was also getting bridge-building business in that period by producing steel to build the George Washington Bridge in New York and the Ben Franklin Bridge in Philadelphia.

But perhaps the defining moment came in 1929. With developers pouring speculative capital into skyscrapers, auto magnate Walter Chrysler and banker George Ohrstrom were in a spirited race for the sky.

Chrysler was determined to build the tallest building in the world, a monument to himself and American capitalism. But Ohrstrom was vowing that his new 67-story Bank of Manhattan would exceed the 808-foot planned height of Chrysler's building.

When Ohrstrom heard rumors that Chrysler now was planning to go higher than 808 feet on his original blueprints, his architects pushed the height of their bank building to 945 feet by making the top steeper and adding a 60-

foot steel cap.

They had won, Ohrstrom declared at the November news conference in which he introduced his bank building as the world's tallest building.

But Ohrstrom's celebration was premature. Four days later, it was revealed that not only had Chrysler tweaked the design of his building to raise it to 860 feet, but workers were secretly constructing a 186-foot spike to be erected on top of the building. Ohrstrom had been outsmarted. The spike vaulted the Chrysler Building's height to 1,046 feet, easily surpassing the height of the Bank of Manhattan and the Eiffel Tower, which had held the title of world's tallest structure for 40 years. With its ornate eagle gargoyles and stainless steel crown glistening in the sun, the art deco monument was well-deserving of that title, Chrysler thought.

Today, former Bethlehem Steel officials look back proudly on that era because they say Bethlehem steel went into both the Chrysler Building and the Bank of Manhattan. There is no dispute that Bethlehem's trademark wide-flange beams helped the Bank of Manhattan go higher.

But just as the two steel giants sparred nearly eight decades ago, U.S. Steel and Bethlehem Steel officials disagree over who produced the steel for the Chrysler Building. For three-quarters of a century, Bethlehem has listed Chrysler — still considered by the architectural community as one of the most striking buildings in the world — as one of its crowning achievements.

U.S. Steel disputes Bethlehem's claim and has provided promotional ads from the 1930s that tout a U.S. Steel subsidiary, Carnegie Steel Co., as a steel provider for the building and U.S. Steel's American Bridge Co. subsidiary as the fabricator. A 1929 New York Times story states that Carnegie Steel was supplying the steel for the landmark, but decades of publications about the Chrysler Building have avoided the issue.

The Skyscraper Museum, the New York Historical Society, the Museum of the City of New York, the New York Public Library and the American Iron and Steel Institute have produced no answers, and even a trip to the Chrysler Building yielded no exposed beams that might bear a company name.

Former Bethlehem Steel officials have not delivered proof, but still contend that while Carnegie Steel might have provided some steel, such as channels and angles, it was the revolutionary Bethlehem beam that propelled the Chrysler Building upward.

The answer to the mystery might lie in the more than 100 dusty boxes of Bethlehem Steel records stored in the basement of the National Canal Museum in Easton. Their keepers say it could take as long as 10 years to organize the documents.

The Chrysler Building would not hold the title of world's tallest building for long. General Motors financier John Jakob Raskob announced he was making a statement of his own. His 102-story Empire State Building would be 202 feet taller, and this time Bethlehem Steel had nothing to smile about. U.S. Steel was willing to bid below market value for the job, which would finally give it a showcase skyscraper of its own.

The Empire State Building opened in 1931, benefiting from plummeting prices that allowed it to come in at half its $50 million budget. But by then the country was mired in the Great Depression and Raskob's victory proved hollow. The building was 77 percent vacant, prompting some to call it the Empty State Building.

Bethlehem Steel quickly countered U.S. Steel's new claim to building the world's tallest building. In 1931, it purchased McClintic-Marshall Corp., the nation's largest steel fabricator. Bethlehem Steel had long provided the steel for the nation's largest skyscrapers and bridges, but with McClintic-Marshall in its stable, it could now build and erect the steel it was selling — a luxury U.S. Steel had been enjoying for years with its American Bridge subsidiary.

After years during which U.S. Steel and Bethlehem honored an unwritten gentlemen's agreement to stay in their own territory, this was an "in your face" move by Schwab. McClintic-Marshall wasn't just the largest steel fabricator; it had plants in Pittsburgh and Chicago, in the heart of U.S. Steel territory.

And with Bethlehem's new acquisition came an inside line into some of the nation's most visionary steel projects. By the time Bethlehem took over McClintic-Marshall, the fabricator already had contracts to build the Waldorf-Astoria hotel and the George Washington Bridge in New York.

It also had the contract for what would stand forever as the crown jewel of Bethlehem Steel's collection.

The Golden Gate Bridge.

"What a magnificent structure," said Beedle, seizing on the expertise he gained during his six-decade engineering career.

After his day on the bridge, Beedle would change his major to engineering, and within seven years he'd be in the South Pacific, working for the Navy, testing the strength of steel against atomic blasts. He'd test the same steel that Bethlehem was producing for warships, and as the longtime director of Lehigh University's Fritz Lab, he'd go on to develop new methods for the design of steel frames for buildings. His "Plastic Design of Steel Frames" theory in the 1950s set off a movement in which a building was designed based on the ultimate strength of its frame, rather than the stresses against it. The Council on Tall Buildings and Urban Habitat, which he founded in 1969, would be not only the clearinghouse for design and engineering innovations worldwide, but the arbiter of debates about the world's tallest building.

His work took him to the roof of the Sears Tower in Chicago, to the top of the Empire State Building and even to the top of the world's second tallest buildings, the Petronas Towers in Malaysia. But none of those experiences surpassed the day he stood on top of the San Francisco tower of the Golden Gate Bridge.

"See, it wasn't just that the Golden Gate was the longest or tallest when it was built," Beedle said. "Its beauty makes it special. To my way of thinking, it stacks up to anything built before or since."

The Golden Gate cost $35 million and took more than four years to build, but by the time it was ready to open, years of heated debate had yielded to a widespread belief that the project was a success. Even the deaths of 10 men working on the bridge, though tragic, were deemed part of the success. The designers pioneered a new safety netting strung beneath the bridge, about 250 feet above the water. The 10 who fell were killed because the netting broke. But the number was far below project estimates of 35 deaths, based on an industry standard at the time that projected one death for each $1 million spent on a wide-span bridge project.

When it opened in 1937, with its 4,200-foot span between two massive towers and an additional 1,100 feet on each side, the Golden Gate was not only the longest suspension bridge in the world, but its towers, extending 746 feet above the bay, made it the highest structure west of Manhattan.

For years, Golden Gate Bridge engineer Joseph Baerman Strauss beat back skepticism from peers who said the Golden Gate could not be bridged, and from residents of the six-county area who said $35 million was too much to spend on a project some of them regarded as a risky publicity stunt. Some said it was too close to the San Andreas Fault; others questioned how the San Francisco tower could possibly be built in 100 feet of rushing water.

E.J. Harrington, designer of the Dumbarton lift bridge over the southern arm of San Francisco Bay and an early opponent of the Golden Gate Bridge, said the bridge could not be built because there was no plant large enough to fabricate the steel needed for construction.

Bethlehem Steel would prove Harrington wrong.

After years of debate, voters in the six-county area overwhelmingly approved the project that would epitomize the conglomerate Bethlehem Steel had become.

The 68,000 tons of steel for the bridge was rolled in Bethlehem and Steelton, transported off the plant property by Bethlehem's subsidiary railroad and taken by train to Pottstown, where McClintic-Marshall fabricated the pieces and built large sections to make sure they fit perfectly. Some of the sections were made at Steelton.

From Pottstown and Steelton, the pieces were shipped by rail to Philadelphia, where they were loaded onto Bethlehem subsidiary Calmar Ship Lines, shipped through the same Panama Canal locks that McClintic-Marshall had fabricated and unloaded in the Bethlehem-owned shipyard in Alameda, Calif., before being moved to the San Francisco Bay building site.

Even then, company President Eugene Grace sensed that the bridge would live on as a symbol of American ingenuity, and he was determined to make sure the Bethlehem Steel name was married to that history.

As he visited the construction site in 1936, Grace stood next to a McClintic-Marshall foreman, admiring the work in progress and noting what a fine job Bethlehem Steel was doing. The foreman suggested it was a McClintic-Marshall project, pointing to the trucks with McClintic-Marshall signs on them.

When Grace returned to Bethlehem, subsidiary McClintic-Marshall was immediately renamed the Fabricated Steel Construction division of Bethlehem Steel.

Bethlehem would go on to build dozens of skyscrapers in Manhattan alone, dozens of long-span bridges and hundreds of apartment complexes, schools, libraries, municipal buildings and office complexes across the nation.

Among its landmarks are the 21-story International-Style Lever House in Manhattan, which in 1957 touched off a new era of skyscrapers encased in steel and glass rather than concrete or stone, and the 59-story Citicorp Center in Manhattan, with its controversial cantilever style that forced contractors to add braces when it was discovered the building was vulnerable to heavy winds.

For 60 years, Bethlehem Steel was the company most responsible for shaping Manhattan, the most recognizable skyline in the world. Its mark is seen all around New York, from the Verrazano Narrows Bridge to Madison Square Garden to the Metropolitan Opera House.

Bethlehem steel stretches across the country from the Chesapeake Bay Bridge Tunnel to the U.S. Supreme Court building in Washington, D.C., to Los Angeles City Hall.

In 1970, Bethlehem Steel thought it had won the steel contract for the World Trade Center when its $117 million bid undercut the only other steel producer large enough to handle the job — U.S. Steel — by $5 million. But the Port Authority of New York and New Jersey rejected both bids, broke the job into pieces and ultimately gave it to a consortium of companies that together underbid Bethlehem by $34 million. The 15 companies that made up the consortium cut some of their costs by using foreign steel.

The loss was devastating for Bethlehem Steel and signaled the end of the era when giant steel companies could dominate major projects. Bethlehem's Fabricated Steel Construction division had long been the flagship of the company. The buildings and bridges it had built were so recognizable that the innovative Grey beam developed many decades earlier had become the company logo.

But developers now realized they could save millions by letting a construction manager break up projects and bid them in small segments. It enabled them to use smaller companies that were not burdened by the type of expensive union workers and top-heavy management structure that drove up Bethlehem Steel's and U.S. Steel's costs. Suddenly, the monopoly was over for the two giants.

About six years later, when Bethlehem executives told nearly 7,000 Fabricated Steel Construction division workers to take a 10 percent cut or risk the division's closing, the workers scoffed.

It's a bluff, they said. The company would never shut the division. We are Bethlehem Steel. Just look at the logo.

Disbelieving union workers rejected the pay cut and instead offered to give up their dental benefits. For Chief Executive Officer Lewis Foy, their offer to give up such a minuscule benefit was like thumbing their noses at the company. The union would pay for calling Foy's bluff.

"Shut it down," Foy said when his negotiators told him what the union was willing to sacrifice.

In the fall of 1976, Bethlehem Steel closed all six plants of its Fabricated Steel Construction division.

Years later, despite a debilitating illness, Lynn Beedle spent many hours sharing his reminiscences of the buildings that were the framework of his career.

As he sat in his Hellertown home in the early fall of 2003, he showed little resemblance to the kid on the bridge. His thick black hair had long since turned silver, and his athletic build had been weathered by 85 years of life.

But some things, he noted, had not changed.

"The steel company is gone, but those structures are still there to be enjoyed by millions and millions of people every day," Beedle said. "That legacy will not be so easily erased."

On Oct. 30, 2003, Lynn Beedle died of cancer.

FIVE

The Grace period

ilbur Kocher points down a path in Bethlehem's old Nisky Hill Cemetery toward a huge stone memorial beyond a rise of modest, tree-shaded graves. Early Moravians who were buried in this city all had the same-size stones to show that they were equals in the sight of God.

But this grave is different.

"He's got chairs around it, although nobody ever sits there. I don't know if it's true, but I heard that they buried him standing up so he could look out at the blast furnaces," the former Bethlehem Steel electrician says when a visitor asks for directions.

Kocher, in his mid-80s, is pruning an azalea for his wife, who has lain under a simple stone since her death a year earlier, in 2002. In life, she kept a beautiful home. "I wanted to keep the area, in case she could see it, like she kept the house," Kocher says.

Two hundred steps away, under a rotunda with a semicircular granite bench that seats 20, lies Eugene Gifford Grace. Son of a New Jersey sea captain turned grocer, he ruled the Bethlehem Steel Corp. for four decades, almost until his death in 1960.

It is a myth that Grace is buried upright. But his grave does overlook the Bethlehem Steel site, today a graveyard of hulking, rusted metal. About 30 feet from where he rests, the cemetery drops off at a high, tree-covered cliff. The Lehigh River flows below, and across it lies the former plant. A visitor on Nisky Hill can see the shuttered, fading 13-story headquarters where Grace reigned.

The company survived him by only 43 years.

Yet during the Grace era, Bethlehem Steel was an empire that changed the nation's face forever and helped the United States win the bloodiest war in history.

With absolute authority and single-minded purpose, Grace and his mentor, Charles M. Schwab, acquired mines, shipyards, railroads and steel plants that helped make Bethlehem the top steelmaker on the eastern seaboard. In the 1920s, when Schwab stopped having an active role in management, his protege carried on with the creed, "Always More Production." He was "the greatest steel man in the country," Schwab marveled.

"Grace charted the course of Bethlehem's growth and prosperity with the solitary and supreme status of a ship captain," said Edmund F. Martin, a Bethlehem Steel chief executive in the 1960s.

But Grace also unwittingly planted the seeds of doom for this great enterprise. He was an autocrat who failed to groom a successor, as Schwab had done. He created a closed culture hostile to outsiders. He sacrificed innovation for short-term profits. He perpetuated the integrated, monolithic structure that worked so well in the early years but one day would surrender to smaller, more agile producers. He paid himself and other executives exorbitant amounts that, while insignificant for a company of its size, betrayed a smug and ultimately misguided belief that the world would always need Bethlehem's steel. He treated organized labor with contempt, fostering a distrust that soured management-union relations to the end.

In his heyday, though, Grace was the master of steel. Fortune magazine gushed in June 1941 that Bethlehem "has geared every unit of its empire to a functional efficiency that Adolf Hitler would envy."

Bethlehem Steel reflected Grace's skill and drive. He had a clear goal to have the company make lots of money because, he said, "The earning of profits is a matter of supreme moment to every executive." He urged on his underlings with the phrase "Onward and upward" and by telling them, "Don't waste time talking about what you have already done. Use the time in planning and executing something new. Dividends are not earned by reminiscing on the past." And this: "Let it be your guiding, impelling aim to take your boss' job away from him."

A penny pincher, he scrutinized accounts to see where the company could save a buck. He could block out distractions and zero in on a problem until it was solved. To stay abreast of business developments, he read newspapers for three hours a day. He saw the advantages of using the press and was among the first industrialists to hold quarterly meetings with reporters. For Christmas 1938, he arranged for CBS to broadcast a live radio show from the drawing room of his Bethlehem mansion. Eight million listeners heard 80 local performers sing and tell the story of how Bethlehem became the Christmas City.

Though shy in public, Grace was often stern and hot-tempered in private. He had deep-set eyes, dark wispy hair and a wiry, athletic build. The New York Times Magazine described him in 1924 as "a slender, rather tall, nervous type of man, very quick and acute in manner, with a knack for piercing the thoughts of his visitors even before they are uttered. He is forceful, energetic, businesslike, impatient of time-wasting and time-wasters, yet pleasant and courteous."

A star baseball player in college, he started playing golf at 32 to stay in shape and talk with his partners about steelmaking. He told an interviewer from the New York World Telegram that "any man who does not talk about his business on the golf course doesn't really care about his business."

Grace's passion for golf extended to his mansion on Bethlehem's Prospect Avenue, nicknamed "Bonus Hill" because of the number of generously compensated Steel executives with homes in the neighborhood. He converted the fourth floor into an indoor course with netting and enjoyed driving shots that bounced off the overhead cross beams.

"The house had a big back yard ... and he would be there every day that he could, hitting golf balls," says namesake Eugene G. Grace III, whose father was Grace's older son, Charles.

Grace bought the house at 1317 Prospect Ave. in December 1923 and named it Uwchlan (pronounced YOO-clin), Welsh for "the land over the valley." Immediately he set out to enlarge it, turning it into a virtual castle during five years of reconstruction.

The home had a ballroom, 23 bedrooms,

15 bathrooms and a basement with a game room. Later, air conditioning would be installed, and the basement would be made into a bomb shelter. The landscaped grounds, as big as a city block, were enclosed by a red brick wall. They had a driving range, a putting green, three greenhouses and a four-car garage with an apartment above it. Grace's own security guards patrolled the grounds around the clock.

A bevy of servants, maids, butlers, underbutlers and cooks waited on Eugene and his wife, Marion, their daughter, Emmeline, and sons Charles and Eugene Jr. Eugene Sr. got along well with his fastidious chief butler, Jack Lund, "because both of them were perfectionists — Grandfather at running Bethlehem Steel and Jack at running the house," Eugene III says.

Uwchlan was the scene of elegant dinner parties on weekend evenings, according to "Eugene Gifford Grace — 1876-1960: As We Remember Him," a privately printed book by Emmeline's daughter, Penny Porter. Guests wore black ties, tuxedos, furs and gowns. They drank vintage wines and champagne. Entertainment was brought in from New York, and regulars included crooner Bing Crosby, one of Grace's golfing buddies.

Today, the Allentown Catholic Diocese owns and operates Grace's home as Holy Family Manor, an elder care facility. The ballroom serves as a chapel.

Marie Gawlik of Bethlehem, who cooked and did other work for Grace, remembers his 50th wedding anniversary party in 1952. Furniture was removed to make way for tables where guests could sit and listen to Gypsy music performed by strolling musicians from New York.

Comedian and musician Victor Borge, whom Gawlik describes as "the comical guy who falls off a chair," once entertained in Grace's home. After such parties, Gawlik and other employees couldn't leave until the inventory of gold and silver was counted. She wasn't insulted; rather, she understood the Graces' concern about theft.

After Marion Grace broke her hip, it was Gawlik's job to follow her around the house carrying a pillow.

The Graces ate well even during the De-

pression, when ordinary Americans scraped for food. Grace was particularly fond of oysters. He had them flown in fresh from Maine and kept a barrelfull on ice in the cellar. He ate them before meals and for midnight snacks, and insisted that others in the family try to enjoy them as much as he did. "He offered each of us a quarter if we could eat a raw oyster whole," says Eugene III. "I never did it."

In winter, the Graces escaped to Aiken, S.C., where they had a home. "In the early days, they used to take a railroad car to get down there. Later, they had the Bethlehem Steel company plane," says Charles Grace Jr., Eugene III's older brother. "A lot of the Aiken people were horsey people, but my grandfather didn't keep horses, just played golf." Among Grace's frequent houseguests in South Carolina were Crosby and golfing legends Bobby Jones, Ben Hogan and Gene Sarazen.

Grace also stayed at Bethlehem Steel's apartment in The Plaza, the swank New York hotel. He had a home in the exclusive Long Island beach community of Southampton, where he golfed with future President Dwight D. Eisenhower and hosted debonair actor/dancer Fred Astaire and other celebrities. "Everyone dressed for dinner," Charles Jr. recalls. "By dressed I mean the gentlemen all wore dinner jackets."

The Graces vacationed at the New Jersey shore and at Buck Hill Falls in the Poconos. They worshipped together at First Presbyterian Church of Bethlehem, where they had their own pew.

"My grandfather was very family-oriented," says Charles Jr., who manages the family's investments. "Just about every weekend we would go either to his home in Bethlehem or to my mother's family home in Bethlehem."

At dinner, Grace was always a commanding presence. "He was a pretty smart guy," Charles Jr. recalls. "He was a Republican and had very strong Republican views."

Charles Jr.'s mother, Nancy Dougherty Grace, found out just how strong, to her dismay. Nancy supported Franklin D. Roosevelt during one of his four presidential campaigns, not realizing how fiercely Grace opposed the Democrat's economic and business policies. Usually she said nothing when politics came up in family conversations, according to Porter's book.

"Finally, one time [he] pierced me with his eye and asked me, 'Who do you plan to vote for, Nancy?' Unable to lie, I told him. Silence."

Several days later, Nancy received a letter from her father-in-law that broke the bond between them forever. "Dear Nancy: From what you told me yesterday, I see that you are not of the proletariat, and I must therefore ask you not to use our apartment in the Plaza Hotel from now on. … Sincerely, Daddy."

Nancy said that as a result of the snub, "the nice side of our relationship did not come back between us. Ever."

Grace loved music, especially old railroad songs and silly tunes about golfers that made him laugh so hard tears came to his eyes. "We would get together and someone would play the piano and we would all sing," Charles Jr. remembers. A record store in New York would send his grandfather all of the latest recordings, adding to a collection of hundreds, and he would return the ones he didn't want.

A 1920 American Magazine profile, under the headline, "'Gene' Grace — Whose Story Reads Like a Fairy Tale," said the steel man's rise to prominence was "a narrative of typical American diligence, vision, forethought, pluck, and unremitting application."

He was born Aug. 27, 1876, to Rebecca and John Wesley Grace in the small town of Goshen on the southern New Jersey coast, near Cape May. The family name was bathed in glory. Eugene's great-grandfather distinguished himself during the Revolution as a scout for Gen. George Washington, marched with the Marquis de Lafayette and witnessed the British surrender at Yorktown, Va.

According to Porter's book:

Eugene's father was a captain of packet schooners trading wheat and coal along the coast and the Delaware Bay and up the Delaware River. He had been sailing for 31 years when his frail wife, Rebecca, urged him to quit.

"We need you at home, Wes," she said. "The boys, 'Gator' and Eugene, are 13 and 11 now. Bess is 15, and you scarcely know baby

Roy. Retire from the sea. You could have a grocery store and warehouse right on the property. And Gator and Gene could help you in the summers and after school."

Gator was John Jr. He got the nickname because of the way he used one hand over the other to catch a baseball — like an alligator's jaw opening and closing.

"Cap'n Wes," as he was called, heeded Rebecca and came home to stay in 1887. He opened a grocery and a wholesale merchandising business that offered grain, feed, coal, bricks and lumber. On his 20 acres, he had cows, a horse, pigs and chickens, and apple, peach, pear, plum and walnut trees.

The boys helped him in the store before and after school and on weekends, with Eugene keeping the books. On Sundays, the family worshipped at the Goshen Methodist Church, where Eugene's favorite hymn was "Will There Be Any Stars in My Crown?"

Eugene was strong, active and smart in school, though he had trouble with spelling. Convinced that "a healthy mind needs a healthy body," he prided himself on how much bagged grain and corn he could carry on his shoulder. He played baseball often and with a passion. He trudged through the local marshes and swamps with a gun in his hand, searching for game. He showed a talent for salesmanship, setting traps for muskrats and selling their skins for 17 cents each.

He was interested in electricity and engineering. In 1892, when he graduated first in his class from the Goshen Public School, he spoke at the Cape May County Courthouse on how industry is "fortune's right hand."

After attending Pennington Seminary, a preparatory school just north of Trenton, he entered Lehigh University with Gator to study electrical engineering. He won a mathematics prize his freshman year and, as a sophomore, a scholarship endowed by Bethlehem Iron Co. Director Elisha P. Wilbur. He was captain of Lehigh's baseball team for two seasons and was considered a fast, smart shortstop.

When the National League's Boston Beaneaters played an exhibition game against Lehigh, Grace hit a home run off one of their best pitchers, Kid Nichols. Impressed, the Beaneaters (later the Braves) offered Grace $200 a month to be their shortstop. But he wasn't interested, figuring that a career on the diamond would leave him washed up by the time he was 35. "I don't think I went to Lehigh to learn to play baseball," he said.

Instead, he accepted an offer to work for the new Bethlehem Steel Co. from company executive Archibald Johnston, a Lehigh graduate dazzled by Grace's play in a game against Lafayette College.

Grace graduated first in Lehigh's Class of 1899 and gave his valedictorian address on the future of electricity. Just days later, on June 29, he started work as an electric crane operator at the South Bethlehem plant for $1.80 a day — 15 cents an hour and a 12-hour day.

At the time, Bethlehem was a small ordnance, heavy forgings and railmaker with 3,500 employees. Just a few months earlier, its directors had formed the Bethlehem Steel holding company to raise money from the sale of stock and to lease the Bethlehem Iron Co. Schwab bought Bethlehem Steel in 1901 and folded it into the U.S. Shipbuilding Co. merger the next year.

Grace's observations on ways to cut waste got him noticed by the bosses, who promoted him to superintendent of yards and transportation.

One day in 1902, according to Porter's book, Grace heard a commotion and a clatter of hooves on one of the brick streets near the mill. Something had spooked a horse pulling a carriage, causing the animal to rear and bolt. Grace ran into the street, grabbed the reins and brought the horse to a stop.

The carriage rider was Marion Brown, daughter of a former South Bethlehem burgess, the equivalent of today's mayor. A courtship began, and on June 12, 1902, Eugene, who was 25, and Marion, 21, were married. The next year, Marion gave birth to Emmeline. Charles would follow in 1905 and Eugene Jr. in 1914.

In December 1904, Schwab grabbed Bethlehem Steel and several other businesses from the failed shipbuilding merger and formed the Bethlehem Steel Corp.

One of Grace's jobs was switching the new owner's lavish private rail car, the Loretto, through the yards on the company's property. While inspecting a blast furnace one day, Schwab was surprised to see the yards landscaped with trees, plants and bushes. He turned to Grace and demanded, "Whose idea was this?"

"Mine," Grace replied. "Why let the mill look like a shambles?"

Schwab agreed, and the greenery stayed. He and Grace then talked about production, and Schwab was impressed with the young superintendent's knowledge.

Early in 1906, when Schwab asked his assistant, James H. Ward, to name the most outstanding employee, Ward replied, "That's a foolish question. There is only one choice. … E.G. Grace."

Schwab had a mission for the 29-year-old: Go to Cuba and "clean up the situation" at Bethlehem's Juragua Iron Mines, which were plagued with high operating costs. Cuban ore made quality steel because it was low in phosphorus and rich in iron and nickel, a natural toughener. Juragua, on the south coast, was Bethlehem's main source of ore. Grace told Schwab he would go, but that he didn't see his future there. "My ambitions," he said, "lie in Bethlehem."

In Cuba, Grace saw that the mine operation was inefficient because it wasn't mechanized. He set it up with machines, which lowered costs and raised productivity. As a result, Bethlehem's cost per ton of iron ore was $4.31, or $3 less than what U.S. Steel paid. A pleased Schwab gave Grace his wish. "You go back to Bethlehem right now, and stay there," Schwab told him. "I shall have work for you to do."

Schwab made Grace assistant to the general superintendent. "Certain management toes were tread on by this arrangement," Grace recalled in 1947 when he gave the first Schwab Memorial Lecture at the American Iron and Steel Institute, the industry trade group in New York. "For the job in Cuba I was paid $500 a month and all living expenses. When I came back to Bethlehem, I found that certain cross-currents had developed. My immediate superiors put me to work at $175 a month and nothing else. Knowing the assurances I had had from Mr. Schwab, that didn't make me quit — as some people were doubtless hoping I would. I felt that I would be given an opportunity ultimately."

Four months later, in June 1906, he was general superintendent. The next year he began supervising construction of the $5 million Grey mill. In 1908, when the mill began rolling the first wide-flange beams for America's skyscrapers, Schwab wanted to take on an advisory role and let Grace run the company as the best of his "Boys of Bethlehem." Grace turned down the post of president, believing Schwab should keep it, and instead became general manager in charge of manufacturing, sales and purchasing. He was also elected to the board of directors.

Grace became vice president in 1911, and five years later, at age 39, president of the corporation. His aims were administrative efficiency, a managerial structure that was taut and intricate, and loyalty to the company. He wanted his managers to consider Bethlehem Steel a career, not just a job, so he rewarded the good ones with transfers and promotions. "When there is a management position open," he told an interviewer, "it is filled by selecting a man who is already working for the company and well-steeped in its practices and philosophies."

In 1922, he set up the "Loop Course," the company's management training program that acquainted college graduates with every facet of the operation. The name derived from the trainees' working in a loop through the plant, with about a week in each department. Each man would be on his own schedule, but there was much criss-crossing and fraternization. In keeping with Grace's emphasis on health and fitness, the 150 men chosen each year not only had to show promise, they had to have good physiques.

Grace continued Schwab's wage incentive system, which rewarded workers who performed better than expected. In the 1930s, he started a public relations campaign to promote the company.

But he was less forward-thinking in other matters and acted in ways that didn't serve the company well in later years. Like Schwab, Grace had no interest in hiring anyone but steel men,

leaving the top ranks dominated by executives who had little business experience outside the industry. The board of directors, too, continued to be run by insiders. And even though the company had enormous resources, Grace discouraged pure research. Both he and Schwab brushed off inventors and tinkerers.

Except for the innovative Grey beam, Bethlehem followed Andrew Carnegie's dictum, "Pioneering don't pay." In the mid-1920s, Schwab and Grace spurned a technological breakthrough, a superior but expensive technique for rolling quality steel up to 3 feet wide and less than a quarter inch thick. This was the continuous hot-strip mill, first installed by the American Rolling Mill Co., later Armco, in 1924 in Ashland, Ky. It was a more revolutionary development than the Grey mill because it provided sheet steel for a bigger product line — the auto, appliance, container and construction industries. Until then, sheet steel had been made at individual mill stands each run by millhands. With the hot-strip mill, that method was antiquated. Bethlehem had to scrap a large hand-sheet mill it was building at Sparrows Point because it couldn't have competed with the hot-strip mill.

When Bethlehem opened a research department in 1926, it was mainly devoted to practical matters aimed at keeping costs down. The kind of inventiveness that tickled Grace was finding a way to make lubricating oil last longer.

Chairman Schwab rewarded Grace generously for making Bethlehem's far-flung enterprises gel. Grace became the highest-paid corporate executive in America, with average annual earnings of $600,000 over 20 years beginning in 1918. Even Elbert Gary, chairman of mammoth U.S. Steel, never made more than $500,000.

When Grace got $1.6 million in bonuses for 1929, on top of his $12,000 salary, incredulous Bethlehem stockholders protested. They didn't know how much he was getting until it came to light during the 1930 court fight over Bethlehem's attempted takeover of Youngstown Sheet & Tube Co. Youngstown stockholders won their fight to prevent the merger in part by claiming Bethlehem had kept Grace's bonuses a secret from their directors. Later, Bethlehem stockholders stripped Schwab of his control over the bonus system.

As Schwab struggled with poor health and finances, Grace stood by him. The "Steel King" got $250,000 a year even though he wasn't doing anything for the company. "There was no sum in my judgment that you could have paid Mr. Schwab that would have adequately paid him for his leadership, devotion and financial risks that he took for the development of Bethlehem," Grace said at the American Iron and Steel Institute.

During a heated stockholders' meeting in 1937, Grace shouted at and had to be restrained from attacking two dissident investors who said Schwab had "outlived his usefulness." After Schwab's death in 1939, Grace scrambled to have the company cover his debts, not wanting his old master's name sullied.

He was equally intense on the golf course at the Saucon Valley Country Club, an office away from the office for Bethlehem Steel executives. A superb golfer within two years of taking up the sport, he was the prime mover behind the founding of the club. It opened as an 18-hole golf course in 1922 with tennis courts, a swimming pool and a clubhouse. In 1951, he enticed the U.S. Golf Association to hold its 51st Amateur Championship on Saucon Valley's links, known as the Saucon Course. Also that year, work began on another 18 holes that would be called the Grace Course.

Stewart S. Cort, who would become Bethlehem Steel's chief executive in 1970, got an early taste of Grace's sober approach to the links. As a teenager in the late 1920s, Cort, a fine golfer and the son of steelmaking operations head Stewart J. Cort, showed up at Saucon Valley one day and asked Grace if he could be part of his foursome. According to the story the younger Cort later told Bethlehem Steel speechwriter John F. Heinz, Grace glowered at him and said, "Cort, I hope you can hit 'em long and straight."

"Well, Mr. Grace, I hit 'em long, but not always straight," the teenager replied. Grace, who liked to golf with better players as a way to improve his scores, dismissed the teen with the words, "Learn to hit 'em straight before you play with us."

When he couldn't keep his golf ball out of a sand trap guarding the fourth hole, Grace complained to Vincent "Pat" Pazzetti, the College Football Hall of Fame quarterback from Lehigh University who maintained the grounds. "Pat," Grace said one day in the late 1930s, "that sand trap at the fourth hole has been giving me a lot of trouble. Maybe it would be a good idea if it didn't do that again." Making it the only priority that weekend, Pazzetti and his staff pushed one mound of ground this way, another mound that way. By the time Grace teed off the following week, the offending trap had vanished. He played on as if nothing had happened. Pazzetti later became general manager of the Bethlehem plant.

In her book, Porter describes how her grandfather's imperious nature and lust for golf kept the Bethlehem police scrambling.

"At 3 p.m. every day, the horn blasted at the steel mill announcing it was time to go home. I am told that at exactly 3:05, Mr. Grace donned his old threadbare camel's-hair coat..., a golf cap, and, wrapping a scarf around his neck regardless of the temperature or time of year, announced he was ready to leave for his daily golf game or lesson at Saucon Valley Country Club.

"Outside the office building, his brown Cadillac waited. And the moment he was seated behind the wheel, the Bethlehem Police Department was alerted to watch for the safety of motorists and pedestrians who might make the mistake of crossing his path. Officers were dispatched to every traffic light between the plant ... and the highway leading to the golf course. No red light was permitted to slow Mr. Grace's progress to his beloved golf game at Saucon. ... Legend assures us he drove 50 mph through every intersection."

When Grace finished his game and got in his car to go home, golf pro Ralph Hutchinson hurried to the caddy shack to call the police. "Mr. Grace just left," he'd say. Officers rushed to keep his route clear.

Grace had a chauffeur, Phil Malone, and a limousine but preferred to drive himself. "He'd just take the keys and make me sit in the back," Malone recalled for Porter's book. "But there were days when ... I just got in and drove, and watched in the rearview mirror as he relieved his tensions by taking putter in hand and cracking golf balls against the opposite door of the limousine.

"One day, the slow traffic and steel business got the best of Mr. Grace. Caught in a traffic jam on the narrow old New Street bridge behind a slow-moving truck, he lost his patience and pulled the hand strap right out from the upholstery."

Grace had the power and influence to stand above the law. He had ample time and money for golf at the country club, as did his associates in Bethlehem Steel's executive offices. Rich men, they breathed the rarefied air at the top of the social pyramid.

Far below them, at the bottom of the pyramid, was the common working man. He worked long hours in the mill for meager pay, under harsh conditions that brought sickness, injury and death. He had no guarantee of health care or job security. His continued employment hinged on whether he could keep his foreman happy with gifts and services that had nothing to do with the work. He got by with little more than the essentials in a shack, a row house or a twin. He was the target of racial and ethnic discrimination and hatred. He was at the mercy of city policemen and officials in the company's pocket. On the streets of south Bethlehem, he had to contend with crime and corruption.

The city of Bethlehem, formed in 1917 by the merger of Bethlehem and South Bethlehem, had 57,900 residents by 1930, four times as many as two decades earlier. Some were coarse-as-sandpaper characters who worked in the mills and contributed to the South Side's reputation for wildness.

In the Roaring '20s, the area around the steel plant was a hive of brothels and smoke-filled, gin-soaked speakeasies. Corrupt police officers chose not to enforce Prohibition, allowing the South Side to become awash in illegal alcohol, and tolerated widespread gambling and prostitution. If an honest policeman tried to do his job, he came up against surly bootleggers and gangsters who weren't about to let anyone stand in the way of easy money and easy women.

South Bethlehem's reputation spread across state lines and drew mobsters and other unsavory visitors in search of a good time, or what they called "a lost weekend." In her pamphlet, "Saturday Night on the South Side," south Bethlehem historian Joan Campion writes: "When the cars with New York license plates rolled across the so-called 'penny bridge,' which stood where the Fahy or New Street bridge is now located, Mr. Santee, the toll keeper, ducked down in his booth and didn't even try to collect from them; he didn't want any trouble."

With violence going unchecked, some called the South Side the "Bucket of Blood." Then-Mayor James Yeakle claimed that 95 percent of the crimes committed in the city happened there. "It is here that we have a preponderance of foreigners. In fact, there are no less than 48 nationalities represented among the labor element of the city. It is among them particularly that all the law violations occur."

A tough new administration took over City Hall in 1930. Mayor Robert Pfeifle, elected on an anti-corruption platform, and his superintendent of police, the Rev. Frederick T. Trafford, succeeded in calming the South Side, though its merchants weren't pleased. "They reacted as they might have done to the threatened closing of a major industry, which vice at that time was," Campion writes.

In its first year, the Pfeifle administration claimed to have shut down 241 speakeasies and "bawdy houses," arrested 190 prostitutes and 105 johns, and seized and destroyed 105 gallons of gin, 2,900 gallons of moonshine, or corn whiskey, and 159 gallons of mash, the crushed malt or grain meal used to make beer and whiskey. They also seized 10 tons of copper that would have been used to make stills and sold it to junk dealers.

The end of Prohibition in 1933 further reduced mayhem, but the South Side would continue to be an unforgiving and dirty place. "Here are the smoke-belching mills, coke plants and begrimed streets of the typical steel town," read the caption to a Bethlehem photo in the 1940 "Guide to Pennsylvania" distributed by the federal government's jobs-creating Works Progress Administration.

Many steelworkers — hot, dirty and tired from their labors — didn't go directly home after their shifts, but to a multitude of corner barrooms where they often fought with one another. They were part of a work force that numbered 10,300 in 1929, the year the stock market crashed. As the Depression deepened, their ranks declined, from 9,500 in 1930, to 8,300 in 1931, to a low of 6,500 in 1933.

In the '20s, Bethlehem Steel had the opposite problem — more jobs to fill than people to fill them. But the company and other producers had a dilemma.

Steelmakers used vast numbers of immigrants from eastern and southern Europe to do unskilled labor. Right-wing groups fighting to keep foreigners out of the country pressured lawmakers to restrict immigration. Though the steelmakers lobbied against the so-called quota laws, Congress passed them in 1921 and 1924. About the same time, the Soviet Union and fascist Italy put their own restrictions on citizens who wanted to emigrate.

U.S. steel companies believed they had only two alternatives. They could employ blacks or Mexicans.

While steelmakers elsewhere turned to blacks to fill the lowest-paying jobs, Bethlehem Steel chose Mexicans. Grace noted there was no restriction on immigration from Mexico. Also, few black men lived in the Lehigh Valley, so they couldn't provide the manpower Bethlehem needed. There was the racial and ethnic stereotyping of the day, a prejudice that was blatant then and illegal today.

"The Mexicans are better, more dependable workers than the Negroes. The Negroes aren't there when you want them; they go south with the cold weather," one Bethlehem executive told sociologist Paul S. Taylor in 1929.

Another executive said, "We have had a more favorable experience with the Mexicans than with the Negroes, but not so favorable as, say with the Hungarians, who are more stable and dependable than the Mexicans."

Bethlehem Steel saw other reasons not to hire blacks. With race riots and lynchings widespread across the country, Schwab and Grace would not have wanted to turn the South Side

into a powder keg. Inside the plant, they didn't want to stir up trouble among other workers, who probably would be angry and resentful because blacks had been employed elsewhere as "scabs," or strikebreakers.

Lehigh University urban planning professor David Amidon doesn't believe there was "some conspiracy on the part of Bethlehem Steel not to hire blacks. I think because there were so few black people around, it did not dawn on them."

Only about 1,000 blacks lived in the Lehigh Valley in the early 1920s, compared with high numbers in other industrial centers. To this day, blacks still make up only a tiny percentage of the local population. About 18,500 live in the Valley, or 3 percent.

Elsewhere, Bethlehem Steel did hire blacks in large numbers. At its biggest plant, Sparrows Point in Baltimore Harbor, a quarter of the work force was black men. Many had come north from Southern farms as part of the "Great Migration" of the World War I era.

That migration passed by the Lehigh Valley. Blacks heading to the industrial North preferred big cities such as Philadelphia, New York, Chicago and Detroit. There, they could live in black communities that already existed and work in factories for higher pay than they would get in Bethlehem.

Even if they had come to the Lehigh Valley, they wouldn't have been welcome. It was an insular place where people felt uncomfortable with anyone or anything different.

A small number of blacks had lived in the Valley since Colonial days. The first came in the 18th century from the West Indies as missionary converts to the Moravian Church. Others were slaves. Though slavery ended in Pennsylvania during the Revolution, blacks born into servitude before 1776 could be held for life. As a result, Pennsylvania still had slaves in the 1850s.

Some free blacks came to the Valley in the 1820s to help build the Lehigh Canal. Part of Allentown's 1st Ward along the Lehigh River was nicknamed Mingo after Santo Domingo, a largely black island nation that today is the Dominican Republic.

When the Lehigh Zinc Co. and the Lehigh Valley Railroad came to south Bethlehem in

A worker in Bethlehem Iron's blacksmith shop makes tools for the company in the 1890s.

John Fritz, an engineering genius hired by Bethlehem Rolling Mill & Iron Co. in 1860, developed the "three-high" rail mill process. Here he looks over a blueprint circa 1900. He retired as plant superintendent in 1892.

Crucible steelworkers gather for a photograph at Bethlehem Steel Corp. in the early 1900s. The crucibles were clay-graphite pots used to melt wrought iron to make alloy steel for metal cutting.

A worker shows the breech of a 14-inch coast defense gun in the No. 2 Machine Shop in the early 1900s. Only a small percentage of guns were made completely at Bethlehem in later years.

Courtesy of National Canal Museum Archives

Courtesy of National Canal Museum Archives

Henry Noll became a celebrated symbol of efficiency at Bethlehem Iron. In 1899, the 27-year-old laborer went from hauling 13 tons of pig iron a day to 48 tons during an incentive program run by efficiency expert Frederick Taylor. Noll's herculean feat was described in Taylor's book, 'Principles of Scientific Management.' A marker on Third Street in Bethlehem pays tribute to Noll, who died in 1925.

From the Archive Collection of Historic Bethlehem Partnership

A postcard shows Bethlehem Steel from the New Street Bridge looking east in 1910, after the Lehigh Valley Railroad's main line was relocated to the bank of the Lehigh River. Before that, the main line went right through the middle of the works.

During the 1910 strike, Pennsylvania State Constabulary officers on horseback patrolled the Bethlehem Steel area.

Steel bars are produced in the 1920s in the No. 3 9-inch mill in the tool steel department. Mill hands, as the rolling mill workers were called, had to catch the red-hot bars as they left the mill and feed them back into the mill. Several passes through the mill were required to reduce a billet to a bar.

Courtesy of National Canal Museum Archives

Courtesy of Lebanon County Historical Society

Bethlehem Steel's Lebanon team had at least one famous player, George Herman Ruth, the 'Babe.' He's the third player from the left in the back row.

Left, President Woodrow Wilson (above) attends an event with Bethlehem Steel Chairman Charles M. Schwab (bottom left) and a riveter of the Hog Island Shipyard in Philadelphia. Schwab ran the government's World War I shipbuilding program in 1918.

Courtesy of National Canal Museum Archives

Bethlehem Steel executives gather during a visit by inventor Thomas Edison (front row, fifth from left). Charles Schwab is in front row center holding a light-colored hat, and Eugene Grace is second from right in the front row.

The main turret made by Bethlehem Steel for the battleship USS Pennsylvania dwarfs workers. The warship was commissioned in 1916. The turret is assembled from several pieces of forged, machined and hardened armor plate.

Women work in the shell shop during World War I at Bethlehem Steel.

Bethlehem Steel fabricators gather for a photograph about 1925.

Courtesy of United Steelworkers of America, Bethlehem

Courtesy of National Canal Museum Archives

A high-pressure cylinder is machined in Bethlehem Steel's No. 2 Machine Shop in 1924. The left end is resting on a planer bed; the right end is being bored by a horizontal boring mill.

James McNally, a Bethlehem Steel employee, holds a brick as he walks away from overturned police cars outside the South Side plant during the 1941 strike. The photo appeared in Life magazine on April 7, 1941.

A woman cuts a steel beam with an oxyacetylene torch. About 2,200 women worked at the Bethlehem plant during World War II.

In a widely used photo from the Bethlehem Steel strike of 1941, a horse ridden by Bethlehem police officer Mel Packard rears as a crowd of strikers presses in. The photo came to symbolize police repression, but Packard contended he wasn't attacking anyone. He said his horse, Chief, reared when a striker came too close.

During World War II, about 200 women carried guns as company security officers, earning the nickname "pistol packin' mamas." Some of the officers are shown at a first-aid class in 1944. Ethel Gasda (standing, second from the right) says she took the job because it almost tripled her pay.

Workers make steel shells in March 1944 at The Steel's Forge Specialty shop.

Bethlehem Steel operated Sparrows Point shipyard in Maryland during World War II. The shipyard was sold in 1997 and renamed Baltimore Marine Industries, which filed for bankruptcy in 2003. The shipyard closed the next year.

Courtesy of International Steel Group

In its glory days, Bethlehem Steel employed pretty young women as escorts to guide visitors through the company's 13-story head-quarters on Third Street in Bethlehem. They were modeled after airline flight attendants. Ellie Zsitek (second row, far left) says New York models were brought in to show the women how to walk and hold their hands. The escorts were part of Bethlehem Steel's effort to project a perfect image.

Courtesy of National Canal Museum Archives

The brakeman signals the narrow-gauge locomotive engineer as Bethlehem Steel ingots go from the mold stripper to the soaking pits in the 1960s.

Nine Check brothers have worked at Bethlehem Steel. In this 1970s photo, the brothers are (from left) John, Bartholomew 'Al,' Steve, Andrew, George, Mike, Emil, Frank and Richie.

In 2003, the surviving Check brothers visit their old stomping grounds at Bethlehem Steel. From left are Bartholomew 'Al,' George, Frank and Richie. Bartholomew 'Al' and Frank died in 2004.

Bethlehem steel went into many of the buildings in Manhattan. A sign in the rolling mill department read, 'Welcome to the Mill that made Manhattan.' Left, New York's Chrysler Building became the tallest structure in the world when it was built in 1930. Bethlehem has listed Chrysler as one of its crowning achievements, but U.S. Steel Corp. disputes that claim.

Right, John S. Wadolny, a former Bethlehem Steel union leader, recalled that just about anyone who wanted a job at Bethlehem Steel during World War II got one. Wadolny worked in the Forge Specialty shop, making shells for the Army and Navy. He died in 2004.

Far right, safety boots, required gear, hang in the welfare room, where Bethlehem Steel workers cleaned up after their shifts. Each steel worker had an open-air hanger so that wet work clothes would not mildew.

Chuck Zovko/
Morning Call
file photos

Courtesy of Joseph Elliott/National Canal Museum Archives

Bethlehem's Blast Furnace C is shown at midnight on the last night of operations in 1995. The end of steelmaking came on a rainy night.

The No. 2 Machine Shop housed lathes and other machine tools. At almost a third of a mile long and 300,000 square feet, it was the world's largest machine shop when it began operations in 1890.

Bethlehem Steel ended steelmaking in Bethlehem in 1995, the year this aerial photo was taken. The Lehigh River is on the left. Bare spots in the foreground show that the No. 3 open hearth and the alloy mills are already gone.

On Nov. 18, 1995, workers on the last shift at a Bethlehem Steel blast furnace gather to watch as the final molten iron is poured into a submarine rail car. For the first time since 1873, steel would not be made in the Lehigh Valley.

An ingot mold is half-buried in debris in the electric furnace melt shop in Bethlehem.

Tom Volk/Morning Call file photo

Bethlehem Steel retiree Kenneth Williams of Northampton (right) talks with a United Steelworkers of America representative about health benefits in March 2003. The company's bankruptcy resulted in retirees losing their free health insurance.

At left, a door machine operator shovels coke spillage into a Bethlehem Steel coke oven in 1995. Facing a chamber heated to 2,400 degrees, he wears protective gear that includes a dust mask and a flame-retardant suit. Coke, a processed form of bituminous coal, is the basic fuel consumed in blast furnaces in the smelting of iron ore.

Today, the former Bethlehem Steel's towering blast furnaces cast a shadow over south Bethlehem.

the 1850s, some of their executives had black servants. In the 20th century, Schwab employed almost all blacks on Loretto, his private railroad car.

"They regarded themselves as a proud elite," notes Amidon, who has interviewed descendants of many Bethlehem blacks. "They were better educated in many cases than the local whites."

Yet blacks were outsiders, as the Valley's Germans had been in the 18th century. Isolated because they didn't speak English, the Germans drew inward. In eastern Pennsylvania, they created a cultural enclave and harbored a distrust of non-Germans. For example, they generally accepted Jewish immigrants from the German states in the 1840s and '50s, but were cool to Russian and Polish Jews who arrived in the 1890s. Any outsider would have had trouble blending into the Pennsylvania German community of that era.

Events in the Midwest reinforced negative feelings toward blacks. In the coal mines of southern Illinois and the lead mines of south central Missouri, they were brought in as scabs during strikes in 1917. Work forces made up largely of white men whose ancestors had migrated from the South rose up against them in a spasm of violence. Word spread that blacks allowed themselves to be used as strikebreakers.

Closer to home was a horrific episode that might have been on the minds of Bethlehem Steel officials — the August 1911 slaying of black steelworker Zachariah Walker in Coatesville, Chester County.

Walker, who had come north from Virginia to work at Coatesville's Worth Brothers' Steel Co., shot and killed a mill security guard. He claimed he did it in self-defense during a scuffle while he was drunk. Captured after a botched suicide attempt, he was held in a hospital shackled to a bed's footboard. A mob encouraged by the sheriff broke in and dragged him away.

Taken to a rural farm, Walker was burned to death, his screams heard up to a mile away. Three times he crawled out of the fire, three times the mob dragged him back until he died. Afterward, some in the crowd gathered pieces of his flesh and bones as souvenirs. The murder made headlines around the world.

Bethlehem executives, led by the image-conscious Schwab, would have shunned that kind of publicity. So early in 1923, Bethlehem Steel advertised for unskilled laborers in San Antonio, Texas, a recruitment center and the gateway for Mexican immigrants not bound for the American West.

According to Taylor in his book, "Mexican Labor in the United States: Bethlehem, Pennsylvania":

Bethlehem Steel and the Mexican government agreed on terms to safeguard the migrants. The cost of transporting them to Bethlehem — $84 per man — would be deducted from their pay in installments, but those who stayed with the company for a year would get the money back. The company would pay to transport the families, and provide room and board for $1.10 a day. It pledged to pay the foreigners 30 cents an hour, the same wage as workers of other nationalities who were doing the same job. The Mexicans would work no more hours than Pennsylvania law allowed, and none would be fired without just cause.

In April and May, trains brought more than 900 Mexican men and a few dozen women and children to Bethlehem, delivering them to the Northampton Heights station east of the steel plant, where police were called out to protect them. The move was a precaution because the company could not know for certain how other workers and the people of Bethlehem would react.

They reacted with shock and alarm.

"This tranquil Moravian city has been surprised over night by a veritable invasion of Mexican and Indian laborers, who have been brought to this town in three long trains, exciting the curiosity of the local population with their characteristic clothing and their broad palm sombreros," read a dispatch from the Universal Service press agency. "This invasion of Mexican laborers has given rise to many comments, and the laboring element here is asking itself thoughtfully what will be the significance of this immigration to the industrial future of the city, the center of whose life is the gigantic metallurgical plant of the Bethlehem Steel Corporation."

Rumors spread that the foreigners posed a "danger of grave labor disturbances." Company executives actually counted on the opposite. The Mexicans added to an already large number of employees who couldn't speak English. That's how Bethlehem Steel liked it. Workers who couldn't understand one another would have difficulty organizing unions and leading strikes.

The migrants were housed in barracks in a section of the city along the eastern edge of the plant and in the labor camp the company had built during World War I on the grounds of the coke ovens. At a company-run boardinghouse, they were provided with Mexican cooks, and a Mexican with a small store sold them groceries and other necessities.

"We wanted the Mexicans to feel that they had a good community," one Bethlehem executive told Taylor. "We wanted them to be happy and feel that we were interested in them as human beings as a matter of good business and good morals."

But the company's concern for the Mexicans' well-being did not go far, according to the book "The Chicano Experience," by Stanley A. West and June Macklin.

The labor camp, a cluster of wood-frame shacks and barracks, was a squalid plot where 250 men, women and children had to endure black soot and noxious odors from the coke batteries and tar pits, as well as rats. Among the residents were Slavs, Hungarians, Portuguese, Poles and Spaniards. Though they had freedom of movement, a fence enclosed the property, and guards stood at the gate.

Still, for most of the Mexicans, the camp was a paradise compared to the dirt-poor life they left behind. Now at least they had buildings to live in, free coke for heat, some furniture and land on which they could have a garden and raise chickens, ducks, pigs and geese.

Mexican men were assigned to the coke ovens because bosses thought they could "take the heat," a stereotype that was also applied to Puerto Ricans who came to Bethlehem after World War II. But the Mexicans worked until they collapsed and were black from head to toe.

A company executive told Taylor that most of the migrants were "good steady workers. As a class, their intelligence is above the Slavish [Slovaks] and Wendish. ... If some people think the Mexicans are dumb, they should see some of our Irish."

But their employment reinforced a prejudice against Mexicans in general. Because Pennsylvania law allowed Bethlehem to hire only Mexicans who were common laborers, all people from south of the border were seen as ignorant and unskilled.

They were also considered dangerous.

"Drunken Mexican goes on rampage with gun," read a 1926 headline in the now-defunct Bethlehem Globe-Times. "Raul Martinez, a Mexican, residing in the camp at the Coke Works, drank moonshine Thursday night and then ran amuck with a revolver." The story didn't say he was celebrating Mexican Independence Day, Sept. 16.

"Can't find bad Mexican," read a front-page headline after a Mexican allegedly knifed a black man.

Mexicans weren't singled out for this treatment. Any ethnic group that was new to the area suffered in the press, which both reflected and pandered to the prejudices of the day. Otherwise, Mexicans were treated no differently from anyone else who went into movies, restaurants, barbershops and other public places.

The problem for Bethlehem Steel was that the Mexicans didn't stay with the company. Soon after they reached Bethlehem in 1923, they began to disperse. Twenty-four percent of those who arrived in the spring were gone by mid-summer, 53 percent by the fall and 71 percent by the end of the year. The average number of Mexicans on the payroll in the 14 months after the original group arrived was 464. Those who left found better jobs elsewhere in the Valley or, homesick and weary of cold weather, returned to the Southwest or Mexico.

Still, Taylor concluded, the results of Bethlehem's experiment "have been sufficiently satisfactory to both Mexicans and executives to maintain a colony."

By 1930, only about 350 Mexicans remained, with a rough balance of arrivals and departures. They lived in the labor camp and along the southern edge of the steel plant. In

1937, those who stayed — a core of about 50 families — formed the Bethlehem Mexican Aztec Society, which became the focal point of community life.

"We didn't have an extended family to fall back on. We had to depend on each other," said Frances Nuno of Bethlehem, a daughter of a Bethlehem Steel worker, in a 1988 Morning Call interview.

The company demolished the labor camp in 1939.

Today, Mexicans make up only a tiny portion — six-tenths of a percent — of Lehigh and Northampton counties' total population of more than 579,000.

Bethlehem Steel's early 20th century workers were overwhelmingly men whose roots were in Europe. Some had followed in the path of their fathers, who had accepted harsh and unfair conditions because they were happy to have a job and eager to prove their manhood. Now there were stirrings among the second generation: Did it have to be this way? Like their fathers, they found themselves groveling for decent treatment.

Public pressure on steel companies had brought workers some relief. Beginning in 1923, workers no longer had an 11-hour day shift, a 13-hour night shift and a 24-hour swing shift on alternate Sundays. The swing shift ended, and workers got an eight-hour day and six-day week. Instead of putting in 84 hours a week, they now worked 56 to 70 hours. With the eight-hour day, the company needed more workers, a major reason it recruited Mexicans.

Hourly employees got no paid vacations, but they didn't have to work Christmas Day and the Fourth of July. Also in 1923, the company instituted a pension plan and employee savings and stock ownership plan. By 1929, the average millworker was earning $2,150 a year, or $22,575 in today's money.

Industrial work meant not only low pay, but dangerous and dirty conditions. A worker could be killed or injured by carbon monoxide, explosions, heavy objects falling, machinery, sparks or boiling steel. Along with coal mining, it was among the most dangerous jobs a person could do. If a man entered the mill at age 20, he could

expect to live seven years less than someone working in an office.

After the strike of 1910, when Bethlehem Steel workers failed to get better pay and working conditions, the Bethlehem community saw the steel plant as unsafe. To ease concerns, Schwab and Grace set up a system that gave each department a safety committee made up of a foreman and three laborers. Those committees reported problems to a central Safety and Welfare Department.

For years, workers injured or sickened on the job had been sent to St. Luke's Hospital in the neighboring borough of Fountain Hill. The company changed that in 1914 by building a dispensary and staffing it full time with doctors and nurses responsible for all except the most serious cases.

But worker safety at Bethlehem still was abysmal. So many employees lost fingers and limbs that some sections of the plant were nicknamed the "chop shop."

From 1905 until the end of steelmaking in Bethlehem 91 years later, 650 workers at the Bethlehem plant died in work-related accidents, including one woman. More than three-quarters died before the Second World War. World War I years carried the biggest toll, with 50 deaths in 1917 and 46 in 1918. Among the 1918 deaths was the woman, Daisy Taylor, whose fate is a mystery. There seems to be no record of what happened to her.

The wife of steelworker Frank Sandor was doubly cursed. After Sandor was killed at the rail mill in 1920, she married one of his co-workers, John Angerman. He was killed at the plant in 1928.

Such unsafe conditions, along with low wages and unfair practices, further demoralized workers at Bethlehem Steel and in plants and factories across the nation when the Great Depression struck. With the stock market crash of 1929, economic misery deepened. The number of jobless people rose from 3 million in 1930 to 15 million three years later, a quarter of America's work force. Only 151,000 had unemployment insurance, and none of those worked in steel.

During the Depression, Bethlehem had a

"spread the work" policy. Hours were divided among the employees based on how much work the mills were getting, and were scaled back as orders dropped. If an employee wasn't laid off, he was working part time. He might work five hours a day, three days a week, for 45 cents an hour, or $6.75 a week. But he didn't know when he'd work, because his days weren't scheduled. He had to show up each day at 7 a.m. along with other workers. A foreman would choose the men he wanted for the shift. "I want you and you and you," he'd say. If a worker wasn't picked, he'd have to come back at 3 p.m. If he again wasn't picked, he'd have to return at 11 p.m. for the next shift. The routine was repeated every day. It grated on the men.

The Depression gripped the U.S. economy in earnest in 1931, starting with the auto industry. With far fewer cars being made, Bethlehem Steel lost most of its automobile sheet and engine market. Then sales to railroads and builders dropped dramatically. Overall, Bethlehem's production fell from 55 million tons in 1929 to 40 million tons in '31.

By 1932, 90 percent of the steel industry's half-million employees were either laid off or working part time.

Mark Reutter, in his book "Sparrows Point: Making Steel," notes that because of its immense size, Bethlehem Steel could make lots of steel economically and rake in high profits when there was heavy demand. But when it was forced to produce less than half its capacity, the economies of scale vanished. Bethlehem had to pay millions just to cover fixed costs and overhead.

In a cry that would resonate among steel leaders decades later, Schwab called on the government to raise tariffs on imported steel, which at the time accounted for little more than 1 percent of American business. "Our markets today are being upset by the dumping of foreign steel at sacrifice prices on American shores," he complained. To economize, Grace cut wages 10 percent in 1931 and 15 percent the next year, taking the base hourly rate from 45 cents to 34 cents.

To hold onto their low-paying jobs, workers understood that they had to stay in the good graces of their supervisors. It wasn't just a matter of knowing the right person. It was also how many pigs, ducks and cigars they could give their bosses.

Soon after he began working in a forge specialty shop in 1934, John S. Wadolny learned that the way to a foreman's heart was through the farm. Each boss had his own garage. Wadolny saw workers from rural upper Bucks County pulling up to the garages on Emery Street in Bethlehem, opening the trunks of their cars and switching chickens, ducks and half a pig over to the cars of the foremen. It always seemed to Bethlehem resident Wadolny that the farm boys got the best machine jobs, known then as the "gravy jobs."

Some bosses loved smoking cigars, so workers showed up with cigars in their pockets. Every other day, the bosses would go up to someone, take two or three cigars from him and continue down the assembly line for more free smokes.

Even away from the plant, foremen got what they wanted. Wadolny got an eye-opening look at the servitude of the workers about two years into his career at Bethlehem Steel. Co-workers invited him to a party at a south Bethlehem Catholic social hall, the Holy Ghost Club, which had a bowling alley. The men and their bosses drank and bowled. Wadolny wondered why the workers were buying the drinks for their bosses and was disturbed by something else he saw.

"I noticed that the foremen were having a hell of a good time grabbing the wives' breasts," he recalled in interviews before his death at age 89 on July 23, 2004. "It just turned my stomach. I thought, 'How the hell can the guys buy them drinks?' It was the system, goddammit. I guess they were afraid to make any trouble with the foremen."

Asking too many questions could get workers fired. Ask for a promotion? They didn't dare. If they didn't call the boss "mister," he would ignore them. If they bothered him too much, Wadolny remembered, the exasperated boss would shout: "Get out! Get out! You're fired!"

Wadolny was at the plant about two years and becoming bored with his repetitive job, tagging and drilling military projectile shells. He respectfully asked his boss to consider him for a vacant position as a machinist. Someone else got the job. Wadolny thought it odd that the new employee had the same name as his boss, until the employee revealed that he was the boss's nephew.

In 1932, Roosevelt's election as president gave workers hope. His New Deal sought to ease the distress of unemployment, get the economy moving again and raise up the working man.

Once seen as America's heroes, business executives were now reviled for failing to end the Depression. Roosevelt believed that given a chance and more purchasing power, workers would save the day. But they would need help from unions.

Trade unions had seen hefty gains in the 1890s and early in the 20th century, enlisting more than 5 million members. But unions declined in the mid-1920s, mainly because the American Federation of Labor failed to organize the bulk of industrial workers. Also, post-World War I prosperity satisfied most workingmen. By 1930, only 3.4 million workers belonged to a trade union.

The Great Depression rescued the labor movement. As unemployment climbed, many Americans saw the cruelty of low wages, long hours, unsafe conditions and unfair practices. They resented the way government sided with businesses and protected them with federal troops and police.

Both Schwab and Grace had battled to keep unions out of Bethlehem Steel, insisting that the in-house program they created — the Employee Representation Plan — adequately served their employees. Grace continued the fight during the 1930s, when Schwab was old and sick and unionism was spreading. To enforce what Grace called the company's "almost sacred policy" against recognizing unions, he held off the government for years with a barrage of legal objections and resorted to dirty tricks, bribery and the stockpiling of weapons.

Still, no amount of resistance would hold back Bethlehem Steel's workers, who in 1941 won the right to join the union that became the United Steelworkers of America. Their triumph was a bitter defeat for Grace, who felt that unions interfered with management's ability to cut costs.

Reutter's "Sparrows Point" book describes Grace's standoff with the Democratic administration:

FDR's secretary of labor, social reformer Frances Perkins, argued that the steel industry's low wages and ban against unions were undemocratic and threatened the nation's stability. All the major steel companies had company unions, such as Bethlehem's Employee Representation Plan, whose representatives could not negotiate on wages or strike. There had to be a balance of power between employers and workers, Perkins said, and to reach it, workers must have the right to organize their own unions and bargain collectively with management.

Roosevelt granted that right under his National Recovery Administration, which allowed industries to write their own codes for compliance. Grace and other steel executives appeared to agree with the labor provision. But in Washington on Aug. 15, 1933, during what was supposed to be a routine meeting on the steel code, Grace and five other steel leaders walked out as Perkins started talking. They had spotted William Green, president of the American Federation of Labor, who was a National Recovery Administration adviser.

"If we sit down with Mr. Green," Grace told Perkins on the way out, "and if we sign a code that he signs, it will be assumed that we are dealing with organized labor. As you know, we have an almost sacred policy that we will never recognize or deal with organized labor."

Perkins was flabbergasted and felt "as though I had entertained 11-year-old boys at their first party rather than men to whom the most important industry in the U.S. had been committed."

When Roosevelt heard about the episode, he was furious over the disrespect shown to one of his Cabinet members and the delay in preparing the code. Schwab and U.S. Steel Chairman Myron Taylor were summoned to the White House. "I scared them the way they never have been frightened before," the president told a visitor later, "and I told Schwab he better not pay any more million-dollar bonuses."

Three days later the industry's leaders signed the steel code, which included a basic eight-hour day and 40-hour week and affirmed a 15 percent pay hike that Bethlehem and most other steelmakers granted in July. A 10 percent raise in March 1934 returned hourly rates to 1929 levels. But Grace sidestepped the code's intent of giving workers freedom to form their own union. He said he interpreted the code to mean that Bethlehem's Employee Representation Plan was the only legitimate way for the company and its employees to bargain.

Perkins thought Grace's argument was ridiculous and that the company unions mocked the code's labor provision. But with legal objections, both Bethlehem Steel and U.S. Steel fended off the administration's attempts to unionize the industry.

In May 1935, the U.S. Supreme Court struck down the National Recovery Administration as an illegal delegation of legislative power to the executive branch and private groups. But the following month, Congress passed a replacement — the National Labor Relations Act, or Wagner Act, which set up a labor board with powers to guarantee workers the right to organize.

Convinced that Roosevelt was on their side, workers started organizing in the steel, auto, textile, rubber and electrical industries, on loading docks, in packing houses and at telephone companies.

United Mine Workers President John L. Lewis formed what would become the Congress of Industrial Organizations and established the Steel Workers' Organizing Committee, or SWOC, to campaign at the mills. The effort got under way in July 1936 and met with mixed results.

But labor won a surprise victory in 1937 when U.S. Steel, the world's largest corporation, signed a contract. The pact met a union demand for 62.5 cents an hour, or $5 a day, and a 40-hour work week with time-and-a-half for overtime.

However, Bethlehem balked at following suit and formed a bloc called "Little Steel"

with four other holdouts — Republic, National, Youngstown Sheet & Tube and Inland Steel. Grace did grant his workers $5 a day and 40 hours a week, but he refused to recognize the steel workers' committee. In fact, he armed Bethlehem Steel to keep the union out by force. The company supplied its policemen with tear gas, pistols, revolvers, rifles, shotguns, machine guns and submachine guns and hired undercover agents to spy on union organizers.

It wasn't the first time Grace had turned vicious in his drive to repulse unions. In 1918, while Schwab was running the government's World War I shipbuilding program, the National War Labor Board condemned Bethlehem's labor practices and cited Grace and his colleagues for anti-union tactics. These included raids on suspected union members by Bethlehem city police. The police chief admitted he ordered officers to enter shops and threaten men or arrest them on misdemeanor charges.

Grace's arms buildup in 1937 belied his public stance that all was rosy. He trumpeted the company union in the March issue of the Bethlehem Review, the employee bulletin: "The Employee Representation Plans which were established in our plants nearly 20 years ago continue to operate with ever-increasing effectiveness. In our company, there is a happy relationship between employees and management which has existed over these many years."

On May 26, 1937, the Steel Workers' Organizing Committee called a strike against Republic, Inland Steel and Youngstown Sheet & Tube. Four days later in Chicago, in what became known as the "Little Steel Massacre," police killed 10 demonstrators and shot or beat 75 others as they marched toward the Republic mill. On June 9, police broke up a union picket line in Youngstown. On June 11, the strike spread to Johnstown, where 8,000 Bethlehem Steel workers walked out, partially closing the plant.

Johnstown's mayor, convicted bootlegger Daniel J. Shields, declared the city under siege and warned that he would "crush the lawless, the communist, the anarchist." His anti-union rhetoric earned him a $10,000 cash gift from Bethlehem Steel the next day. Pleasantly surprised, he asked for more. He continued his torrent of invective and ended up getting a total of $36,450 in bribes from the company.

Attempts at mediation failed. Grace hung tough and broke the Johnstown strike.

The union petitioned the National Labor Relations Board in August 1937, accusing Bethlehem of intimidating workers who wanted to join or help. Hearings lasted into April 1938, with Bethlehem twice demanding that the case be dismissed. Grace swore he would fight any labor board finding that he interfered with the "freedom" of his employees and their Employee Representation Plan.

In November 1938, a trial examiner ruled that Bethlehem had engaged in unfair labor practices. Grace appealed, inundating the labor board with legal briefs. But the decision on the appeal in August 1939 supported the Steel Workers' Organizing Committee. The labor board found that for many years, Bethlehem had intimidated employees interested in forming a union. It also found that the Employee Representation Plan violated the Wagner Act by failing to serve the "will of the employees."

The labor board ordered Bethlehem to stop the unfair practices and dismantle the company union. Grace appealed again, this time in federal court.

There would be no ruling for almost two years. In the meantime, the Employee Representation Plan continued, pending the appeal. Union activists responded by forming the Bethlehem Organizing Committee and kicked off a unionizing drive in 1940, setting the stage for the strike the next year.

In March 1941, the Employee Representation Plan at Bethlehem was scheduled to elect new officers. More than a week before the elections, the 15 members of Bethlehem's organizing committee warned that the company union was illegal and that they would strike if balloting began. Members called the company union representatives "the brownies" and considered them stooges with close ties to the bosses and

plant manager.

Howard T. Curtiss, director of the Bethlehem Organizing Committee, claimed a majority of the plant's 18,000 production workers belonged to his group, but he was bluffing on a grand scale.

John Wadolny was a member of Curtiss' committee. The one-time amateur baseball pitcher said that by the time of the strike, just a few thousand workers had indicated an interest in joining the union, and only 140 were dues-paying members. The company's managers, he said, didn't know how many workers sympathized with the union. The committee's members gambled that worker support would gather momentum.

The company union elections went on as planned in six departments on Monday, March 24. At 5:45 p.m. that day, SWOC struck. By midnight, about 2,000 workers had walked out.

An explosion of violence followed on Tuesday, as more than 50 cars were overturned and many people were injured, including three Bethlehem police officers. Gov. Arthur H. James declared an emergency, closed all local saloons, clubs and liquor stores and sent 125 troopers wielding nightsticks to restore order.

"They brought in the state police," Wadolny said, "and they were sneaky. Two boxcars came in, and all of a sudden, state cops came out of the boxcars riding their horses ... and start swinging their clubs at everybody — women, children. Swinging, didn't give a goddamn who they might hurt."

It was unclear how many men were on strike. Curtiss said 16,000 employees had walked out, while the plant's general manager, R.A. Lewis, said 6,500 were still on the job. Representatives from the company union appealed to authorities to protect their rights in the face of "lawless agitators, many strangers to our city."

At the Emery Street gate and the main gate on Fillmore Street, a half-dozen strikers at a time were overturning strikebreakers' cars. Wadolny and others picketed and held signs at Emery Street. A strikebreaker with two other men in his car drove fast down Third Street, honking his horn at the last minute to try to get strikers to move. Men in line got out of the way, but a boy was struck and his leg hurt. Furious, the strikers took it out on others who tried to enter the plant, overturning car after car.

An officer at the main gate tried to break up the picket line so employees could get through to go to work. Pickets told him to go to hell. Some officers shot tear gas into the crowd, but strikers went on another car-flipping rampage.

Jim Cox, in his mid-80s and still fit from years of playing tennis, remembers that he had to do his job as a maintenance foreman in the midst of the strike. He got a few men into the plant by boat. The men were getting hungry, but they couldn't go into the mob outside. So Cox asked a worker who was known as a good scrounger if he could round up some food. The scrounger returned with a ham, onions and a bag of potatoes that Cox later found out were stolen. The workers cooked up a ham stew over a blacksmith's fire.

Sated, the millworkers then had other things to worry about. The strikers outside saw through the windows that work was being done, so they began throwing bricks through the glass. Cox called for a welder. As bricks and glass showered over them, the welder and the tall, lanky Cox installed wire mesh over the windows. The mill kept operating.

The families of those who continued working felt the brunt of the strikers' fury. Five-year-old Ellie Prizznick was whisked to her grandmother's house when her father, a straightener at the steel company, chose to ignore the picket line. Strikers drove a tow truck to his house, hitched up his car, a LaSalle, and dumped it into Saucon Creek. Little Ellie wondered why Daddy's car was filled with mud. Going to her grandmother's house didn't get her away from the violence because strikers broke her Grammy's windows.

Even those not directly involved in the strike were affected by it. Ethel Bogunovich was 19 and living in nearby Hellertown. Her mother, a native of Hungary, forbade her to go into Bethlehem. "Uh-uh, you are not leaving Hellertown," ordered the mother as news of the overturned cars spread.

"I want to see what's going on," Ethel begged.

"No! You stay home!"

On Wednesday, March 26, the impact of the strike still wasn't clear. Plant manager Lewis said the plant was operating at full capacity, with almost 80 percent of workers on the job. But the Bethlehem Organizing Committee said 80 percent of the plant was shut down. According to the company, the union had imported "toughies" to upset cars and cause other mayhem; the union said the vandalism was the work of company agents. State police raised their force to 250.

On Thursday, Mayor Pfeifle said he had organized a secret law and order committee to help the state police "suppress vandalism and depredations in our city."

After five hours of talks, a settlement was reached at 5:40 a.m. Friday, March 28. It deferred further voting on the Employee Representation Plan's officers until the federal court case over Grace's refusal to disband the company union was resolved.

"This is the greatest victory in the history of our relations with Bethlehem Steel," crowed John Riffe of the Steel Workers' Organizing Committee.

Wadolny and other jubilant workers said to one another, "Let's parade down the streets of Bethlehem. A victory parade!"

Steelworkers who didn't belong to the union joined the Bethlehem Organizing Committee's members on the street. The local leader of the International Ladies Garment Workers Union brought 80 flag-waving women with her. In all, about 4,000 men and women marched past the company's headquarters on Third Street, while Mayor Pfeifle grumbled that the strike had "brought about 500 to 1,000 gangsters to Bethlehem."

Suddenly, nonunion workers were eager to sign up.

Though the strike had lasted less than four days, it was highly publicized across the country. One of its most dramatic images was a photo of a policeman on a horse that's rearing, surrounded by many strikers. Bethlehem mounted officer Mel Packard recalled that a striker came up to him and said, "You'd look funny under that horse." Packard replied, "You'd look funny with this club over your head." The crowd pressed in and Packard's horse, Chief, reared. Someone snapped a picture, which appeared in national news magazines and came to symbolize police repression. But Packard said he hadn't attacked the man. Rather, he escorted him to the nearest bus stop. Later, SWOC members asked Packard, who was sympathetic to the workers' plight and whose four brothers were striking steelworkers, to escort them in their victory parade.

Less than two months after the strike ended, on May 12, 1941, Grace's legal firepower against the union was silenced. U.S. District Court dismissed Bethlehem Steel's appeal of the National Labor Relations Board ruling. The union asked the labor board to set elections on representation. In June, talks between the labor board and Bethlehem resulted in an election schedule, a step in the process of reaching a collective-bargaining agreement.

Grace did not challenge the government this time. His long, hard battle made Bethlehem Steel the last major company in the industry to yield to the steel workers' union.

Why did he give in when he could have kept fighting?

One possible reason was that Roosevelt's National Defense Commission ruled in the spring of 1941 that only companies complying with the Wagner Act and other laws could get U.S. military contracts. But it's questionable whether America could have become the "arsenal of democracy" without a powerhouse like Bethlehem Steel.

Reutter, the "Sparrows Point" author, suggests there was a combination of reasons: Grace was cautious by nature, unwilling to take risks. Roosevelt, a tough adversary, had shown he wouldn't back down. Wall Street might cut off Bethlehem's purse strings for furnaces and more expansion, Grace's overriding goal. And Grace probably thought he could break the infant union.

Roosevelt, though he agitated Grace on labor issues, actually was good for Bethlehem's business. Almost from his inauguration in 1933, he started placing orders for the buildup of the Navy. He loved the sea, kept a place at Campobello Island in Canada and had been assistant secretary of the Navy under President Woodrow Wilson.

It was steel work for the Navy that powered the Bethlehem Iron Co. near the end of the 19th century. It would power its successor, Bethlehem Steel, out of the Great Depression.

By 1937, the Navy had finished design work on a new class of big-gun warships — the battleships USS North Carolina and USS Washington — and boosted a program to build more ships. As a result, Bethlehem Steel got an increasing number of government orders for ordnance, armor plate and propulsion machinery parts. The company began to expand and upgrade its forging and treatment operations.

The steelmaker returned to longer hours, and employment at the Bethlehem plant rose to 10,900 in 1938, to 13,000 in 1939 and to 18,200 in 1940. When World War II broke out in Europe in September 1939, orders for ships and ordnance began pouring in from France and England.

Against this backdrop of rising fortunes, Bethlehem Steel workers voted decisively in the fall of 1941 to make the Steel Workers' Organizing Committee their exclusive bargaining agent. In 1942, the committee changed its name to the United Steelworkers of America.

Grace felt nothing but contempt for the USW. That would never change.

In the mid-1950s, as his health deteriorated, he was frequently betrayed by heavy eyelids at board meetings. His directors would wait for the slumbering chairman to awaken — sometimes for as long as an hour — before continuing the meetings as if nothing had happened.

"Everyone had far too much respect for Mr. Grace and his accomplishments to do any different," Edmund Martin said in his memoir.

It was a sign of the extraordinary power Grace wielded from the first decade of the century, when he participated in Schwab's gamble for the Grey mill, to the end of his life, when he ruled a vast empire of steel. But in all those years, his strict stewardship of the company was never more necessary than during the most terrible conflict in the history of the world.

The Second World War was Bethlehem Steel's biggest challenge. It took the company to its greatest heights.

Bethlehem goes to war

n the Bethlehem Steel forge shop where John Wadolny worked, the usual complement of 400 men was beefed up to a thousand men and 500 women. Stenographer Althea Kulp and others at the Bethlehem plant office reported to work at staggered times to prevent crowding in halls and elevators. Ethel Bogunovich and 200 other women, toting guns as company security officers, got the nickname "pistol packin' mamas" while keeping watch for saboteurs.

Along Third Street, whistle-blowing police officers manned intersections to ensure a smooth crossing for the streaming host of people wearing Bethlehem Steel photo ID tags. One playful officer got the nickname, "The Whistler," for the ditties he tweeted while directing traffic with grand, theatrical gestures.

The Victory Restaurant, near the company's Third Street headquarters, resembled an assembly line. So did the Palace Theater, where newsreels preceded the movies. Fabric shops and furniture and music stores were packed. A few days each week, farmers brought their vegetables and chickens to a bustling market. New parking lots were cleared to accommodate employees, but some still couldn't get their cars closer than eight blocks from their departments. Big houses that had stood almost vacant or went unsold during the 1930s were divided into apartments or rooms and rented to workers.

World War II had come to south Bethlehem. It was a busier, noisier, more crowded place than ever before.

Employment at the Bethlehem Steel plant more than doubled from 13,055 at the start of the conflict in 1939 to an all-time peak of 31,523 in 1943. Though women worked there during the First World War, they now reached large numbers, with 2,200 in the ranks.

Nationwide, Bethlehem Steel's employment swelled to 283,765, including about 25,000 women, at the company's mines, railroads, shipyards, fabricators and other steel plants.

Up on South Mountain, the Star of Bethlehem went dark. The plug was pulled after the Japanese bombed Pearl Harbor in Hawaii on Dec. 7, 1941, plunging America into the war. The 91-foot-high electric star, installed in 1937, had become a symbol of hope to a Depression-battered region. It was part of a campaign by the Chamber of Commerce and the administration of Mayor Robert Pfeifle to revive Bethlehem's holiday retail trade.

But the star, which could be seen for miles when lit at night, had to be blacked out. Bethlehem Steel was the nation's top military contractor during World War II, making the city a potential high-profile target for the enemy. It would have been a cruel irony if the symbol of Christ were used to guide Axis bombers to the Christmas City.

The enemy never reached Bethlehem or seriously threatened the continental United States. Bethlehem Steel was free to help meet President Franklin D. Roosevelt's challenge, made a year before Pearl Harbor, that the United States become "the great arsenal of democracy" by supplying its allies and building up its defenses with planes, tanks, guns and ships. Earlier than that, Bethlehem Steel was an engine for the Allied cause. But it also provided raw materials for America's future enemy in the Pacific.

Bethlehem Steel began selling pig iron and scrap metal to Japan in 1936 under a contract with the emperor, who needed the imports to bulk up his armed forces. The next year, Japanese troops invaded China, and their leaders were buying alloy steel products from Bethlehem. Not until 1940 did the United States shut off all exports of war-essential goods to Japan.

This dispassionate pursuit of profit also came through when Bethlehem Steel President Eugene G. Grace heard on Sept. 3, 1939, that France and England had declared war on Germany. He told his golf partners in his regular foursome at the Saucon Valley Country Club, "Gentlemen, we are going to make some money."

Bethlehem soon got $300 million worth of orders from England for shrapnel, big guns and warships. Combined with the work the company already was doing for the U.S. Navy, Bethlehem was producing more than it did at any time during the First World War.

Among those who benefited from Steel's surge in business was John Umlauf of Ashland, Schuylkill County. In the summer of 1940, he rented a room near Packer Avenue on the South Side and worked in the company's press forge shop with his brother, Chuck. John was 22 and among the first graduates of Muhlenberg College in Allentown to take the company's "Loop Course" for management trainees. He and Chuck helped forge 18-inch-thick armor plate and 40-foot-long gun jackets for warships.

Steel ingots under the huge hydraulic presses had temperatures between 1,800 degrees and 2,400 degrees, says Umlauf, now living in west Allentown. "Large flatbed furnaces surrounding the entire shop kept us wearing long underwear and heavy leather gloves to keep the heat out, and taking 10 to 20 salt tablets a day to replace body salts lost in sweating. The tablets were put on girders in the shop for us."

Ten-men gangs worked the hydraulic presses, shaping 20- to 50-ton red-hot steel ingots "like someone squeezing a banana," says Umlauf, who wrestled and played football at Muhlenberg and now is a solidly built octogenarian. With Bethlehem's production running at capacity, the gangs alternated shifts every two weeks, and each press was down for maintenance for only one eight-hour shift a week.

In Washington, Roosevelt foresaw America's entry into World War II. His administration initially called on Bethlehem Steel to build more than 70 warships and nearly 100 cargo carriers, 20 times as many ships as Bethlehem had built in any recent year.

It was the beginning of the largest and most diverse shipbuilding program ever undertaken by a private corporation. Rallying as it never had before, Bethlehem Steel assembled and trained an immense work force, expanded its shipyards and built new ones on both coasts. The company's Shipbuilding division employed 175,362 people in 1943. Its 15 yards had a total of 37 dry docks, 11 miles of berthing space and 76 ways, the inclined structures that support ships while they're being built and launched.

Leading the effort was Arthur B. Homer, vice president in charge of shipbuilding. A dour numbers-cruncher riveted to the task of producing ships, he had majored in economics and engineering administration at Brown University and served in the Navy Submarine Service during World War I. After a brief time at sea, he was assigned as engineering officer of the Navy's first submarine fleet being built by Bethlehem Steel at its Fore River Yard in Quincy, Mass., near Boston. In 1919, with the war over, Bethlehem hired Homer, then a civilian, to take over the shipyard. Two years later, he became manager of the company's diesel engineering and sales department, where he became known for the gas turbines he designed. In 1939, he prepped Bethlehem for the rush of orders after hearing about the Navy's plans for a two-ocean fleet.

With experts predicting a severe shortage of steel, the government paid for an additional 1 million tons of steelmaking capacity at Bethlehem, most of it to expand the company's Baltimore Harbor plant at Sparrows Point.

Ship construction was the top priority because German U-boats were sinking Allied cargo vessels faster than new ones could be built. To boost output, Bethlehem got a contract in February 1941 to build a shipyard at Fairfield, across Baltimore Harbor from Sparrows Point. The Fairfield Yard had the most employees of any Bethlehem shipyard — 44,625 in 1943 — and one of the finest construction records of the war. Its workers would build 384 Liberty ships, ungainly but easily mass-produced cargo vessels nicknamed "Ugly Ducklings." One Liberty could carry 2,840 jeeps, 440 tanks, or 230 million rounds of rifle ammunition.

The first Liberty, the SS (Supply Ship) Patrick Henry, was built at Fairfield in 1941 and ready for service in 244 days. Within two years, a Liberty could be delivered in just 41 days. Because the cargo ships were prefabricated, they were half built before they reached the ways. Builders could work on them indoors around the clock; they didn't have to depend on daylight.

But the slow "ducklings" were easy prey for submarines. Early in 1944, Fairfield began building a swifter merchant vessel, the Victory ship. By war's end, the yard would launch 79 Victorys.

A few weeks after the Pearl Harbor attack, Bethlehem Steel had more than $1.3 billion in orders to make bomb casings, armor-piercing shells, gun forgings, airplane parts and warships. It boasted that no other company harnessed America to fight in the air, on land, at sea and beneath the sea.

Bethlehem made parts for the radial, air-cooled engines mounted on all Navy planes, including the Dauntless dive bombers that battered the Japanese carriers in the Battle of Midway, and the Wildcat, Hellcat and Corsair fighters. It made engine parts for all Army Air Force bombers, such as the B-25 Mitchells that Lt. Col. Jimmy Doolittle used in his raid on Tokyo, and the B-17 Flying Fortresses that pounded Nazi-occupied Europe. Among Army Air Force fighter planes, the rugged P-47 Thunderbolt used Bethlehem engine parts. Bethlehem also made parts for military cargo planes such as the C-47 "Goonie Birds" that towed troop-carrying gliders and dropped paratroopers into enemy territory.

The company made air-flask forgings for submarine torpedoes. An employee who worked on the flasks, A. Richard Metzger, later would come into contact with some of them halfway around the world. Metzger had joined the company in the spring of 1941 as a Loop Course graduate and was assigned to the Heat Treatment Department, Manufacturing Division. In early 1942, he became a foreman in the No. 2 Treatment Shop, where air flasks were tempered. Each flask got a number. Metzger joined the Navy, went to submarine school and served on a sub that fired a number of torpedoes during patrols in the South China Sea.

"Upon review of the records which accompanied each torpedo," says Metzger, now of Essex, Conn., "I found to my surprise that I had in fact helped to heat-treat some of the air flasks."

Bethlehem Steel also made forgings for flasks used to store compressed air for starting submarine engines, blowing water out of ballast tanks and other purposes.

The company produced airfield landing mats, fabricated steel structures, forged armor, gun-elevating mechanisms, large-gun forgings, marine oil burners and strainers, railway equipment, sheet steel, ship shafting, small-arms gun barrels, tank forgings, turbine rotors and casings, wire ropes and cables, benzene for parachute nylon and other materials.

It built American defense plants such as the Chrysler Tank Arsenal near Detroit, five city blocks long and two blocks wide, and the almost mile-long Consolidated Vultee bomber plant in Fort Worth, Texas.

But it was Bethlehem's shipbuilding program that took the most time, energy and resources. The company had to hire and train thousands of men and women to become sheet-metal workers, welders, painters, riveters, electricians, pipe fitters, cabinetmakers and machinists. These were people, as Grace later put it, "who had never seen a steel plant or a shipyard before."

The company indoctrinated job seekers in groups, screened them with aptitude tests, instructed them in advanced shipbuilding techniques and put them to work in the yards.

"America Needs Ships to Sink the Rising Sun," a company poster read, referring to Japan. "Let's Go, Bethlehem."

During the 1942 and 1943 battles for Guadalcanal island in the South Pacific, it was possible for a sailor to be on a ship built of steel from a Bethlehem Steel yard, propelled by engines constructed at the Bethlehem plant, protected by armor plate from the plant and firing guns and shells produced at the plant.

Bethlehem's Fore River Yard in Quincy produced some of the mightiest vessels of the war. One was the battleship USS Massachusetts. Another was the carrier USS Lexington, a source of tremendous pride for its builders.

Launched in 1925, the "Queen of the Flat-tops" was sunk by the Japanese in May 1942 during the Battle of the Coral Sea — the first U.S. carrier lost to the enemy. Employees petitioned the government for permission to give another carrier the same name. The new Lexington, bigger and more powerful, was launched

from Fore River in September 1942. Designated a national historic landmark in July 2003, the Lexington is preserved as a museum in Corpus Christi, Texas.

Another carrier from the Fore River Yard was the USS Wasp. Called the "One-Ship Task Force" for its work in the Pacific, it was torpedoed by the Japanese off Guadalcanal in September 1942. Just as they had done with the Lexington, Fore River workers built a second Wasp that the company described as "twice as big, four times as formidable." They also turned out three other carriers — the Hancock, the Bunker Hill and the Philippine Sea — and 31 light and heavy cruisers.

The Sparrows Point Yard mainly produced tankers, which carried the fuel for bombers, tanks, jeeps and ships. The Bethlehem yards at Staten Island, N.Y., and San Pedro in Los Angeles Harbor launched destroyers. Staten Island also had a foundry that specialized in making propellers for all of Bethlehem's other yards. The Hoboken Yard in New Jersey built command ships for amphibious forces. Just outside Boston Harbor and a few miles from Fore River, Bethlehem's new Hingham Yard mass-produced destroyer escorts, the antisubmarine vessels used to protect Allied warships, tankers and transports. The San Francisco Yard built destroyer escorts. The Baltimore Yard joined Fairfield in building Liberty ships. The Hingham, Fairfield and Fore River yards turned out landing craft to carry troops and tanks ashore.

The crush of orders at Bethlehem's shipyards and steel plants came after a prewar period in which Americans cared little about the escalating violence in Europe and Asia. In the late 1930s, most Americans felt that the world's problems were not their concern and that their country was safe behind its ocean ramparts. Build up a "Fortress America," many argued, but let the foreigners fight it out among themselves.

As late as August 1941, four months before Pearl Harbor, U.S. Rep. Francis E. "Tad" Walter, whose district included Northampton County and Bethlehem, told a group of World War I veterans that the best thing the United States could do, after Hitler's invasion of the Soviet

Union in June, was to let the two regimes battle one another.

In fact, the Valley's ethnic Germans and Austrians were pleased to see Germany seeking a proper place among nations, even if they were uncomfortable with Hitler's persecution of the Jews and other extremism.

The late Randolph Kulp, a Muhlenberg College student in the mid-1930s, recalled hearing professor Preston Barba, a local historian and expert in German folk culture who regularly conducted student tours of Germany, say that although he did not approve of everything Hitler was doing, "you have no idea of how bad things were and how demoralized people in Germany were" before the Nazis came to power in 1933.

After Pearl Harbor, though, the region and the country united behind the war effort.

Joseph Silverman, chief clerk of Bethlehem's Draft Board No. 1, noted "an unprecedented rush of young men to the offices in the South Side municipal building seeking to enlist in the armed forces of the United States." Bethlehem had no recruiting office, so Silverman sent them to Allentown, but the South Side would soon get its own station.

Bethlehem Steel union leader John Wadolny did not leave to join the military. He was 27, married and had a child, and his work was deemed vital to the war. The Selective Service system put off inducting men older than 26 who were "contributing to essential agriculture, war production or war-supporting activities."

Wadolny, who had been working five days a week, was now working six — 48 hours at 90 cents an hour. His post was in the No. 3 Forge Shop, also called Forge Specialty, where he and others made shells for the Army and Navy. The total of 1,500 workers in the shop was almost four times the usual number in peacetime, and a third of them were women.

He remembered that just about anyone who wanted a job at Bethlehem Steel during the war got one. Some new workers came to Bethlehem from across eastern Pennsylvania and found places to stay so they wouldn't have to commute. Trolleys and buses were heavily used, but many employees drove to work despite gasoline

rationing, and a few made use of a new practice called car-pooling. But with hundreds of vehicles converging on the plant, traffic problems were common.

"You had many people who had to park on the street and walk as far as eight to 10 blocks to get to the gate," said Wadolny, who at the time lived in south Bethlehem on a hill overlooking the blast furnaces. He would walk to the plant for his 8 a.m. to 4 p.m. shift with one or two workers from his neighborhood, or take a trolley for 10 or 12 cents.

Trolleys usually were crowded with steelworkers, Wadolny recalled. The cars moved on tracks, got their power from electric lines slung overhead and were operated by motormen. Though widely used in the 1920s, trolleys had lost their popularity in the '30s. The Lehigh Valley Transit Co. had phased out some service and scrapped dozens of passenger and utility cars by 1940. But then wartime gas rationing spiked ridership, and service between Allentown and Bethlehem became especially busy. Businesses, taking advantage of the new reliance on public transportation, advertised their proximity to bus and trolley routes.

With the large number of men joining or being drafted into the military, Bethlehem Steel faced its first labor shortage since the early 1920s, when quota laws had cut off immigration from Europe and prompted the recruitment of Mexicans. Wadolny and other employees who were declared essential to war production stayed, and other men were too old to be drafted. All were given longer hours, and some even worked seven-day weeks, which wore them down.

Randolph Kulp, who had worked in the company's cost accounting office since 1940, recalled hearing a story about a confrontation between a forklift operator and a naval officer assigned as an inspector at the Bethlehem plant. It was early on a Sunday morning, and the worker was so tired he couldn't stay awake. Seeing him nod off, the officer shouted, "Hey you! Wake up! Don't you remember Pearl Harbor?"

"Sure, I remember Pearl Harbor," the worker replied, "That was the Sunday morning the Navy slept late."

The furious officer tried hard to get the worker fired for the remark, but there was too much work and too few people to do it, and he kept his job.

Hiring women was the obvious solution to the labor shortage. Women had been working in the local silk and textile industry since the 1880s, and Bethlehem Steel had employed some during World War I. But defense work during the Second World War drew them to the steelmaker and other local plants in large numbers for the first time.

As many as 10,000 women made war materials in the Lehigh Valley, which had about 346,500 residents in 1940. A quarter of the women workers were at Bethlehem Steel, while others were on the payroll at such major employers as Roller Smith in Bethlehem, maker of aircraft instruments and other electrical products, and the Bonney Forge & Tool Works and American Armament, both in Allentown.

In a 1985 survey of 50 women war workers at Bethlehem Steel, Carol Baylor, a journalist doing a program for National Public Radio, found that many were living at home with their parents when the war broke out. Those who had children had friends or relatives to take care of them while they worked. Most had never worn pants, still regarded as mannish, a la Katharine Hepburn, and had never thought of working outside the home.

By May 1943, Dorolee, a women's clothing shop on W. Fourth Street in Bethlehem, was advertising coveralls for $4.25 and overalls at $2.69 as "No. 1 Favorites With Women In War Jobs." By the next year, 53 types of manual labor at Bethlehem Steel, from assemblyman to wrapper of nuts and bolts, were being done by women.

"The introduction of women to work that heretofore has been exclusively men's domain has been planned with great care," the company said in a 1944 newsletter, which went on to note that Bethlehem "enabled the women to feel 'at home' in their new surroundings."

Feeling at home was important. One of the innovations provided at Bethlehem was the hiring of older women in the role of matron. They were assigned primarily to help insecure women adjust to their jobs and responsibilities. Decades later, women fondly remembered the matrons.

Many men resented the women, who heard comments like "Why don't you go back to the sweatshop where you belong?"

One aspect of work at Bethlehem Steel that angered women was disparity in pay. Many felt cheated when they learned they were making 10 to 12 cents less an hour than men who were doing the same jobs. But working with representatives of the United Steelworkers of America, the former Steel Workers' Organizing Committee, the women got their back pay.

Althea Kulp began working at the company as a stenographer in January 1942 for $95 a month. The 21-year-old Allentown High School graduate had heard from her older brother, Randolph, the accounting office employee, that opportunities for women at Bethlehem Steel had widened after Pearl Harbor. She quit as a clerk at Allentown's Hanover Acres housing program and signed on with the steelmaker, becoming a secretary to the machine shop superintendent.

Like her brother and many other Steel employees, Althea rode to and from work on the trolley. Her father was a motorman for Lehigh Valley Transit's south Bethlehem line, though not for the 6:30 a.m. trolley Althea took every weekday from her south Allentown home.

Althea wore suits she made herself and carried a thermos bottle of cold milk and a bag lunch that her mother had packed for her. A 45-minute ride that included other stops brought Althea to Broad and New streets in Bethlehem. From there, she walked the eight blocks to the main plant entrance at Third and Fillmore streets.

Along the way, she passed stores selling goods other than refrigerators and washing machines, which couldn't be produced under the government's wartime restrictions.

A Victory gas range sold for $49.95. A complete bedroom — a bed with mattress and box spring, a chest and a dresser or vanity "just as you want it ... in neat waterfall walnut veneers" — sold for $119.

Among clothes, a hot accessory for women in the spring of 1943 was the Montgomery beret. It was inspired by the jaunty headgear of the famous British Gen. Bernard Montgomery, victor over German Field Marshal Erwin Rommel in North Africa. It cost $2.95 and came in black, brown, navy, red, kelly, turf, pecan, gray or brown.

Hess Brothers in downtown Allentown, north of the Little Lehigh Creek from Althea's home, was offering Nunn-Bush Oxfords for $10.85 and women's felt slippers for $1.69 — "These slippers not rationed," an ad noted. Summer dresses were selling in Hess's bargain basement for $2.69.

But Althea couldn't dally at storefronts; to be on time, she had to reach the steel plant by 8 a.m. There was, and still is, a clock on the wall above the main gate.

The company sought to keep employees from bunching up at entrances, hallways and elevators by having them report at 20-minute intervals. Althea had to be at her desk on the second floor of the No. 4 Machine Shop by 8:20. Once inside the plant, she and many others had to wait for trains and vehicles to pass in the yards, and stood in lines as they made their way to their workplaces.

Lunch breaks also were staggered, and Althea's was at 12:30. She ate at her desk, usually a sandwich of ham or peanut butter and jelly, an apple, a banana and some cookies, and went for a stroll. Then it was back to work until her 4:40 p.m. quitting time.

One rainy day, while walking through the plant on her way to the machine shop, a blast furnace "spouted off."

"All this soot came down. When I went in the office, they laughed," says Althea, now a trim and cheery grandmother in her 80s who lives in Allentown. "I said, 'What's the matter?' They looked at me and said, 'Look in the mirror.' I went in the ladies room and saw that my face, my navy blue coat and white collar were all black. My boss said, 'You try to get cleaned up.' But we didn't have hot water, and there wasn't much you could do with cold water."

About six months later, when a six-story plant office opened, Althea moved there and worked in an office on the first floor. She didn't have to walk past the blast furnaces anymore.

While some Bethlehem Steel women did manual labor alongside men like John Wadolny,

and some were secretaries like Althea Kulp, others had a role that reflected the company's urgent need for security. These women carried guns and kept watch for saboteurs.

Ethel Bogunovich of Hellertown, whose mother wouldn't let her go into Bethlehem during the riotous steel strike of 1941, was working in a security office at the plant two years later. But the feisty 21-year-old was eager to try something else. She wanted to be transferred to the outdoor security patrol, a job that would pay her nearly three times her current salary of $60 a month.

She had to learn to shoot, but caught on quickly. During a training session for prospective patrol women in 1943, Ethel hit the bull's-eye the first time she pulled the trigger of a .38-caliber revolver. The sure shot earned her a citation from the patrol chief and a spot on the force.

On the radio, country singer Al Dexter — and later Bing Crosby and the Andrews Sisters — had a song called "Pistol Packin' Mama" that shot to No. 1 like a bullet.

Lay that pistol down, babe,
Lay that pistol down.
Pistol packin' mama,
Lay that pistol down.

The women patrolling the plant liked the sound of it and called themselves the "pistol packin' mamas."

"I worked specifically at the main gate, checking in employees as they came in, checking their lunch bags and making sure they didn't carry any contraband or anything to that effect," says Ethel, whose married name is Gasda. The method of checking lunch bags for knives was to flatten the bags like a pancake.

Some security staff searched cars entering the plant for guns or knives. Ethel doesn't recall the company finding contraband but is certain that the security force was a deterrent to potential saboteurs.

Another duty was to prevent employees from working when they were drunk, which frequently happened on payday. Yet another was patrolling the plant in darkness, a task that

Ethel, now in her 80s and living in Lower Macungie Township, found unpleasant.

"Well, during the night shift, say from 11 o'clock to 7 in the morning, it was rather dull. After all the employees were checked in, we had to do turns walking up and down the carpenter shop. There were lots of rats running up and down. … Of course I was afraid of them. But as the elderly gentleman on the police force said, 'What are you afraid of? You have a gun, a .38. You can shoot them.' But you were charged 5 cents for each bullet you used."

Ethel had wanted to become a nurse, but her mother deemed nurses to be "pot wallopers" who did little more than carry bedpans, and Ethel canceled her job interview at nearby St. Luke's Hospital. Her mother didn't approve of Ethel's job at Bethlehem Steel, either.

"My daughter is a pistol packin' mama! My daughter!" she exclaimed to friends. "I'm ashamed to tell anybody what my daughter's doing."

Ethel's father, Frank Bogunovich, a Bethlehem Steel furnace repairman, was supportive. "Honey," he said to his daughter, the fifth of six children, "you do what you want."

The flood of women and other wartime steelworkers led to new homes outside south Bethlehem. It also prompted property owners, nudged by public officials, to offer rooms and apartments for rent.

Working with Bethlehem's banks, the U.S. government encouraged housing conversions. In May 1943, the National Housing Agency for Properties announced it had arranged a lease with two property owners to provide space for war workers, the first of what agency officials hoped would be many more. The next day, Bethlehem's First National Bank and Trust Co. announced its "Remodeling for Victory" campaign, reminding property owners that "idle houses and rooms are slackers in this war." Owners could get loans to make conversions.

The big mansions of Bethlehem Steel's founders — Robert Sayre's residence and the house where Robert Linderman and Charles Schwab had lived — were divided into rooms and apartments.

But like the company's earlier luminaries, its chief executive during the 1940s lived in a large house and kept a regal presence.

In 1941 and 1942, Eugene Grace's annual pay was $537,724, the highest in the nation after Hollywood mogul Louis B. Mayer. In April 1943, while announcing that Bethlehem Steel's first-quarter earnings were only slightly higher than those for the same period in 1942, Grace said he was taking a 58.8 percent pay cut. That brought his total compensation for the year to about $221,600.

It was still a princely sum, and Grace was treated like a feudal baron. His comings and goings at the Bethlehem offices on Third Street were a finely orchestrated dance of precision and security.

A Bethlehem Steel police officer perched on the building's roof, binoculars in hand. When he spotted Grace's motorcade, which consisted of Grace's chauffeur-driven car escorted by motorcycle policemen, a signal was buzzed to elevator operators in the headquarters building. The elevator attendants stopped at the nearest floor, and everyone got off and out of sight. The elevators descended to the granite-and-marble art deco lobby to await Grace's arrival. Emerging from his car, Grace chose an elevator and rode up by himself.

Determined to golf, he had his chauffeur drive caddies who couldn't get to the Saucon Valley Country Club because of gasoline rationing.

But if Grace was at times lordly, he was also respected, and at no time was that respect greater than during World War II. As the ultimate steel production man, he gave the country and its allies what they sorely needed: a rapid outpouring of steel in unprecedented quantities. The shortage that experts feared in 1941 never happened.

Grace, who fought bitterly with Roosevelt over labor unions throughout the 1930s, cooperated with the administration on several fronts. At the president's urging, he served on the board of a program called the Controlled Materials Plan, the central clearinghouse for the allocation of steel. He developed a way to quickly assign priorities for civilian and military use of the metal.

In the labor arena, Grace and union leaders found common ground with the president in meetings at the White House. Philip Murray of the Steel Workers' Organizing Committee, soon to be the USW, agreed to no strikes. Grace and the presidents of the other major steel companies pledged not to lock out employees in the event of a dispute.

Though Murray tried to get 12.5-cent raises for workers at Bethlehem Steel and other "Little Steel" companies, the National War Labor Board limited pay hikes to 5.5 cents in 1941. After that, wages were frozen for the duration of the war.

In his annual report to employees, Grace said the average hourly wage for all employees in 1943 was $1.30. Laborers, who made up a third of the work force, made significantly less. The top skilled workers, who represented 10 percent, got the highest pay. Grace said the average number of weekly hours for all employees was 45, but millworkers put in longer hours.

When they had free time, Bethlehem Steel employees with a few coins in their pockets went to the movies or live shows.

Castle Garden, the dance hall at local amusement venue Dorney Park, was a major attraction for big-band fans. On July 17, 1943, civilians could pay 75 cents and servicemen 35 cents to hear and dance to Ken Keely and his Royal Manhatters, whose chief draw, according to one local critic, was "the hottest drummer boy on the road."

Moviegoers in 1943 could spend a quarter to see "Destination Toyko," a submarine drama starring Cary Grant and John Garfield that was as "big as the broad Pacific, violent as a China Sea typhoon." George Raft, Sydney Greenstreet and Peter Lorre stood toe to toe in the spy drama, "Background to Danger," in which "the Gestapo gets it from the G-men."

Lloyd Nolan charged up the beach in "Guadalcanal Diary," and Pat O'Brien, "a lovable fighting American," showed that both football and war could be hell in "The Iron Major."

People who wanted to forget about the war could go to the movie theater and catch "Happy Land," which was "as American as an ice cream soda." If Westerns were their interest, they could see John Wayne and Martha Scott taming the West in "In Old Oklahoma." Lon Chaney Jr. had given up his hairy wolfman role and now wore the vampire's cape as "Son of Dracula." Claudette Colbert and Fred MacMurray showed they had "No Time for Love" in the romantic comedy.

Radio was a cheaper form of entertainment. On a typical Sunday, listeners could hear comic Jack Benny, ventriloquist Edgar Bergen and his wooden pal Charlie McCarthy, Walter Winchell's theater and nightclub gossip and a host of big-band broadcasts. But the war was never far away, with radio programs such as "Labor for Victory" and "Report from Washington: On Rationing."

Rationing was the biggest reminder for the vast majority of people that war had changed their lives. It affected everyone.

The system, overseen by the federal government's Office of Price Administration, was designed to deal with the wartime allotment of scarce goods.

The first task given to the OPA was to stabilize prices of goods, services and rental housing. In May 1942 it froze prices at March 1942 levels for almost all everyday goods and about 60 percent of all foods. During World War II, most rents also were frozen and rose by less than 5 percent.

This "price freeze," as the agency called it, was only partially successful. Noncontrolled prices and wages continued to rise. Partly in response to that, Roosevelt gave the OPA rationing power. To administer the program, the agency established local volunteer-staffed rationing boards. People went to these boards to register themselves and their families.

By late 1943, Bethlehem shoppers, like those across the country, were preoccupied with the system of ration cards, coupons and stamps. The local boards issued certificates for seldom-purchased items, such as tires, and books of ration coupons for frequently needed commodities such as gasoline and sugar.

Ration stamps were required for about a third of food items. A letter on the face of each stamp indicated the ration period. The number on each stamp corresponded to the points each was worth. Point values of various foods were announced by the government. The point value of an article changed as it became scarcer or more plentiful.

Human nature being what it is, people cheated on the rationing system. This led to creation of the black market, where gasoline and meat were the most valuable commodities.

No matter what diversion or hardship people on the home front faced, the war was always uppermost in their minds. At Bethlehem Steel, Grace believed that victory would come sooner if the company ratcheted up its production to give the Allies overwhelming superiority at sea.

In January 1943, Grace told reporters he wanted to bring the company to the point where it was completing a ship a day, a goal that some in the press considered fanciful. But that year, Bethlehem Steel built 380 ships, more than one a day. Naturally, Grace wanted to boast, so he arranged for a ceremony that was the ultimate radio broadcast.

"All of our different yards, plants and mines are connected by radio for this year-end ceremony," Grace said at 1:30 p.m. Friday, Dec. 31, 1943, from the Staten Island Yard. "I believe this is the first time anywhere that a nationwide hookup both inside and outside of every plant and office has been used by a company to review its year's work, and to get set for the task ahead."

Grace said he was speaking "from aboard a big destroyer in New York Harbor." In a matter of days, he said, "this destroyer will be speaking a different but more persuasive language to our enemies."

He thanked the 67,000 former Bethlehem Steel employees who were on battlefronts around the world. "Our work is for you. Our effort is small beside yours, but we are going to keep up everlastingly at it, so that you may have the supplies you need when and where you need them."

Grace, a staunch Republican whose relationship with the pro-labor Roosevelt administration had been frosty when not hostile, praised the government for its cooperation with industry.

But most of all, Grace wanted to talk about what Bethlehem Steel had accomplished.

"You may recall that last January, I pledged that Bethlehem in 1943 would build a ship a day, a major-size ship a day, with several to spare . . . . I don't mind saying that there were many times during the year I was doubtful of reaching our goal. And I know that our shipyard managers at times thought that it just couldn't be done.

"The total number of fighting and cargo ships which Bethlehem delivered this year is well above a ship a day," Grace said. Seventy percent were battleships, aircraft carriers, light and heavy cruisers, destroyers, destroyer escorts and landing craft for the Navy, and the rest were for the Merchant Marine.

"I believe that Bethlehem was able to handle this enormous shipbuilding job because of the way we are set up as an integrated company. By 'integrated' I mean we are a company which produces materials all the way from the ore in the ground to the complete ship. This helps us understand how each part fits together. So I say to you men in the mines in Michigan and Minnesota, in Pennsylvania and in West Virginia that your work is the starting point."

Grace ended with bittersweet words of encouragement. He told his workers that 1944 "may be a year of greater hardship and sorrow than our country has ever known. But it can be made happy for all of us, in doing our part toward victory."

Five months later, on D-Day, June 6, 1944, the Allies made their long-awaited landings in occupied France. It marked the beginning of the end of Nazi Germany.

"Many people spent the day at their radios," according to The Morning Call story filed from Bethlehem. "Others who could not remain at home stopped to listen to every radio which they passed. It seemed that there wasn't a set in the business sections of the city that was not tuned in to the newscasts."

Associated Press and United Press International bulletins were posted in the newspaper office's window. Throughout the day, people lined up to look at them.

A Bethlehem Steel official noted that "the materiel being expended in one day of the invasion represents a month's work on some items and a year's work on others."

Among the servicemen who took part in the landings was John Umlauf, who went to work in the Bethlehem plant's press forge shop soon after the war began. He left the company to join the Navy in 1943 and became an officer. On D-Day, he was second in command of a gunboat that raked the German defenses off Utah Beach on the Normandy coast.

Hopes that the war would be over soon were dashed in December 1944 with the German offensive at the Battle of the Bulge. But by the following spring, Hitler's regime was collapsing.

Roosevelt, the nation's indomitable commander-in-chief, would not live to see the end. He died at 63 on April 12, 1945. Since 1933, a whole generation had come to maturity never knowing another occupant of the White House. In Bethlehem, the grief over his passing was as deep as it was anywhere in the nation.

From his office at Bethlehem Steel, Grace paid tribute to his nemesis: "It was President Roosevelt's destiny to guide this country in the great contest to preserve freedom throughout the world, and his death is a tragedy in that he did not live to see its final accomplishment. ... His passing will in no way lessen, but if possible will increase the determination and efforts of all the people of the United States to prosecute the war to final victory and the establishment of a permanent peace."

Harry S. Truman became the nation's new wartime leader. By May, Soviet troops were entering Berlin, and U.S. soldiers had driven deep into Germany and Austria.

On May 3, the day the U.S. 3rd Army seized Hitler's birthplace town of Braunau in Austria, The Morning Call's banner headline read, "NAZIS SAY HITLER DIES IN BERLIN." Above a photo of the late dictator giving a speech was the word, "KAPUT!"

That same day, Mayor Pfeifle warned Bethlehem residents against a premature celebration of victory because the fight against Japan was still raging. So after Germany surrendered on May 8, the local observance was heartfelt but subdued. Church services were held, but public schools remained open. Some retail businesses closed early at 3 p.m.

At Bethlehem Steel, workers gathered at the windows between shifts to shout their pleasure. But C.P. Newell, head of the United Steelworkers local, urged members not to slack off. "To all steelworkers I say, 'Come on, you steel men, pour it on and give those Jap rats the works.'"

The final peace came on Aug. 14, 1945, days after American B-29 bombers dropped atomic bombs on Hiroshima and Nagasaki.

News of the Japanese surrender "ran like an electric current through the sidewalk crowds," noted The Morning Call. "Men and women bared their heads and hurried to churches and prayed. ... Men who fought and bled on the world's battlefields took the news quietly when the whistles and sirens sounded to bring relief to aching hearts in millions of American homes."

Bethlehem steelworkers celebrated by blowing a whistle from the French luxury liner Normandie, which caught fire at a New York pier in 1942 while being converted to a troop ship and had to be scrapped. The steam-powered brass whistle, which weighed 620 pounds and stood atop Steel's No. 1 Boiler House, was used to announce shift changes.

In a statement the day after the surrender, Grace held out a hand to returning veterans, promising "to help them readjust to civilian life." But not everyone at Bethlehem Steel wanted to hear it. For women, it meant they would largely be phased out of the work force.

Many women welcomed a return to peacetime roles. Others were reluctant to give up what had become an exciting and challenging career. But it mattered little what they wanted because they had no choice. One Rosie the Riveter recalled hearing a male co-worker shout joyfully in her ear when Japan surrendered, "Now you girls can go home!"

Ethel Bogunovich Gasda says the feeling among women all along was that they were just standing in for the men. Both she and Althea Kulp left Bethlehem Steel within a few years after the war ended, but not because they were forced out.

Althea quit to marry a returning veteran, a New Yorker named William Coe. She had corresponded with him while he was serving with the Army in the Pacific and met him for the first time when he came home in the fall of 1945. At the time she left the company, a few days before their wedding in July 1946, she was making $160 a month, $65 more than when she started in the same job four years earlier.

The newlyweds moved to New York, where Althea was a secretary at the Time-Life publishing company and William an assistant manager at an advertising firm. Unhappy in the big city, they moved to Allentown in 1950 and ran a grocery store just a block from Althea's girlhood home.

Ethel Bogunovich grew tired of being a pistol packin' mama and wanted out, so in 1945 she took a job in the company's claims office. She stayed until 1948, when she married a war veteran who worked in Bethlehem Steel's accounting office. The marriage ended in divorce in 1964. Ten years later, Ethel married Quentin Gasda. He died in November 2003.

In the late 1960s, Ethel returned to Bethlehem Steel to work in its public affairs department. She was as much of a straight talker then as she had been a straight shooter in the '40s.

When an executive groused about the steelworkers union, Ethel, whose father was a Bethlehem Steel union organizer, lashed out: "If it wasn't for those guys out in the plant, you wouldn't have a job. Who the hell would produce the steel? You wouldn't last an hour out there."

For Bethlehem, a symbolic end to World War II came on Dec. 1, 1945, nearly four months after the Japanese surrender. The city paid tribute to its first Gold Star mother, Johanna Silvoy, whose son Stephen was missing in action with the Navy in March 1943. He was among 1,167 Lehigh Valley servicemen and a nurse who lost their lives in the war. His mother was given the honor of flicking a switch on the Hotel Bethlehem's Zinzendorf Square.

All at once, seven miles of Christmas decorations extending from west Bethlehem along Broad Street through the business section of Main Street lit up. They shone across the Hill-to-Hill Bridge, down Third and Fourth streets and on Wyandotte Street. A huge tree created out of 40 separate spruces stood at the bridge's center, its multicolored lights aglow.

Over them all was the Star of Bethlehem. High on its South Mountain perch, it shone once more after four years of darkness.

Down the slopes to the north, stretching for 4.5 miles along the Lehigh River, stood Bethlehem Steel, a major force in making the peace. It had produced 73.4 million net tons of steel, a third of the armor plate and gun forgings required for the Navy. It had made 80 percent of all parts for radial, air-cooled engines on planes used by the Army Air Forces and the Navy. Its yards had built 1,085 fighting ships, cargo vessels and tankers, making it the world's biggest shipbuilder of the war. They also had repaired, converted or serviced 37,778 ships.

As Grace had predicted, the company had made money. Sales in 1945 totaled $1.33 billion, with a net income of $34.9 million. Shareholders had gotten common-stock cash dividends of $6 a share, tops since the 1920s.

Grace reveled in what he called "the miracle of American production that spelled the doom of the Axis." In his statement after the Japanese surrender, he said the world now needed steel to rebuild, and that Bethlehem Steel — the nation's seventh-largest industrial company — would provide it.

Indeed it would.

The company would grow fat in the postwar years, but trouble would lurk beneath the prosperity.

SEVEN

Good times, bad omens

Her eyebrows were plucked. Her blond hair was perfectly coiffed. Her face was painted with the same expensive makeup worn by New York models.

In the tradition of the pretty young Bethlehem Steel escorts who guided visitors through the company's 13-story headquarters on Third Street in south Bethlehem, she stood in front of the elevator with the proper posture: one hand under an elbow, one foot in front of another.

Ellie Prizznick didn't know what she had done to be summoned to her boss's office shortly after she began working as an escort in 1954. Her misdeed turned out to be the small shaving cut on one of her legs.

Bethlehem Steel had an image to uphold, and Prizznick wasn't doing her part. She had neglected to hide the razor nick on her calf. The boss made her put makeup on the cut, risking an infection but covering up anything that could be perceived as a blemish on the company.

Yet Bethlehem Steel came out of World War II without any such visible blemishes. It had helped the nation win another world war, it was one of the largest companies in the world, its profits were unwavering and the demand for steel was high, with American steel exports outnumbering imports five to one. In 1953, Bethlehem Steel alone produced more steel than Germany and doubled the output of the other vanquished enemy, Japan. Its sales of $2.1 billion that year were five times the total in 1939.

This golden era for Bethlehem Steel was reflected not only on the balance sheets, but in the perks its executives enjoyed. They had gold nameplates, kept afternoon tee times for golf at the plush Saucon Valley Country Club and ate lobster and filet mignon prepared by company chefs.

In answer to a suddenly prosperous America hungry for the good life after years of deprivation, Bethlehem Steel refocused itself from building war materials to producing steel for cars and appliances.

But like the rest of the nation, Bethlehem Steel was vulnerable in ways that were not so visible. A national strike would give employees the power to demand higher wages and open the door to foreign steel and domestic mini-mills that would ultimately steal Bethlehem's customers.

A national civil rights movement would force the company to examine why few minorities could climb more than a few rungs up the company ladder.

Bethlehem Steel's habit of granting big contract increases, then raising steel prices to pay for them, forced it into several confrontations with American presidents who thought the industry was run by greedy profiteers.

A burgeoning Cold War gripping the country would find its way into Bethlehem Steel's plants, as company executives tried to root out communists in their work force.

Through it all, the steel industry was evolving as other companies and other countries developed more efficient ways to make steel, always with a cautious Bethlehem Steel lagging. It was too busy making money to innovate. While other companies anticipated the future of steel, Bethlehem was surprised by it.

Steel's executives were simply blinded by profits. In the quarter century after World War II, a seemingly boundless prosperity made it easy to live, work and spend as if the profits would never end.

For escort Ellie Prizznick, the daughter of a Bethlehem Steel straightener who taught her the value of saving money, it was exasperating in the mid-1950s to see company executives immersing themselves in extravagance.

"They had bowls in the center of their tables, I don't know what it cost, if they were $1,000 apiece or what," says Ellie, a widow whose married name is Zsitek (pronounced ZY-tech). "This is what aggravates me today, because there were so many executives and so

much money spent. It's aggravating because I saw this, and it was overwhelming. They had their nameplates in 18-karat gold. Why is this necessary? They had special meals. I mean, lobster tails, filet mignon. That was nothing for them to have."

Executives wanted to eat only the freshest steak, so black Angus were raised on the grounds of the Saucon Valley Country Club. Thirty-two executives dining in two shifts drank from crystal glasses, ate with engraved silver off the highest-quality china and sat on leather chairs.

Everything had to be perfect, including the escorts.

Mostly in their late teens and early 20s, they were modeled after airline flight attendants. They couldn't be more than a size 12, Marilyn Monroe's proportions. They were instructed how to gracefully open an elevator door. New York models were brought in to show them how to walk and hold their hands.

Ellie Zsitek, who is in her mid 60s, lives in Bethlehem, has piercing blue eyes and still keeps her hair impeccably, likens the escorts to a "pretty picture" on a wall. The sight of them in their elegant cranberry or green glen plaid dresses from New York boutiques stopped traffic.

They could keep their jobs until they became pregnant, or as Zsitek puts it, "our bellies popped."

When a Japanese ambassador, an African prime minister or other dignitaries were guests of Bethlehem Steel at the country club, the escorts had to be there.

When Chairman Eugene G. Grace pulled up to headquarters in his shiny black limousine, escorts and other employees scurried. A spotter who had been watching the parking lot relayed a message that Grace was about to enter the building. The escorts made sure that Grace had an elevator to himself. When he stepped into it, the nonstop button assured that he would have a quick ride to his sixth-floor office.

If the escorts were the working world's version of high school cheerleaders, the "loopers" — college graduates who worked as Bethlehem Steel management trainees after being taken around a loop of the plant — were the would-be football captains.

A woman did well to marry a rising star and was treated in accordance with her husband's place on the company totem pole.

The wives had their own role, and in the eyes of company executives, their job was to appear proper and respectful. They were expected to know their place.

"The wives were very important to the husbands. They were important by the way they entertained the bosses, and they were important by the way they behaved in public," says John Strohmeyer, a Pulitzer Prize-winning former Bethlehem Globe-Times editor whose book "Crisis in Bethlehem" chronicled Steel's decline. "Some wives were drunks or loudmouths, and that would affect your promotion. The wives had a lot of power. As their husbands' power grew, their power grew."

Victoria "Lala" Leach hasn't forgotten what a vice president's wife told her in 1954, before her husband, Ed, had risen to vice president of mining.

"She'd say to me, 'Don't forget. If you see me tomorrow night at the cocktail party, you don't come and talk to me unless I come over and talk to you,'" says Leach, now in her mid-80s and a widow living in the same stone Tudor house in Bethlehem that she and Ed shared in the 1950s. "I must not presume that just because she called me up and we chatted on the telephone all the time that we were great friends. She was the boss. They were up there, and I was down here."

Some executives carried the extravagance home with them. Wilbur Kocher, an electrician who worked at Bethlehem Steel during the World War II and Korean War eras, says the higher-ups routinely called in Bethlehem Steel employees on company time to remodel their homes or make improvements at their playground, the Saucon Valley Country Club.

If an executive's roof was leaking or the furnace failed, there was plenty of skilled labor in the plants to take care of it. Kocher says the executives told the workers to take off their company hard hats, making it more difficult for outsiders to identify them as Bethlehem Steel employees.

Many employees had their hands in the till, too. Kocher says it was commonplace for workers to fill out forms for tools they needed, while at the same time requesting additional tools that supposedly were for their jobs but really were for their homes. "People used to drag things out of the plant," he says.

Security workers didn't interfere, provided they were given some tools of their own, Kocher recalls.

After World War II, it was easy to justify dipping into the company's wealth because Bethlehem Steel was making so much money. It hadn't had a losing year since 1933, and the war had kept its plants going full tilt. As the company reduced its record wartime work force by half, its profits exceeded $40 million a year.

While Bethlehem Steel was preparing for business in peacetime, the country was celebrating the return of its triumphant troops.

No one captured the national mood locally quite like Allentown department store owner Max Hess Jr. Returning G.I.'s were greeted with a Hess Brothers ad in The Morning Call that showed a G.I. in full battle uniform on one side. On the other was the same figure now dressed in a snazzy civilian suit from Hess Brothers.

The message was clear: Now that the fighting was over, the boys were back to enjoy the post-war promise of peace and prosperity. Throughout the war, "Nothing is too good for our boys" was the common cry. Now the country had to make good.

But to Grace and others who ran American industry, there was a long memory back to the end of World War I. The sudden end of that conflict had brought disruptive strikes and other labor troubles. These captains of industry feared it would happen again. They didn't have long to wait.

Bethlehem workers had made great strides since unionizing in 1941, but as the company made huge profits, grimy, soot-covered men were still toiling at dangerous jobs that paid them less than $1 an hour.

On Oct. 18, 1945, two employees were overcome by carbon monoxide in a pit under a heat treatment furnace at the No. 3 Tempering

Plant, where huge barrels for battleship guns were heat-treated to give them greater strength. One man after another went in to check on the missing co-workers, and none returned. Eight workers were killed by gas that day. It was the deadliest accident ever at the Bethlehem plant but accounted for only half the deaths at the plant that year.

Even without the dangers, the conditions in the plants were a stark contrast to the comfortable offices enjoyed by executives at the headquarters building on the edge of the plant lands.

"You wore long underwear in the winter and summer — in the winter to protect you from the cold and in the summer to protect you from the heat. It insulates you," says Glenn Snyder, who started his 28-year machinist career years later. "The only thing you have to watch is, if you get too close to liquid iron, it would turn the perspiration on your body into steam, and it would go back in and burn you."

As 1945 ended, millworkers decided it was time for them to get a bigger piece of the Bethlehem Steel pie. No sooner was New Year's Day 1946 over when Philip Murray, head of the United Steelworkers of America, was calling for a wage increase of 19.5 cents an hour. Representing the steel companies, U.S. Steel CEO Benjamin Fairless offered 15 cents. President Harry S. Truman presided over steel talks at the White House, but couldn't get Fairless to agree to a compromise of 18.5 cents.

On Jan. 19, 1946, about 800,000 steelworkers in Bethlehem and across the nation walked off the job in the biggest strike in American history to that point. On Feb. 16, Bethlehem Steel joined the other steelmakers and agreed to the 18.5-cent increase. It raised the average hourly wage of the steelworker to $1.09. Bethlehem simply passed on its cost to consumers, charging an extra $5 a ton.

The steel strike was just one of many labor actions that hobbled the economy in 1946. There were also coal and rail strikes. But as the nation was preoccupied with labor problems, another problem surfaced.

America and the Soviet Union had been allies against Germany during World War II. But with war's end, the frictions between communist and capitalist countries re-emerged. On March 5, 1946, former British Prime Minister Winston Churchill told Americans in a speech at Westminster College in Fulton, Mo., that they faced a new danger.

"From Stettin in the Baltic to Trieste in the Adriatic, an iron curtain has descended across the Continent," he said. All of the nations and peoples behind that curtain, he noted, "are subject in one form or another not only to Soviet influence but to a very high and increasing measure of control from Moscow."

Many Americans were stunned to hear this from Churchill, a man widely respected in this country for warning the world about the menace of Adolf Hitler. Now he was issuing a warning about a former ally.

But even as Churchill was providing America with a new reason to worry, Detroit was providing a reason to celebrate, as the first civilian automobile produced by Detroit since 1942 rolled off the assembly line.

It might have seemed shallow and superficial, but to a public starved for consumer goods — a public weary of four years of gasoline and tire rationing — prosperity was overdue. America was the economic superpower of the world. Germany and Japan were in ruins. No one expected them to have any industrial power for years to come. Although the Soviet Union, England and France had won, their industry was in little better shape than that of their enemies.

Bethlehem Steel was geared to meet the challenge. If the Soviet Union were to become America's enemy, Bethlehem was ready to provide the tools of war. If peace were in America's future, Steel would gladly turn its might into producing steel for office buildings, automobiles and refrigerators.

As the Cold War escalated, it was clear that America was on the verge of both good times and heightened anxiety.

By 1948, few people doubted that a rivalry between the United States and the USSR was on. The risks rose even more in 1949 when the Soviet Union exploded an atomic bomb and communists prevailed in China.

In June 1950, the Cold War went hot when communist North Korea invaded the non-communist South. Caught off guard, the United States quickly sent troops doing occupation duty in Japan into the fighting.

Once again, Bethlehem Steel provided much of the ordnance for U.S. armed forces. Its shipyards refitted ships they had built for World War II.

In April 1952, after Korean War peace talks had started but before the fighting had stopped, Truman took action that judges, lawyers and political scientists argue about to this day: He headed off a strike by seizing control of America's steel mills, something that no other president ever has done.

Steelworkers, who hadn't gotten a raise since 1950, forced Truman's hand by asking for a wage increase of 35 cents an hour. The steelmakers, Bethlehem included, wouldn't even discuss it. The union announced that its 650,000 members would walk off the job on Dec. 31, 1951, if they didn't get the raise.

On Dec. 22, Truman turned the dispute over to his Wage Stabilization Board. The union agreed to hold off going on strike until April 8 the following year, while the board tried to arrange an agreement. After weeks of hearings, the board announced its support of a compromise wage increase of 26 cents. The union agreed, and the steel companies were willing to oblige as long as they could raise the price of steel by $12 a ton.

But because the government was buying much of that steel, Truman opposed the price hike and extended the negotiations into April 1952. The interests of the nation in wartime were too important to be jeopardized by a work stoppage, Truman decided.

So when a strike by the United Steelworkers of America appeared imminent, the president known as "Give 'em hell, Harry" took over the mills to keep them running.

"Under similar circumstances, the president of the United States has to act for whatever is best for the country," Truman said.

The national press compared Truman to Hitler, Josef Stalin and Benito Mussolini and accused him of stealing private property. Inland Steel Chairman Clarence Randall called it an "evil deed."

Two months later, on June 2, 1952, the U.S. Supreme Court called the takeover illegal and voided Truman's order.

"We cannot with faithfulness to our constitutional system hold that the commander in chief of the armed forces has the ultimate power as such to take possession of private property in order to keep labor disputes from stopping production," wrote Justice Hugo Black.

Steelworkers almost immediately hit the picket lines. The strike lasted seven weeks. It was the longest, most costly steel strike to that point in U.S. history. The industry lost 21 million tons of production, workers lost $400 million in wages and 1.4 million workers in related industries were idle for at least part of the strike.

The steelworkers ultimately settled on a pay increase of 21 cents per hour.

In North Korea, the fighting stopped on July 27, 1953. By then, Truman was back home in Independence, Mo., and Dwight D. Eisenhower, a Republican and the general who led the Allies in Europe during World War II, was in the White House.

Elected on the slogan "I Like Ike," he was seen as the genial grandfather figure who won the White House because of public reaction to the wars, strikes and tensions of the Truman years.

Some historians look back on the 10 years from 1953 to 1963 — from the start of the Eisenhower presidency to President John F. Kennedy's assassination — as a time of political and cultural consensus, when a wealthy nation run by big institutions gave prosperity and peace to more people than ever before.

But in the 1950s, even great prosperity was filtered through the prism of the Cold War, as Congress began a war of its own against the communist threat. The Smith Act of 1940 provided the weapons to do it. The law banned membership in any political party that advocated the overthrow of the U.S. government by force.

On the bulletin boards at Bethlehem Steel's plants were fliers urging workers to turn in anyone believed to be a communist.

By 1950, hearings conducted by U.S. Rep. Richard M. Nixon had alleged that State Department official Alger Hiss had spied for the communists. Meanwhile, the junior senator from Wisconsin, Joseph McCarthy, was claiming that the State Department was riddled with communists.

Bethlehem Steel employees were encouraged to testify before subcommittees run by Nixon and McCarthy, and anyone found to be a communist was dismissed.

The Lehigh Valley's first brush with the communist threat came in May 1954, when Herman Erwin Thomas, a 42-year-old delicatessen owner from Allentown, testified at the trial of nine men accused of being communists. It was held in Philadelphia before federal Judge J. Cullen Ganey of Bethlehem. Among the accused was Joseph Kuzma of Easton, a former Bethlehem Steel worker and union activist.

When Kuzma was arrested on July 29, 1953, he didn't deny being a communist, and the local media were unrestrained in telling the story.

On the day of Kuzma's arrest, The Evening Chronicle of Allentown featured a cartoon that showed a large flyswatter labeled "FBI" whacking communist insects. The article on his arrest said federal agents had labeled Kuzma "the Mr. Big of Communists in eastern Pennsylvania." The Chronicle's editorial that day referred to Kuzma as a "Kremlin termite."

Thomas, who had been a communist from 1937 to 1939, was asked by the FBI to go undercover to rejoin the party in 1944 and attend meetings of communist groups such as the Easton Fur Club and the Bethlehem City Club.

On the witness stand, Thomas said Kuzma not only ran the meetings but told members that communists arranged the Bethlehem Steel strike of 1946. According to Thomas' testimony, Kuzma went on to tell members that the only way to establish a government of the workers in the United States was to overthrow the government in Washington. Thomas named several other local residents as having attended the communist meetings.

On Aug. 14, 1954, the jury found all nine men guilty of being communists. They were sentenced to five years in prison and ordered to pay $10,000 fines, but they appealed. The courts threw out the verdict and declared the Smith Act unconstitutional.

Months later, in December 1954, Thomas was called to Washington to give testimony in a private session to McCarthy's subcommittee. The hearing testimony and the responses by those Thomas named weren't made public until May 2003. Transcripts show that Thomas claimed Bethlehem Steel was the "main concentration center" for the Communist Party in eastern Pennsylvania and employed hundreds of communist sympathizers.

McCarthy wasn't at these private hearings. Earlier in the year, he had accused the Army of coddling an alleged communist sympathizer, and his attack backfired. By December 1954 he was trying to stay out of the limelight. But one of the people at the hearings was a bright young attorney named Robert F. Kennedy, the brother of John F. Kennedy and a future attorney general.

The committee got almost nothing from Bethlehem Steel workers called to testify. Some denied ever belonging to the Communist Party; others used their constitutional right not to incriminate themselves. But pleading the Fifth Amendment had its consequences. Bethlehem Steel fired workers who refused to cooperate with the subcommittee.

Communists were blamed for a lot in the 1950s, including matters for which they weren't responsible. In 1951, Bethlehem Steel President Arthur B. Homer told members of the American Iron and Steel Institute, the industry trade group, at a meeting in Philadelphia that communists caused America's rising inflation.

Homer's logic was that a large part of inflation was brought on by government spending. He hastened to add that he was referring only to the "failure to reduce unnecessary nondefense spending." Apparently defense spending, which helped carry Bethlehem Steel's bottom line, was acceptable.

"American inflation could indeed be Russia's secret weapon," he said, referring to Russian communist leader Vladimir Lenin's call for worldwide revolution against capitalism. "There are, in fact, many who believe that in line with the Lenin formula, the real aim of Russian threats is to worry us into spending ourselves into bankruptcy."

Homer's language reflected the great fear of the era: that the "Reds" could even be neighbors of patriotic Americans, undermining the country as they sat in on the local parent-teacher association meeting or attended the firemen's ball. Hollywood's 1956 film "Invasion of the Body Snatchers," about people in a small town who are duplicated and replaced by aliens hatched from pods, mirrored the era's paranoia.

But Homer had bigger things to worry about than the communist threat. After leading Bethlehem Steel's shipbuilding effort during World War II, he took over as corporation president in December 1945, when Grace was elevated to chairman. He was the first of the new generation of Bethlehem managers. Twenty years younger than Grace, he had no memory of the Bethlehem Iron Co. of the Robert Sayre era or the more flamboyant times of Bethlehem Steel Corp. founder Charles M. Schwab.

On Nov. 1, 1957, Grace retired at the age of 81 and Homer took over as chief executive officer. The title of chairman of the board that had been used by Grace was abolished. But Grace was named honorary chairman, a title created just for him, and he retained his seat on the board.

Homer was a departure from past leadership, but his arrogant view of the company's untouchable place in the world market was the same as his predecessors'. When it was suggested that European steel methods were technologically ahead of America's, Homer replied, "I don't believe it."

As Homer ran the company that locals simply referred to as "The Steel," Grace adopted a role as the grand old man of steelmaking. In one of the many opinion pieces he wrote for The Evening Chronicle, he addressed the question of whether the end of the Korean War and a government slowdown in spending would plunge the nation into a recession.

Grace said it was true that as the steel industry goes, so goes the country, but the war's end didn't have to mean plummeting activity for The Steel.

"Steel is basic to our industrial civilization," said Grace. "It follows that the nation has a very real interest in a healthy steel industry capable of meeting all of its demands. Today we have the plant to do the job."

It was clearly the view of a man whose answer to almost everything was more production.

But Stanley Ruttenberg, director of the Congress of Industrial Organizations, the federation of industrial unions formed in 1935, had another view in an Evening Chronicle article that appeared next to Grace's. He believed that what America needed was for its workers to be paid more. If they had more money, they would be more active consumers. And it was consumers, especially middle-class consumers, Ruttenberg argued, who would fuel the economy.

The idea of paying workers higher wages never appealed to Grace, and he was unwilling to accept its importance in the growing role consumers were playing in the economy of the 1950s. But it was there, and it was gaining ground.

Television had created a mass market for those with a suddenly raised disposable income. Housewives were promised a kitchen where steel machinery would lighten their workload.

Advertising on 1950s television created as near a "perfect" world as was possible. Families were perfect, homes were perfect, hair was perfect. Husbands and dads did not work at dirty, dangerous places like Bethlehem Steel blast furnaces. They had nice middle-class office jobs like Ward Cleaver on "Leave It To Beaver" or Ozzie Nelson on "The Adventures of Ozzie and Harriet."

Moms didn't work as clerks in department stores or in knitting mills helping to make ends meet when strikes put dads out of work. On TV, they wore pearls and dresses even when they vacuumed the floor.

Unlike the multi-ethnic neighborhoods that the children of Bethlehem Steel millworkers knew, television families lived in an all-white world inhabited by people with Anglo-Saxon names.

Unions, layoffs and strikes were also absent from the TV America of the '50s, but they were part of the reality for Bethlehem Steel workers. As the decade wore on, they saw themselves being written out of the perfect life promised to other Americans. All they were told was that higher wages would bring inflation.

By 1956, steelworkers were no longer buying that excuse. In July, they struck for 35 days before they were given an industry-wide three-year contract that granted the first cost-of-living escalator clause. Bethlehem Steel was the last of the major steelmakers to sign. Its local unions had held out for a seemingly simple little passage known as 2B, the past practices clause. Three years later, that single letter and number would spur the longest strike in the company's history.

The past practices clause was designed to address labor fears of workers being replaced by machines. It provided that if a job required three workers to perform it, three workers would always be assigned to that job even if the technology available did not require it. The company also couldn't change the pay rate.

This clause, which would cause Bethlehem Steel so much trouble in the future, was not part of the national steelworkers agreement in 1956. It was agreed on separately by Bethlehem and its union locals.

Why did Bethlehem Steel allow the clause to be added to the contract? At least one reason was that the company was in a hurry to start producing steel again. The economy was white hot. Every day of a strike was a day when the company was losing money and market share. During the strike, the Bethlehem plant alone lost $43 million in production.

At the same time, European steel was starting to come into the American market. To Bethlehem Steel executives in a hurry to get going again, it seemed foolish to argue over what seemed at the time a very small point. They were more concerned about turning out more steel than they were about responding to the technological advances of their foreign competitors.

"What, me worry?" asked Mad magazine's goofy-looking Alfred E. Neuman, and that was The Steel's position. The good times were seemingly never going to end. In 1957, the company netted a record $191 million.

The next year, as an economic recession led to layoffs and job cuts in Bethlehem's work force, Fortune magazine put six Bethlehem Steel executives in the top 10 on the list of the nation's highest paid executives. Homer topped the list with $511,249 that year, and chairman of finance R.E. McMath took home $394,322.

Steelworkers at the time were making an average of $1.96 an hour. As the expiration of the 1956 contract neared, they were tired of Homer's argument against higher wages.

"We are approaching a fork in the road," Homer wrote to employees in 1959. "One route leads to greater efficiency with resulting lower costs, means a wider demand for steel and products made of steel, without the threat of further inflation. [The other route] leads deeper into inflation with the disastrous consequences of falling employment and further rises in living costs. Make no mistake about it, inflation spares no one."

Homer, leading a company that made $137 million in profit in 1958, proposed that workers take a one-year wage freeze. To most, the proposal was arrogant, insulting and almost unbelievable. Workers were determined to get their share.

Jim Lynn was a fourth-generation Bethlehem Steel worker in a family that boasted five generations of them. Like many workers at The Steel, he was brought up to believe there were two types of people in Bethlehem: bread-eaters and cake-eaters.

The bread-eaters lived on the South Side, in the shadows of the steel plant that employed them. They lived in houses with windows tinted by steel-plant soot, in tightly knit ethnic neighborhoods that had churches and social clubs on nearly every corner.

Homes were practically on top of one another, and the Pennsylvania Germans controlled many of the neighborhood shops. The Hungarians labored in the mills. The Slovaks sweated in the blast furnaces. The Italians worked in the labor crews. The Irish operated in the open hearth department. The Poles strained in the shops and foundries. The Puerto Ricans toiled in the grimy coke works.

The conditions for all of them were brutal.

"It was dirty and it was dusty and it was greasy and it was crummy," says Barry Stein, who spent 27 years as an electrician in the blast furnace shops. "You had to work in all different weather, all different conditions and all kinds of shifts. You gotta do what you gotta do when you want to raise a family."

The cake-eaters worked in neatly kept offices and lived on the north side, away from the dirty plants, in spacious homes with tightly cropped lawns.

Now, the bread-eaters believed that the cake-eaters were trying to deny them the few extra crumbs they were seeking.

On July 15, 1959, steelworkers at Bethlehem and across the nation went on strike.

John Wadolny, a machine shop worker and president of USW Local 2599, one of three USW unions at the Bethlehem plant, said the strike began over the usual issues: wages, paid vacations, incentives and pensions. All of that could have been settled in a week, maybe two, he said.

The big point of contention was Clause 2B.

Bethlehem executives, having woken up to the implications of what they had agreed to just three years earlier, said the clause handcuffed them and robbed them of the flexibility the company needed to thrive, while providing a safe haven for loafers.

Strohmeyer in his book cites the example of an engineer who ripped up the newspaper of an employee who worked a crossword puzzle for a few hours a day instead of answering the office phone. The office worker replied that doing crossword puzzles was a "past practice" and thus should be allowed under the past practice clause. The engineer was scolded for not respecting an employee's personal property.

Maintenance foreman Jim Cox saw the past practices clause at its worst. After a crane broke down, a man who specialized only in electrical repairs and another who specialized only in mechanical repairs sat on the bridge of the crane arguing about why the other worker was supposed to fix it. Cox sent the two men home and docked their pay. They filed a grievance, and Cox lost. He had to pay the workers a full day's pay.

Mike Pron, who worked in the beam yards, agrees that work was becoming much too specialized. He remembers that a request to put an air conditioner in a room meant that an electrician would install it and a carpenter would build the frame. Asking the electrician if he could handle the frame would get a reply of: "That's not my job."

Kocher, the longtime Steel electrician, says the clause sometimes held up work. "If you were an electrician, you didn't dare pick up a brick," he says. "That was the bricklayer's job. And it might have taken two or three days to get someone to the place."

As the strike of 1959 wore on, it taxed the patience of everyone: the company, the workers and the country. Pron always tried to put away a few extra dollars in case of a strike, but there was no way he could have saved for 116 days. So when he wasn't on the picket line that year, he laid blacktop in nearby Bath.

During the strike of 1941, the union hadn't received much sympathy from local business owners, who sided with the company. But 18 years later, the union was so well established that grocers, business owners and butchers gave it food and supplies. A food bank was set up, with different unions donating potatoes, beans and canned goods to the striking workers. But the workers had to picket to earn the donated food.

Richie Check, an apprentice rigger whose eight brothers and a sister worked at The Steel, wanted to get by without help from the union.

At 26, Check was married and the father of two boys. He rented a second-floor apartment at 540 Selfridge St. on the South Side — the same street where he grew up — for $30 a month. Throughout the strike, he had to live without his pay of $1.12 an hour, or $45 a week.

In exchange for meals, he helped remodel the Catholic church he attended, Ss. Cyril & Methodius, and build a three-car garage there. The Rev. Felix Labuda, the pastor, had asked for volunteers after Mass one day. As many as 30 men, almost all idled steelworkers like Check, worked up to 12 hours a day, six days a week. Labuda couldn't pay them, but he fed them. He offered cold cuts and Coke for lunch. If the men kept working into the evening, he served them dinners of ham, chicken or Hungarian goulash, with maybe a glass of wine or a beer.

Any food that was left over, the men took home to their families.

Check usually worked at the church from 9 a.m. to 4 p.m. and brought leftovers home to his wife and two young sons. He cleaned up a neighbor's back yard in exchange for fruits and vegetables and helped paint a home in return for a hot dog.

For money, he collected empty soda bottles and sometimes stole them from the back of stores. The deposit on each bottle was 5 cents, so that three bottles collected was enough to pay for a quart of milk. The milkman from Lehigh Valley Dairies would arrive with a bill for $8. Many weeks, Check could only pay him $5. The milkman told him there were people who owed much more than that.

Check's oldest brother, Steve, was a foreman who kept working at the blast furnaces, which continued to produce iron during the strike. His seven brothers who were on strike were better off than Richie; they had worked longer and managed to save some money. They eased the crunch a little. "My brothers would give me a buck or two," Check says.

The Check family — nine sons, five daughters — symbolized how life in Bethlehem revolved around The Steel. Even Richie's sister Irene worked for the company; she was in the billing department. Altogether, 11 family members logged 439 years at the plant.

Michael Check, Richie's father, had started at The Steel in 1912 after moving to Bethlehem from his native Slovakia. He raised his family on Selfridge Street. From the second floor of their house, the children could see the blast furnaces. When his boys got old enough to join the company, they followed his advice to work in different departments so that a layoff in one department wouldn't affect all of them.

One summer night in 1943, 10-year-old Richie awakened and couldn't get back to sleep. He sat on his bed. His father put his big hand on the boy's shoulder and asked what was wrong.

"Pop, why's there gotta be all that bangin' and boomin'?" he asked.

"Rishy," his father said in his thick accent. "Be happy that you hear that banging and

booming, because that means that people are working. When you don't hear it no more, you're gonna cry."

When the banging and booming stopped during the strike of 1959, Check wasn't ready to cry, but he was getting desperate. Thinking the strike would never end, he applied to be a policeman. But he never took the exam because he couldn't fool himself.

"I'm not a cop," says Check. "I'm a steelworker."

It was the only thing his family knew. His father died of a heart attack at Blast Furnace G in 1954.

As for Richie, he tells people he worked at The Steel "43 years, five months and 15 days." His years evident in the deep creases in his face, he can talk for hours about his experiences on the job, saying "Jiminy crickets!" and "Honest!" to emphasize a point. He still lives on Selfridge Street, where he has a view of the blast furnaces that sustained his family.

In mid-September 1959, while Richie Check was collecting bottles and his co-workers were walking the picket lines, Steel negotiators were huddled in Room 965 of the Roosevelt Hotel in New York.

This was not like the Bethlehem Steel strikes of old, when Charlie Schwab could tell workers that he could hold out as long as they could and bring in the state police if necessary. This was a national strike with a national union against all the major steelmakers in the country. And it was having a national impact.

For President Eisenhower and those around him, there was fear that the strike would affect the nation's defense at the height of the Cold War.

"The Department of Commerce reported to me that its effects were becoming more apparent throughout the economy," Eisenhower wrote in his memoir, "Waging Peace: The White House Years 1956-1961."

"Work weeks were shortening, plants were shutting down, and a shortage of alloy steel plates and beams threatened to delay the construction of missile bases."

The strike dragged on. Shortages were beginning to delay deployment of a new unit of the Polaris missile, a two-stage ballistic missile powered by solid fuel rocket motors. In 1960, the Navy's successful test-firing of the Polaris would allow the United States to base much of its nuclear deterrent forces on submarines, where they would be safe from a successful first strike by the Soviets.

Eisenhower asked for an injunction that would force the employees back to work for 80 days, and on Oct. 21, 1959, a federal court granted his request. As a result of Eisenhower's intervention, steelworkers returned to work on Nov. 8 after 116 days on strike.

"We don't like the idea of having to go back to work with a bayonet in our backs, and we have no intention of returning to the old era," said local union leader Wadolny.

Wadolny didn't know it then, but labor had an unlikely ally in the talks for a new contract. Vice President Richard Nixon, who was getting ready to run for president in 1960, was keenly interested in the outcome of the strike.

On Dec. 30, 1959, Nixon and the secretary of labor flew to New York to meet with industry negotiators. Nixon, Eisenhower writes, "laid it on the line" for steel executives. If the strike resumed, the vice president said, "the country will have no place to go for a remedy but to the Congress, which as you know, the Democrats control. In an election year, management won't like the labor-management legislation such a Congress will produce."

A series of almost nonstop meetings began. Ten were held at Nixon's Washington home. The final one lasted 22 hours. The result was an agreement that the industry predicted would cost it $1 billion.

The contract provided substantial insurance and other benefits, plus pay increases of 7 cents an hour in 1960 and 1961. It called for increased pension benefits for workers. Most damaging for Bethlehem Steel, Clause 2B stayed.

For the first time, union workers got wages that took them out of the working class into a decent quality of life and gave them the promise of cradle-to-grave security. For the first time, the bread-eaters could move across the street from the cake-eaters.

The headline in the Jan. 5, 1960, New York Times left no doubt which side won the strike of 1959: STEEL SETTLEMENT IS REACHED/UNION VICTOR, PRICE RISE SEEN/NIXON, MEDIATOR GAIN STATURE.

After that watershed settlement, steelworkers were so used to winning labor disputes that they asked for — and received — benefits they couldn't have dreamed of getting, such as 13-week vacations for senior workers and United Nations Day, Oct. 24, as a paid holiday.

Lance E. Metz, historian for the National Canal Museum in Easton and an authority on Bethlehem Steel, says no other event had as much impact on the social environment of the Lehigh Valley. Because other big local industries considered Bethlehem Steel the pacesetter for the entire Valley, the settlement led to a better quality of life for workers at Mack Trucks, Air Products and Chemicals, Western Electric, Dixie Cup, Ingersoll-Rand and other area industrial companies. It was the heyday of secure middle-class manufacturing jobs here and throughout the country.

But the long, severe strike had also opened a path that would lead to the rust-belt grimness of later decades. Because American companies didn't make steel during the strike, U.S. manufacturers turned to foreign steel out of necessity. Those manufacturers soon found that steel made elsewhere was of a higher quality than they had been led to believe, and it was cheaper. Ships were lined up outside Philadelphia for miles to bring in steel from other countries.

Foreign steel imports exceeded 5 million tons in 1959, their highest level to that point. That number would double in the next six years, as some customers never returned to buying domestic steel and others cut back on it even after the steelworkers returned to the mills.

The new labor contract that U.S. steelmakers took on made it more difficult for them to compete with the new stream of foreign steel.

Jim Cox's father, John L. Cox, was the chief engineer at Midvale Steel, Bethlehem Steel's biggest competitor in the armor-piercing shell and gun business. Jim grew up listening to his father complain about Bethlehem Steel. But when Jim was receiving offers from Bethlehem Steel,

U.S. Steel and other companies as an engineering graduate of the University of Pennsylvania in 1939, his father noted that Bethlehem Steel was a better-managed company and offered a broader field than U.S. Steel.

By 1959, however, the well-managed company that Cox's father lauded was making questionable decisions.

Jim Cox thinks the past practices clause and the lack of flexibility it caused Bethlehem Steel hurt the company's overhead and gave more ammunition to mini-mills. He wondered how Bethlehem could improve its operation and cut costs when the past practices clause prevented it from making changes and improvements.

But as long as the steel industry could keep raising prices, there wasn't any compelling need to cut costs and streamline operations. The profits kept coming anyway.

Just as Bethlehem Steel was pulling out of the crippling strike yet celebrating $80 million in profits the first half of 1960, Eugene Grace died in his Prospect Avenue home on July 25. He was 83.

Under Grace, The Steel had grown so big that it had more police officers than the city of Bethlehem. It paved Bethlehem's streets, plowed its snow and helped build Bethlehem's water system, the best in the Lehigh Valley.

To mark his funeral, flags flew at half staff in Bethlehem. The steel plant's machines fell silent for two minutes. A fleet of limousines carried dignitaries to Packer Memorial Church at Lehigh University, where Grace had studied and played baseball in the 1890s and served as president of the board of trustees from 1924 to 1957. Among the mourners were David Rockefeller, vice chairman of Chase Manhattan Bank, and U.S. Steel Corp. President Leslie Worthington.

The Rev. Elam Davies of Bethlehem's First Presbyterian Church said Grace's will was "indomitable without being inflexible." Benjamin Fairless of the American Iron and Steel Institute cited his "invaluable services to industry." Earle W. Bader, president of the Bethlehem Chamber of Commerce, declared that "future generations will rise up and bless him … for his unselfish services to the city." Local USW union leader

Wadolny lauded him as "a worthy and honorable opponent."

With that, Grace was taken to his tomb at Nisky Hill Cemetery.

Just as one era was ending for Bethlehem Steel, a new one was beginning for the nation with the election of John F. Kennedy as president in 1960.

Kennedy was an internationalist. He believed the future was in free trade and open markets. Where steelmakers were traditionally protectionist, calling for high tariffs to keep foreign steel out, Kennedy wanted to encourage global competition.

Steel industry leaders never bought Kennedy's claim that he wasn't opposed to business. Arthur Schlesinger Jr., the Harvard University historian and Kennedy adviser, says in his memoir of the administration, "A Thousand Days":

"Though [businessmen] doubtless admired Kennedy's intelligence, were impressed by his knowledge and were generally conciliated in his presence, they felt he stood at a distance from them. The fact remained that he was outside the business ethos, that he did not regard the acquisitive impulse as man's noblest instinct, nor the pursuit of profit as man's highest calling."

Ultimately, Kennedy clashed with the steel industry over prices. Fearful that a round of steel prices and wage increases might lead to inflation, Kennedy in September 1961 wrote to the industry's leaders. He told them that because steel was "a bellwether as well as a major element in industrial costs," he would urge that they "forgo a price increase." He then wrote to steelworkers union head David J. McDonald, asking that wage demands be kept "within the limit of advances in productivity."

Early in 1962, Secretary of Labor Arthur Goldberg, who once had been general counsel for the steelworkers union, negotiated a new contract between the union and the steel industry.

On April 10, four days after the agreement was reached, a reporter at the annual Bethlehem Steel stockholders meeting in Wilmington, Del., asked company President Edmund F. Martin if the industry intended to raise prices.

"Hell no, this isn't the time to raise prices,"

said Martin, Steel's No. 2 executive. "We should be trying to reduce the price of steel, if at all possible, because we have more competition, particularly from foreign sources."

About six hours after Martin's statement, U.S. Steel, Bethlehem Steel's rival, increased the price of a ton of steel by $6. Bethlehem Steel followed its lead the next day, and four other companies responded by raising prices, too.

Kennedy was livid.

"My father always told me that all businessmen were sons of bitches, but I never believed it until now," the president told his closest advisers. He called the steel price increase "a wholly unjustifiable and irresponsible defiance of the public interest."

And he applied some federal muscle.

At 10 o'clock that night, three FBI agents banged on the door of Martin's Prospect Avenue home.

"Mr. Martin's office hours are 8 to 5. If you want to see him on business, you can see him tomorrow at his office," his wife told them.

But Martin, in his pajamas, talked to the agents for about half an hour. They wanted to know exactly what he said at the stockholders meeting. He repeated what he was quoted as saying.

The next day, Bethlehem Steel issued a statement saying Martin was "indefinite about the matter of prices."

Bethlehem Steel secretary Bernard Brocker was subpoenaed to appear before a federal grand jury in New York a week later with all his records and documents.

Kennedy addressed the nation about the crisis.

"In this serious hour of our country's history ... when we are asking reservists to leave their homes and families for months on end and servicemen to risk their lives — and four were killed in the last two days in Vietnam — the American people will find it hard as I do to accept a situation in which a tiny handful of steel executives, whose pursuit of private power and profit exceeds their sense of public responsibility, can show such utter contempt for the interest of 185 million Americans."

Kennedy went on to note that costs for the steel industry had actually gone down since 1958 and that the most recent wage agreement with steelworkers was not inflationary. He noted that the industry's cash dividends had exceeded $600 million during the previous five years.

"Some time ago, I asked each American to consider what he would do for his country, and I also asked the steel companies," Kennedy said. "In the last 34 hours, we had their answer."

Some Bethlehem Steel executives didn't take Kennedy seriously. They jokingly wore buttons on their lapels stating, "I'm an SOB by order of the President."

But Kennedy pressured the steelmakers to back off. The Department of Defense began to shift its contracts to smaller companies that had not raised their prices.

On April 13, Kennedy's strategy began to pay off. Like falling dominoes, Bethlehem and other steelmakers announced they wouldn't raise prices.

But the government's business with Bethlehem wasn't over. On Oct. 25, 1962, as the Cuban missile crisis brought the United States and Soviet Union to the brink of nuclear war, a federal judge fined two Bethlehem Steel executives for bid rigging.

Erb A.P. Gurney, sales manager of Bethlehem Steel's forgings, casting and special products division, was ordered to pay $7,500. Robert Barnes, assistant manager of the same division, was fined $1,500. Three executives from two other steel companies were also fined. All had pleaded no contest to the charges brought by the Justice Department, led by Kennedy's brother Robert. It had accused Bethlehem Steel, U.S. Steel and two smaller companies of conspiring between 1948 and 1961 to fix prices and rig bids in sales of steel forgings to the Army, Navy, electrical companies and other buyers. Barnes told the judge, "I know now your honor I did wrong, and I assure you it won't happen again."

But his admission was dwarfed in the news by the enormity of the missile crisis.

Labeled "circles of danger," an Associated Press map of North America showed the range of the Soviet missiles in communist Cuba. The Lehigh Valley was well within one of the circles. It was no secret why: Bethlehem Steel was a leading defense contractor.

It was also still a company producing steel and profits with equal proficiency. By the time Homer was ready to pass the baton to Edmund Martin in April 1964, the company's ledger sheet looked good. It netted $102 million in profits the previous year — its 12th $100 million-plus year in the past 14 years — and was already on pace to increase that in 1964.

Imports were trickling in and mini-mills were chipping away at The Steel's business, but Bethlehem's leaders regarded both as woodpeckers assailing a block of granite.

Bethlehem's plans for the future were to follow Grace's formula. More capacity equals more profits. It was a formula that was only reinforced in 1964 by a record production of 19.4 million tons of raw steel. And the company was poised to take advantage of that winning formula.

Grace had long coveted the Midwest market, dating to Bethlehem Steel's attempt to acquire Youngstown Sheet & Tube in the early 1930s. That attempt was blocked by a federal judge, who ruled that Youngstown was undervalued and Bethlehem wasn't being straightforward with Youngstown's stockholders.

In 1954, federal judges again blocked Grace's attempt to acquire Youngstown, ruling that the merger of the second and fifth largest steel companies in the country ran afoul of antitrust law and would give Bethlehem an unfair monopoly.

Bethlehem fought the decision in the courts.

"If the law in its present form is interpreted to prevent a merger like ours, then they'd better change the law quickly for the good of the economy and the good of the country," Grace said.

In his autobiography, Martin notes that if Grace had been well, the company might have taken the case to the U.S. Supreme Court.

But in 1957, the company dropped its appeal of the ruling after Grace suffered a stroke and Homer replaced him as chief executive. Homer didn't see the merits of another long legal battle. On Jan. 26, 1959, Bethlehem and Youngstown officials announced they were dropping all plans to merge.

With its bid to acquire Youngstown blocked, Bethlehem decided to build its own plant to take on U.S. Steel in the lucrative Midwest market. Construction of the $400 million plant in Burns Harbor, Ind., began in 1962 on 3,300 acres on the banks of Lake Michigan, 30 miles southeast of Chicago.

Sprouting from a piece of land nearly twice the size of Bethlehem's flagship property, Burns Harbor would be an integrated mill that could increase The Steel's capacity by 6 million to 10 million tons a year. Being integrated meant that the plant contained the entire steelmaking process, from ore to finished steel, all on the same property.

While Steel officials touted the plant as the future of the company, it met with opposition in Indiana, where residents protested the plant's location in the middle of the scenic Dunes, the miles of beaches, sand dunes, bogs, wetlands and woodland forests along the Indiana National Lakeshore.

It was also met with mixed reviews back in Bethlehem, where workers and residents began to question the company's commitment to the Lehigh Valley.

"It is encouraging that the company has both the confidence in the future of this nation's economy and the resources to undertake such a gigantic expansion," a Morning Call editorial stated in 1962. "There are also regrets it was necessary to bypass the area in which the company has its deepest roots."

But The Steel was taking its investment — roughly $500,000 a day during construction — where the market was, and there was no question it was the Midwest. The Burns Harbor plant would give the company direct access to the automotive industry and the Chicago building markets.

Burns Harbor primarily was designed to make cold-rolled sheet steel, the product used for everything from automobile bodies to television chassis to refrigerators.

The location of Burns Harbor in the Great Lakes region meant the plant could get exceptional ore from Minnesota and, via the St. Lawrence Seaway, from Labrador, Canada. Almost next door to Burns Harbor is Gary, Ind., home of U.S. Steel's major plant. The Great Lakes was the place to be.

Bethlehem's largest plant would be on a waterway approachable by cargo ships, eliminating the need to haul materials from the ports by rail. Transportation costs — and particularly those for rail shipments — were becoming costly for landlocked plants such as the one in south Bethlehem.

"It actually cost us less to ship ore from Africa to the ports of Philadelphia than it did to move it by rail from Philadelphia to the Bethlehem plant," says Robert Wilkins, who started with Bethlehem Steel in 1954 and became vice president of finance in 1982. "Being on Lake Michigan was a huge savings."

Burns Harbor began producing steel in November 1964, touching off four consecutive years in which The Steel's raw steel production pushed past 20 million tons and helping the company net a half billion dollars in profit in the final half of the decade.

No one could have imagined then, but Burns Harbor would be the last integrated plant built in the United States.

With the new capacity and the new modern plant, profits were not a problem. But as the three-year labor contract neared expiration in 1965, the company and the country feared another strike like the one of 1959. This time, President Lyndon B. Johnson, using the heavy-handed style he was noted for, stepped in.

The country was still recovering from the assassination of President Kennedy, a growing sense of unease was building with the increased involvement in the Vietnam War, and Johnson wasn't going to let another steelworkers strike plunge the country into a recession.

With the strike deadline of Aug. 31, 1964, just hours away, Johnson locked negotiators from both sides in a room at the White House. First he persuaded them to accept an eight-day extension, then he explained — in the colorful language he was prone to use — that they had two choices: Either come to an agreement or face a president determined to make them pay for the damage they would cause the country.

Legend has it that Joe Moloney, then vice president of the United Steelworkers of Amer-

ica, peered out of a window and observed workmen digging holes to plant trees on the White House lawn.

"I think we'd better settle," Moloney said. "LBJ is getting the graves ready."

On Sept. 3, 1965, steelworkers got a new three-year deal that gave them a wage increase of 16 cents an hour, twice what industry negotiators said they were willing to settle for before Johnson sequestered them in the White House.

Johnson's iron fist and the fear of another strike prompted steel industry negotiators to agree to a contract that cut into profits. The outcome also continued a tone in which labor asked for the moon and management grudgingly gave it.

But Bethlehem was again lifted by war. It was producing small armaments for the military, this time for American troops fighting in Vietnam, and its plants were running at nearly 90 percent capacity. Its production, at a record 21 million tons of steel, brought the company its largest profit in a decade. In fact, the $170 million it netted made 1966 the third most profitable year to that point.

That same year, a small nuclear instrument and electronics company struggling to regroup after nearly going bankrupt began to redirect its core business away from electronics to steel joist manufacturing and ultimately toward steelmaking. Nuclear Corp. of America (Nucor) took on a new management team, moved its headquarters from Phoenix, Ariz., to Charlotte, N.C., and built its first bar mill.

Nucor executives decided to use electric furnaces pioneered by a few small companies a decade earlier and built its first electric furnace mini-mill in 1969 in Darlington, S.C. The furnaces were fed by inexpensive scrap, stripping away the costly overhead of ore mines, coke ovens and blast furnaces. Nucor combined its furnaces with a continuous casting method that allowed workers to shape steel directly from its molten form into billets, eliminating the need for large, expensive mills. Then it combined those savings with a cheaper, largely nonunion work force.

Integrated steelmakers such as Bethlehem Steel and U.S. Steel had been using early versions of electric furnaces for decades, but only for high-grade products such as alloy and tool steel and for low-tonnage specialty products such as generators, rolls and propeller shafts. The big companies regarded electric furnaces as having too low a volume to be widely used.

But Nucor and a growing number of mini-mills challenged that belief, making electric furnaces the heart of the operation and becoming a new breed of steelmakers. And Nucor's new and aggressive president, E. Kenneth Iverson, offered workers a profit-sharing plan that persuaded them to shun unions.

In 1969, Nucor's total sales of $46 million weren't even a blip on the radar screen. But Bethlehem would come to regret ignoring Nucor's arrival into the steel market.

Bethlehem already was a step behind — even with its newest technology. In 1968, the Bethlehem plant was opening its first basic oxygen furnaces, a technology that other companies had been using for more than a decade. The advantages of this type of furnace were that it could process metal more quickly than open-hearth furnaces, was cheaper to operate, controlled more easily and could be fed by up to 30 percent scrap.

The furnace was developed in Austria in 1952. Yet five years later, when Bethlehem needed to increase capacity at Sparrows Point, it built an open-hearth shop instead — the last built in the United States. It was evidence that the company that pioneered the beam that revolutionized construction in the United States had given way to Grace's methodical caution.

For Bethlehem, building new furnaces meant spending tens of millions of dollars. It wasn't easy for such a large company to buy into the latest wave. It would have required abandoning hundreds of millions of dollars Bethlehem had invested in technology now obsolete.

Rather than pour money into a new technology without a proven track record, Bethlehem followed 19th century steelmaker Andrew Carnegie's dictum that "Pioneering don't pay." The company had adopted a habit of waiting until that technology was advanced and perfected before investing in it.

Even when Bethlehem Steel did invest in innovation, it was too cautious to take advantage of it. Other companies did. The process of continuous casting is an example. It was a revolutionary method of pouring molten steel directly from the ladle into a billet, bloom or slab instead of first making ingots. Bethlehem helped develop the method but didn't capitalize on its own work.

Yet Bethlehem's foreign and domestic competitors refined the process and began using it. Bethlehem later reconsidered its belief that continuous casting could not mass-produce.

In 1969, while continuous casting was already being used in Japan and at domestic mini-mills, Bethlehem decided to build a casting machine of its own. Despite advisers suggesting it be built at one of the company's more progressive plants such as Burns Harbor or Sparrows Point, Martin decided to put it in Johnstown. However, after spending millions of dollars to prepare the site and build the foundations for the casters, Johnstown's modernization abruptly ended, further delaying Bethlehem's foray into new, more efficient technology.

The company would build casters at Burns Harbor in 1975 and 1986 and at Steelton in 1983 but not at Bethlehem. The technology never became the foundation of the company's steelmaking process.

Even when Bethlehem Steel officials tried to stay a step ahead of competitors, they often misfired. In the early 1970s, they conducted a study of worldwide iron ore supplies. The study determined that the steel industry was headed for an iron ore shortage.

Company forecasters knew that Bethlehem's Cornwall mines in Lebanon County would run out soon. They knew that the supply in the Grace Mine near Morgantown, Berks County — one of the most modern mining operations in the nation — would last several years.

Hoping to prepare for the more distant future, Bethlehem signed several long-term contracts to buy ore from mines in New Jersey, Venezuela and Chile. The plan rested on the core belief that steel demand would continue to rise.

It didn't, and instead of an iron ore shortage there was a glut. So Bethlehem closed the one mine it controlled completely: the Grace Mine. The company abandoned it despite its state-of-the-art diesel locomotives, plentiful supply of high-grade iron ore and the tens of millions of dollars it invested years earlier.

Charlie Taylor, general superintendent of the Grace Mine, kept water pumps running for four years after the mine was closed to keep it from flooding.

"I couldn't believe they had done such a dumb thing," Taylor says. "I kept the pumps going, because I figured one day they'd come to their senses and reopen it, but they never did."

While Bethlehem Steel was losing the battles of prognostication and innovation, its labor costs were escalating. The company averted another labor strike in the 11th hour by giving steelworkers a three-year deal that included a record 44-cents-an-hour wage hike and big increases to the pension and benefit packages.

There was also a rising sense of worry about imports. On July 31, 1968, the day after the labor contract was signed, Bethlehem Steel raised prices 5 percent to pay for it, putting the company at an even bigger disadvantage in the face of foreign companies penetrating its markets.

Foreign imports that were insignificant before the 1959 strike accounted for 12 percent of all steel consumption in the nation nine years later. But Bethlehem Steel wasn't changing the way it did business to compete with foreign countries that were taking advantage of cheaper labor and new technologies. Instead, it wanted the federal government to protect it.

"Recent trends, if allowed to continue, will seriously weaken the domestic steel industry and therefore threaten national security," Martin reported in 1968, urging Congress to set quotas on foreign steel.

The pleas of Martin and other industry executives were not ignored. In early 1969, steel producers in Japan and Europe agreed to voluntary quotas that would limit imports into the United States to about 14 million tons a year, about 4 million less than the previous year. The countries opted for the voluntary limits in hope of avoiding legislated limits by Congress.

It was the first time foreign countries ever agreed to limit their sales in the United States, and as the 1960s closed, domestic steelmakers were optimistic.

Imports had become a growing concern, but trade limits would help keep them in check. Mini-mills were providing new competition, but the real money was in beams, sheets and raw tonnage. The electric furnaces never would be able to pump out steel of high enough quality to threaten those markets and never would be able to produce enough tonnage to be a serious threat.

All this, The Steel's officials believed.

The $156 million in profits in 1969 convinced them they were right. The company was building a new, impressive headquarters as a pledge to the city where the company got its name, and it was shunning any suggestions that it move the headquarters to a bigger city.

"We have done a lot of thinking about the probable future of the city of Bethlehem and the Lehigh Valley," Martin said during groundbreaking for the headquarters on Aug. 26, 1969. "It looks good to us. … In short, it is evidence that we are here to stay."

In November 1970, Martin handed the company to his trusted second-in-command, 59-year-old Stewart S. Cort. He was a tall man with the sleek frame of an avid golfer, who had a Yale University economics degree and a Harvard School of Business graduate degree that helped carry him quickly up Bethlehem Steel's sales department ladder.

Though 1970 was a down year in which profits dipped below $100 million for the first time in eight years, the biggest immediate battles ahead for Cort were not against his competitors but against the U.S. government.

The Labor Department was investigating allegations that Bethlehem Steel was discriminating against minorities.

The executive offices in Bethlehem, occupied solely by white men, first came under public scrutiny in 1964, when Philip B. Woodroofe was discharged from his job as supervisor of municipal services. Woodroofe, the white son of an Episcopal minister, said he was asked to resign after he refused to end his involvement in the Bethlehem Community Civic League, a newly formed citizens group dedicated to the advancement of blacks in the community.

His boss, F.C. Rabold, told Woodroofe he would have to either give up the group or leave the company. The company felt that his group would cause trouble rather than prevent it, he was told.

Woodroofe told his boss that neither he nor his wife would leave the league.

"I think you're making a big mistake," Rabold said.

Woodroofe was shaken by the reception he got when he arrived at work the next morning.

"I'm surprised that you are here," Rabold said.

"Do you mean to say really I'm through?" Woodroofe asked.

"Yes, you're through," Rabold said.

That month, after Woodroofe's dismissal, Martin explained to the press that the company employed 13,254 blacks, accounting for 12.6 percent of the work force throughout Bethlehem Steel's plants, railroads, mines and shipyards. Blacks made up 11 percent of the work force at all other businesses across the nation, Martin argued.

He added it was difficult to find minorities with enough training for top jobs. The company had never discriminated against black people, he said; there just weren't many black engineers.

"We would like to employ Negroes in top jobs, but we can't get them," Martin explained on Woodroofe's last day of work. "There aren't very many who are metallurgical engineers. We are trying to train them ourselves and bring them up to better jobs."

Martin said his fear was that Woodroofe's civic activities might be seen as the policy of Bethlehem Steel.

Woodroofe never claimed that racial prejudice in the upper levels of Bethlehem Steel led to his firing, he told author Strohmeyer. Rather, he believed his dismissal was the result of office politics. He went on to become a real estate executive in Philadelphia, and there is no record that he ever took legal action against the steelmaker.

But in 1973, Labor Department findings of racial bias had more serious consequences. Beth-

lehem had to correct discriminating practices. The charges focused mainly on the Sparrows Point plant and were based on the Civil Rights Act of 1964. The plant, just below the Mason-Dixon line, was charged with having a seniority system that locked blacks into inferior jobs. While blacks were placed in dirty, low-paying coke oven or waste disposal jobs, whites were assigned to timekeeper or sheet metal posts, Labor Department lawyers said.

Investigators soon targeted U.S. Steel as well, and the Justice Department and the Equal Employment Opportunity Commission were brought in to determine damages. In the end, Bethlehem Steel and eight other steel companies agreed to pay $56 million in back wages to 40,000 minority workers who were underpaid in the previous 30 months. They also agreed that half the future openings for skilled jobs would go to minorities and women until their numbers equaled their overall percentage of employment at each plant.

Guillermo Lopez Jr., who started working at The Steel in 1973, didn't need the government to tell him that his employer was behind the times. While thankful for what the company did for the community and for the paychecks that supported him and his family, he doesn't have fond memories of the way minority workers were treated.

Before he went to work with his father and other Puerto Ricans in the coke works, which he later found out was a polite term for "chemical plant," Lopez hoped to get a craftsman job. After the 1973 settlement, such jobs were set aside for minorities for the years in which they lost out on jobs that went to supervisors' relatives or cronies.

Lopez would soon come to believe that the minority job program was set up to fail. His first day on the job, he hoped that some brotherly co-workers would show him how to run a machine. Instead, he was put in with a big Pennsylvania German, who said: "I'm here to make money, so you just stand in that corner there and stay out of my way."

So Lopez watched.

After three weeks of standing there for eight hours a day and getting grunts when he hoped for conversation, Lopez talked the man into letting him clean the machine. By the 13th week, the two were having conversations. Soon the man let Lopez run part of the machine while he walked around smoking his cigar and bragging, "This kid is making all my money for me. I don't have to do nothing. I come into work and watch him work."

They were getting along — until Lopez's last day of work.

It was the second part of what the man said to Lopez that unleashed months of pent-up resentment.

"I have really enjoyed you being here, and I'm really sorry to see you go. It's not what I expected at all," the man said.

Then came the crack: "You're not like all the rest of them."

"What are you, a ... wise guy?" Lopez retorted.

Lopez had been part of a Puerto Rican migration into Bethlehem Steel's work force that had started decades earlier.

Beginning in 1948, migrants from Puerto Rico came to the Lehigh Valley as seasonal contract farm workers. The orchards and potato fields of the region had depended on a supply of cheap labor that had always been met by the large families of the Pennsylvania German population. In the Depression-era 1930s, there had been plenty of workers.

But after World War II, farmers discovered their traditional source of labor was unwilling to work the long hours for the wages they wanted to pay. So Puerto Ricans filled the void in the garment mills of Allentown and at Bethlehem Steel's coke works, where they occupied the same rung on the employment ladder that the Mexicans had in the 1920s. The largest number lived on the south side of the Lehigh River near the Bethlehem Steel plant. Others lived in public housing in a project in the northeast corner of the city.

Migrant job seekers, usually young men, came first to look for work. When they found it, they sent word back to their rural home villages, such as Patillas and Corozal, that there was work in Bethlehem.

By 1960, when 56 percent of the Lehigh Valley's work force was in either the textile or metal industries, Puerto Ricans were well represented.

Most of these early migrants from Puerto Rico were unskilled. At first they were welcomed because they filled the kind of jobs in a booming economy that most whites didn't want.

But by the early 1960s, tensions between Puerto Ricans and south Bethlehem's older, more settled ethnic European community were rising. The same prejudice and ethnic stereotypes that were directed at the Mexicans — that they should have the hottest jobs because they could stand the heat— were directed at Puerto Ricans.

Yet Puerto Ricans continued to come to south Bethlehem, where they formed such cultural civic groups as the Puerto Rican Beneficial Society and the Council of Spanish Speaking Organizations. In 2003, they made up a large part of the South Side, and more than 33,000 lived in the Lehigh Valley and worked in virtually every facet of the job market.

Bethlehem Steel might have been having difficulty moving minorities into every level of the company, but that wasn't affecting the bottom line. Its $206 million profit in 1973 made the company and the industry an easy target for a steelworkers union that had learned to bully management. In 1971, steelworkers again threatened to strike and again got big wage and benefit increases.

This time, a full year before the three-year contract was ready to expire, negotiators began discussing what would be deemed the Experimental Negotiating Agreement. Industry negotiators had grown weary of what had become an unbroken string of strike threats followed by 11th-hour contract increases. The long-term Experimental Negotiating Agreement prohibited steelworkers from striking for financial reasons but guaranteed that wage increases were pegged to inflation. Senior workers were made eligible for 13 weeks of vacation every fifth year.

All other non-wage parts of the contract, such as pension or benefits, were handled through arbitration.

The agreement prevented strike threats in 1974, 1977 and 1980 and was hailed as revolutionary by industry negotiators who thought they were sparing the country a steelworkers strike. Some workers protested losing their right to strike, but as the years wore on, they weren't complaining.

No agreement put more money in the pockets of steelworkers and more red ink on the balance sheets of steel companies. In the 10 years in which the Experimental Negotiating Agreement was in effect, annual inflation hit double digits five times, including one year when it was 13.5 percent. Steelworker wages nearly tripled.

"That's where we made all of our money," says Tom Jones, a new steelworker in 1973 who went on to become the union business agent in Bethlehem. "Before that we were getting raises of maybe a dime an hour, but that changed everything."

Still, in 1974, there was no reason to believe Bethlehem couldn't afford the agreement, even though imports continued to penetrate American markets, mini-mills were sprouting up across the country and The Steel's signature Fabricated Steel Construction division would have to be closed because it was losing money.

When the 63-year-old Cort decided to retire, he was turning what appeared to be a company at its peak over to new Chairman Lewis W. Foy.

One look at the ledger sheet had Foy, a Johnstown native who had scaled the corporate hierarchy through its purchasing department, thinking big. Not only were the plants running at full tilt, but 1974 brought $342 million in profit, by far the largest in company history.

In August of that year, 17 days after Foy had taken the helm, the new chairman fell back on Grace's advice.

"The job we have to do now is expand the industry as rapidly as possible so we don't get into a [shortage]," Foy said. "I think we are in a new day. I really do."

Bethlehem Steel was heading into a new day, but not the one Foy envisioned and certainly not the one he wanted.

Douglas Benedict/Morning Call file photos
With a pull of its pillars, a Bethlehem Steel landmark fell within a matter of seconds on Jan. 31, 1998. The basic oxygen furnace plant, which opened in 1968, allowed the company to process metal more quickly than open-hearth furnaces. Workers had cut the building's supports over two months to prepare for the demolition. About 100 people watched the structure fall.

CHAPTER
EIGHT

The bitter end

Lorraine "Cookie" Burkhardt struggles to look through tears to find her car in the lot outside Martin Tower in Bethlehem.

Until now, it had been an exciting month for her. She bought a new car — a shiny 1977 Ford Pinto with a snazzy red pinstripe — moved to a suburban ranch home twice the size of her old house and just returned from taking her two children on their first trip to Disney World.

But at this moment, on Friday, Sept. 30, 1977, as Burkhardt scurries across the tree-lined lot with the remnants of her brief career at Bethlehem Steel tucked into a cardboard box, Martin Tower is far from the happiest place on Earth.

As she makes her way out of The Steel's headquarters, she is among 2,500 shell-shocked, white-collar Bethlehem Steel workers, including 800 from Martin Tower, who were sent packing from the jobs that had helped them live the American dream.

A few weeks earlier, while the country mourned the deaths of Elvis Presley and Groucho Marx, 7,000 plant workers were dismissed. But the layoffs at the headquarters were the first time white-collar workers were let go. It was their Black Friday.

Seemingly overnight, Bethlehem Steel had gone from industrial titan to struggling dinosaur, and this was the day its workers realized the company they thought was invincible was in serious trouble.

"We all went to Danny's, got terribly drunk and cried in our beer, literally," Burkhardt says. "Then we went back to my big new house and cried some more. We never saw it coming."

Burkhardt and many of the employees laid off in 1977 would be called back to work over the next two years, but Black Friday would forever be known as the day Bethlehem Steel's long era of plenty ended.

No one factor was to blame. Rather, Black Friday — and ultimately the demise of Bethlehem Steel — was the confluence of decades of mistakes that caused the former behemoth to collapse under the weight of its own corporate obesity.

Maybe things would have been different if the 1959 steelworkers strike hadn't opened the door to foreign steel and paved the way for years of labor contracts the company couldn't afford.

Or maybe if The Steel's inbred board of directors had allowed members from outside the company before 1965, it would have realized sooner that the demand for steel would not always grow and that the company needed to diversify rather than dump billions of dollars into outdated steel plants.

Maybe if Bethlehem had not been so certain that foreign countries and upstart mini-mills couldn't compete with its product, it would have been better prepared when both started stealing its customers. It could have been quicker to buy into technologies such as basic oxygen furnaces and continuous casting, quicker to respond to the competition of plastics and aluminum and quicker to abandon a corporate culture that emphasized conformity over innovation.

By the time the consequences of those decisions converged in 1977, nearly 10,000 shocked and angry employees were out of work, suddenly left with too much time to ponder what happened.

"What are we supposed to do now?" Burkhardt says to a restaurant full of unemployed colleagues as they gulp pitcher after pitcher of Lehigh Valley-brewed Schaefer beer that does little to help them forget their fate.

For Bethlehem Steel, there would be years when profits would return, and there would be occasional signs of hope. But overall, Black Friday signaled the start of a quarter-century decline in which jobs were lost, dreams were shattered and an industrial icon plodded toward a slow, agonizing death.

Even if the realization that The Steel was in trouble had come sooner, there was little it could have done to prevent much of the pain that would follow Black Friday. It wasn't just Bethlehem that was sick; it was the entire steel industry.

In the final 25 years of a century in which steel had become king, nearly 1.5 million steelworkers worldwide lost their jobs. Half were from the foreign countries that U.S. steelmakers blamed for eliminating American jobs. While the United States was losing 73 percent of its steel jobs in that span, Japan was losing 57 percent and Germany was losing 67 percent.

Only a few years before Black Friday, in 1972, Bethlehem Steel had built a new headquarters on the city's west side. At 330 feet, it was the tallest building in the Valley, reaching 8 feet higher than the Allentown headquarters of electric utility PPL.

But the extravagance didn't stop with its size. The building was constructed in the shape of a cross rather than a traditional square to create more corner and window offices for the glut of vice presidents in the company's top-heavy executive hierarchy.

These weren't just any offices accented by two walls of windows. The executive offices, specially designed by New York decorators, were adorned with ornate furniture, wooden doorknobs engraved with the company logo and handwoven carpet. When the executive boardroom's carpet was damaged in transit up the elevator shaft, the weavers were brought to Bethlehem from New York to fix it.

"Only the best decorators and the best furniture would do," says Craig Bartholomew, a senior buyer who ordered much of the materials and furniture for the office complex. "After all, this was Bethlehem Steel."

The 21-story Martin Tower was a monument to one of the most powerful companies in the nation. Bethlehem was on a 39-year run of annual profits, including the $134.6 million it netted the year its imposing new headquarters opened. Its profits continued right through 1974, when they hit a record $342 million. Demand was high and the money was flowing. Life at Bethlehem Steel was good.

But Ethel Gasda was getting suspicious. A former "pistol packin' mama" who brought bullets to work as part of the plant security patrol during World War II, Gasda was nervous about what she saw while working as a secretary in a Bethlehem Steel vice president's office.

She had been at Bethlehem Steel for parts

of four decades, but in the months leading up to Black Friday, she was worried. The company where employees thought they had a job for life, the company known for its philanthropy, was slashing its charitable offerings. It reduced its matching grant donations to Lehigh University. It cut its annual donations to the Metropolitan Opera in New York. Gasda realized there was a rising sense of panic in the executive offices of the 21st floor.

"When they started cutting all that down, you knew," Gasda says in the flawless diction she honed in The Steel's perfectly proper executive offices. "They didn't stop it completely, but it was going down, down, down."

Gasda had reason to be nervous. By the time the company closed out its record year in 1974, the mini-mills it regarded as a mere annoyance were cutting deeply into its business. Nucor of Charlotte, N.C., with its electric furnaces and streamlined staff of nonunion laborers, had seen its sales increase tenfold in the previous decade.

When Nucor started in 1966, the inferior steel from its furnaces could only chip away at Bethlehem Steel's low-grade steel wire, rod and bars business. But now, new technology had Nucor producing a better product and stealing Bethlehem's structural business, too.

As Nucor and its copycats pecked at companies such as Bethlehem and U.S. Steel from one side, imports came at them from the other. Bethlehem had spent the past 15 years arrogantly ignoring both threats, and now it was too big, too fat and too unwilling to abandon its culture of conformity to respond quickly enough.

Two decades earlier, Chairman Eugene G. Grace declared that Bethlehem Steel could sell all of the steel it could make, and company executives had been predicting increases in demand every year since.

While demand more than tripled between 1950 and 1973, Grace looked more like a genius than an optimist. But then demand hit a plateau. With fenders, dashboards and bumpers being made of plastic, cars needed far less steel. Some bridges and buildings were being made with precast concrete, and aluminum companies had begun to steal Bethlehem's frozen orange juice, soda and beer can business. With too many steel

companies possessing too much capacity, the industry had become a matter of survival, and Bethlehem Steel eventually would prove it was not among the fittest.

All the trends that had been building since the 1950s hit hard, and bad luck heaped on to make 1977 a nightmarish year for Bethlehem Steel. In January, nearly 14 feet of snow had already fallen on the banks of Lake Erie, where its Lackawanna plant operated, when a three-day storm brought 70 mph winds and several more feet of snow.

Hundreds of workers were stranded in the plant, while others using high-wheeled payloaders cut through the drifts to rescue workers marooned at the ore storage pits, John Strohmeyer says in his book, "Crisis in Bethlehem." No workers were lost, but the blizzard halted production, costing the company more than $10 million in sales and plant repairs.

A week later, on Feb. 7, an underground fire struck Bethlehem's Cambria division coal mines, 40 miles outside Pittsburgh. The fire in Mine 32 quickly grew out of control, spread to Mine 33 and burned for weeks until workers built concrete walls to isolate the two mines and flooded them with water. Mine 33 remained closed for two months, and Mine 32 didn't reopen until the following year. The fire caused about $15 million in damage, but that was on top of the coal business Bethlehem lost and the money it spent to buy coal from elsewhere to run its plants.

As the company cleaned up the mine fire wreckage, torrential storms pounded Johnstown on July 20, dropping a foot of rain on The Steel's Johnstown plant. The Stonycreek and Little Conemaugh rivers washed over their banks, sending water as deep as 8 feet flowing through the downtown streets. Seven earthen dams failed, including one break that killed 44 people. In all, 78 people died, 413 homes were lost and 1,363 were damaged. Floods wracked the plant and deluged Bethlehem's coal mines, dealing it an additional $40 million in cleanup and repair costs.

By December, the company's executives had nothing to celebrate. Nevertheless, they gathered for a lavish black-tie Christmas party in the guest house at the posh Saucon Valley Country Club's Weyhill Golf Course.

As Bethlehem Steel's elite sang Christmas

carols and listened to piano tunes, word came that the company's miserable year wasn't over. Two company-owned supertankers had collided in a remote shipping lane off the southern coast of Africa.

"Just when we thought things couldn't get worse, they did," says Robert Wilkins, Bethlehem Steel's vice president of finance. He had gone to the party hoping that for at least one night he could forget the year Bethlehem was having. "We all looked at each other and said, how do two ships hit each other in an ocean that big?"

The oil cargo was contained, but two seamen were killed and both tankers were out of commission for eight months. The explanation at the time was that the tanker crews didn't realize they were in the same area, but some steel executives later said the crews were trying to wave to each other and simply got too close.

However it happened, the disaster was just another log on the fire engulfing Bethlehem Steel's financial house. By the close of 1977, the company's 43-year run of profits was over. Despite layoffs and plant closings, the disastrous events and a $750 million write-off resulted in a $448 million loss for the year.

That write-off in unprofitable assets — the largest in corporate history — represented a major change in philosophy under Chairman Lewis W. Foy and led to Black Friday. Rather than continue pumping money into outdated, unprofitable plants, Foy chose to shut down several mills in Johnstown and Lackawanna.

Only a few years earlier, he had proposed more than $200 million in upgrades for Johnstown, including new basic oxygen furnaces. Some of Foy's advisers were telling him then to close the landlocked plant. They knew that the steel market had moved to the Midwest. Plants that cargo ships couldn't approach — such as those at Johnstown and Bethlehem — were logging huge transportation costs to move raw materials from the East Coast ports and finished products into the Midwest.

But the soft-spoken Foy, who rose through The Steel's purchasing department, was a Johnstown native who couldn't bring himself to inflict pain on his own people.

"I can't shut down mills in my hometown,"

Foy told his advisers in 1974. "We can make those plants profitable again."

By the time floodwaters washed into the Johnstown plant, Bethlehem Steel was already building the basic oxygen furnaces there. Much of the work was destroyed, but Wilkins says it was not the financial disaster the company portrayed.

"The Johnstown flood, while tragic, was the best thing that happened [financially] to Bethlehem Steel that year, because it caused us to rethink the upgrades we were planning there," Wilkins says. "Putting more money into Johnstown would have been like dumping money into a hole, and most of us knew it. That flood saved the company hundreds of millions of dollars."

With the steel industry in a free fall and Johnstown severely damaged by the flood, Foy conceded that the company shouldn't proceed with most of its plans to modernize Johnstown. But even then he tried to cushion the blow to his hometown. Rather than close the entire Johnstown or Lackawanna sites, as his captains were advising, Foy spread the pain evenly between the two.

Gone were the plate mill, several other outdated mills and 3,800 jobs at Johnstown. Lackawanna lost four blast furnaces, five rolling mills and 3,500 jobs.

It was a strategic downsizing plan cobbled together by Foy's new financial adviser, Donald H. Trautlein. He was a Price Waterhouse & Co. accounting firm partner who had handled the Bethlehem Steel account for more than a decade. As The Steel's accountant, Trautlein attended executive meetings, quietly sitting in the back, speaking when he was spoken to and making suggestions only when he was asked. Foy brought him into the company as comptroller when losses started to pile up in 1977.

When Trautlein joined the company, his no-nonsense approach and analytical view of the bottom line had Foy taking his suggestions to heart. The bloodletting Trautlein advised, while painful, seemed to stop the hemorrhaging at least temporarily. Bethlehem Steel posted a combined $500 million in profits in 1978 and 1979, as Trautlein vaulted from comptroller to senior vice president to executive vice president in less than three years. In a rigidly traditional company where high-level promotions usually came only when someone retired or died, Trautlein's rise was meteoric — and it wasn't over.

In April 1980, the 65-year-old Foy triumphantly dipped into the company till to fly 250 Bethlehem Steel managers and their wives to the posh Boca Raton Country Club in Florida. He congratulated them for the reversal of fortunes since 1977 and turned them loose to enjoy the Atlantic oceanfront, golf on the club's four 18-hole courses and drink — free of charge.

The trip closed with an extravagant banquet in which Foy introduced his successor, Trautlein. Looking every bit the accountant in his three-piece suit as he stepped to the lectern, Trautlein quickly brought the celebratory crowd back to Earth. Bethlehem Steel is entering an era of change and pain, he told them matter-of-factly.

"We are not in the business of making steel," Trautlein said, challenging the company's staunch traditionalism. "We are in the business of making money."

The banquet became known as The Last Supper. The popular Foy left with a multimillion-dollar retirement package and went off to his estate in the exclusive Elms neighborhood of Saucon Valley. Like many of The Steel's retired top executives, Foy would spend the next two decades "going to work" in Suite 310 of the Hotel Bethlehem, in the offices kept by Bethlehem Steel for its most prominent executives. Like the others in Suite 310, he'd get a consulting fee for a while. But the offices were more about giving powerful men a way to continue to feel powerful than they were about running the company.

Bethlehem Steel was now heading into one of its most agonizing periods.

Trautlein was an outsider. Unlike previous chairmen, he wasn't carefully groomed. He had never worked in a steel mill, never sold steel, never managed a company-owned shipyard or coal mine. To the lunch pail-carrying men who breathed coke dust in south Bethlehem, he was a bean counter who didn't know an I-beam from Jim Beam.

But the unimposing numbers man with a photographic memory and a seemingly tireless attention to detail had his defenders. Foreman Jim Cox says an accountant was exactly what the company needed at the time. The way Cox saw

it, there was no denying that the low-cost mini-mills were duplicating the material coming out of Bethlehem.

Bethlehem Steel had the overhead burden of ore mines, coal mines, limestone mines, ships to move the material, all the transportation facilities, coke ovens and the blast furnaces needed to convert pig iron and scrap into steel. Grace had trumpeted this control of steelmaking from start to finish as the reason Bethlehem could build more than 1,000 ships during World War II. But now it was hobbling the company because mini-mills didn't need all of those things. They just put scrap into their electric furnaces and out came steel.

Someone had to figure out how to turn Bethlehem's lumbering giant into a lean production machine that could compete with the mini-mills, imports and new products such as plastic and aluminum.

"I don't think it was fair," Cox, a maintenance foreman who spent 42 years at Bethlehem Steel, says of his colleagues' harsh view of Trautlein. "Trautlein was an accountant, and what the company needed I think at that time was somebody who could sort out the changing business world."

Closings and layoffs came in flurries. By May 1980, the 18-inch rolling mill in Bethlehem was downgraded to part-time status. By June, 108 workers at the ingot mold foundry were out of work, and by the end of Trautlein's first year, Bethlehem Steel was 8,000 workers lighter. That was just the beginning.

As the company lost more money, about 30,000 workers were let go over the next two years, a third at the Johnstown and Lackawanna plants that Foy tried to spare a few years earlier.

Two days after Christmas 1982, as pop star Billy Joel appeared at a news conference before a concert at Lehigh University's Stabler Arena, The Steel's assistant vice president of public affairs, Bruce Davis, hopped a flight to Lackawanna.

Joel appeared with Allentown Mayor Joseph Daddona to become an honorary citizen and to soothe fans offended by his song "Allentown," which portrayed the Lehigh Valley as a struggling region devastated by The Steel's decline. Joel opened and closed his concert before 6,000 fans with "Allentown."

Well, we're living here in Allentown.
And they're closing all the factories down.
Out in Bethlehem they're killing time
Filling out forms, standing in line.

Meanwhile, Davis' nonstop flight from the Lehigh Valley had just touched down in Buffalo, N.Y., six miles north of the Lackawanna plant. As he went to the lectern in the auditorium of Lackawanna's headquarters, he could come up with only three sentences to open the meeting.

"The industry is in trouble. The company must take corrective action," Davis said, as a coat of fresh snow covered the plant outside. "For Lackawanna, that will mean the loss of 7,300 jobs."

That day, Davis decided he wanted out of the steel business.

"It was the wrong time for the announcement, and I was the wrong guy to make it," Davis said later. "I resented being deemed the executioner."

Davis left Bethlehem Steel three years later to practice law, and most of the employees laid off never returned to work at Bethlehem Steel.

Trautlein took a 10 percent pay cut and ordered cuts for 22,000 other white-collar workers, but in the eyes of the union he was the most hated man in the company's history.

"I guess I was one of the guys chucking spears for him, but he did what had to be done, what should have been done much sooner," says Gary Millenbruch, a vice president under Trautlein who rose to chief financial officer and ultimately vice chairman. "There was no avoiding it. The company was sinking fast."

In fact, the industry was sinking. By 1982, nearly 200 steel plants were closed nationwide, 200,000 jobs were eliminated and another 140,000 workers were laid off. Plants that once ran full and still had trouble meeting demand now were running at 48 percent of capacity. Imports made up 26 percent of all steel sold in the United States.

The domestic steel industry lost $3 billion in five years, and Bethlehem Steel did more than its share to contribute to that. In 1982, The Steel broke its dubious 1977 record by posting a $1.5 billion deficit, largely based on a $1 billion write-off of more closed plants in Johnstown and Lackawanna.

Massive layoffs, plant closings and restructuring weren't enough. So on an otherwise typical Monday morning in late 1982, Trautlein called his senior managers into the executive boardroom to ask them if they were in the mood for a fight.

"Illegal imports have become a serious problem," Trautlein told executives who had been living that fact for years. "It is time for us to take on the world."

In the coming months, Trautlein would lead an industry offensive on imports, but he wasn't willing to go to war without ammunition. If he had any chance of persuading the independent U.S. International Trade Commission and President Ronald Reagan to restrict foreign steel, he knew he would need concessions from the United Steelworkers of America.

Without concessions, it would be too easy for the International Trade Commission to divert the blame from trade and pin it on labor. There was no hiding the fact that as demand for steel flattened between 1970 and 1980, the average hourly wages for Bethlehem Steel employees had nearly tripled, from $4.96 per hour to $13.64. With vacations, health care, pension and other benefits added to that, it was costing the company $26.12 per hour for each worker.

But getting concessions from the union would not be easy. American steelworkers had never before agreed to them, and two attempts to renegotiate the deal that was to expire in July 1983 had already been rejected by the union rank and file.

Through the 1970s, steel salaries skyrocketed because hourly increases were based on annual inflation rates. In 1973, when company officials agreed to cost-of-living increases in return for the union's pledge not to strike, they didn't foresee that inflation would hit 13.5 percent during the worst 10-year stretch since World War I.

Ed O'Brien, a raspy-voiced straight-talker with the crooked nose of a boxer, knew the industry was hurting. But the man who rose from coke works laborer to local union president didn't trust Trautlein.

"The bottom line," O'Brien told Bethlehem Steel negotiators in January 1983, "is we won't insist on any more than we've got, but we won't take any less, either."

A month later, O'Brien and two other local union presidents voted against a contract that included concessions, but they were outnumbered by union officers across the nation. On Feb. 27, United Steelworkers voted 169-63 to ratify the first concessionary contract in the history of the steel industry. The 41-month deal lowered wages by $1.25 per hour, and with benefit concessions, the hourly savings to steel companies would approach $3 per hour per worker. In all, it was a 9 percent reduction.

Also gone were the 13-week vacation that senior steel employees got every fifth year and the United Nations Day paid holiday, Oct. 24, that had come to represent an embarrassment of benefits.

Company executives projected the industry would save $2 billion over the life of the contract. For their part, union employees got increased benefits for laid-off workers, some of their lost pay was offset by company stock and management promised to use the contract savings to rebuild the industry.

"It didn't give our laid-off people enough," a dejected O'Brien said after the vote. "There was no real guarantee of putting people back to work."

Despite the cuts, the union did not budge on the past practices clause, or Clause 2B, that had been introduced in the 1956 contract. The clause barred the company from combining jobs to reduce the number of workers needed to do a task. Teams of high-paid union workers would continue to do jobs that one nonunion worker was doing at foreign plants or in domestic mini-mills.

Though Bethlehem executives couldn't rid themselves of Clause 2B, the salary and benefit concessions gave them and other steelmakers the ammunition they needed to ask Washington for protection from steel imports.

Trautlein planned to wage his fight through the U.S. International Trade Commission by filing a petition of injury under the provisions of the Fair Trade Act. The commission holds hearings on claims of unfair trade and has the power to recommend remedies to the president. Best of all, the Fair Trade Act required that the process be completed in eight months. If Trautlein and his allies won their case with the commission, Reagan would have to decide on tariffs or quotas in the fall of 1984 as he was campaigning for a second term.

Trautlein was convinced it would be easy to prove that foreign countries were "dumping" excess steel in America by selling it for less than it cost to make, a clear violation of international trade laws passed in 1976.

But a battle against dumping meant jumping into a sticky political arena of international relations. The United States had sought trade quotas before, but enforcement had always been lax, partly because of international politics. If the United States put restrictions on foreign steel, it risked foreign countries putting restrictions on American goods.

Opposition from Japan and Germany was expected, but Bethlehem also had foes among some of its best customers. Caterpillar and General Motors opposed trade restrictions because they would drive up steel prices. Even U.S. Steel, the nation's top steel producer, refused to back Trautlein, arguing that his plan could upset voluntary restrictions that some foreign countries agreed to only a few years earlier.

But Bethlehem Steel's controversial leader was undaunted, and he had allies. Most of the nation's other steel companies were with him, as well as the union. Outside union headquarters at Van Bittner Hall on Lehigh Street in Bethlehem was a 45-foot beam with the words "Stop Illegal Steel Imports" painted on it.

On this issue, the union chose to look past its disdain for Trautlein. In January 1984, he and the union filed a petition with the U.S. International Trade Commission on behalf of the steel industry.

"There is absolutely no free trade in steel," Trautlein said in announcing the petition during a news conference at the Hotel Bethlehem, a landmark that was built at the urging of Bethlehem Steel Corp. founder Charles M. Schwab. "Damages caused by dumped and subsidized imports are undermining [the industry's] very foundation."

With Steelworkers International President Lynn Williams at his side, Trautlein estimated that Bethlehem had lost nearly $2 billion in revenue in four years to dumped steel, and asked that the trade commission and Reagan limit imports to 15 percent of steel consumed in America. Williams was quick to add that the union had done its part by taking concessions.

Later at hearings, two trade commission members questioned whether the steel industry was merely using foreign trade as a convenient excuse for its own high wages, outdated plants and unrealistic projections of increased demand.

"Imports do not come close to being the most important problem," said Paula Stern, a trade commission member appointed by President Jimmy Carter. "No. 1 is the general decline in demand."

Nevertheless, by a 3-2 vote the commission found in favor of Trautlein's petition, and Reagan — further nudged by a letter-writing campaign orchestrated by Bethlehem Steel — agreed to limit imports to 18.5 percent by striking "voluntary" deals with several foreign countries. Trautlein didn't get everything he wanted, but Reagan's decree was a huge victory for American steel. To those who opposed the petition, it was a gross violation of free trade.

The trade deals slowed the stream of imports for a while, but they were never stringently enforced, and imports never dropped to 18 percent. It didn't take long for foreign countries to find loopholes. Countries that agreed to the voluntary limits, such as Japan, simply made it appear that the goods were coming from countries that struck no deal, such as Canada and Mexico. Others used clever labeling to skirt the restrictions.

William Tattersall, a longtime Bethlehem Steel attorney and manager of its state government affairs office who moved on to work for the International Iron and Steel Institute, had an overarching view of the world trade situation from his institute office in Belgium.

"The tariffs on finished products were higher than unfinished, so foreign companies would relabel a shipment of bicycles as steel tubing," Tattersall says. "Or they'd label it from Mexico or Canada. All they did was alter the labels. The U.S. either didn't have the agents to monitor it, or they simply chose not to for political reasons."

It was soon clear that the industry's problems went far beyond imports. Trautlein had closed dozens of plants, trimmed the work force by more than 50,000 people and tried to replace a culture of entitlement with one of productivity.

He tried to modernize the plants and diversify the company by buying nonsteel operations such as Kusan Manufacturing Co. of Nashville, Tenn., a plastics maker that could help boost Bethlehem Steel when steel faltered. He cut The Steel's payroll by 40 percent while nearly doubling the tonnage production per worker.

Still, the company had lost $1.7 billion over the six years Trautlein was at the helm, its future looked even more tenuous than when he had arrived, and he was worn out and despised by many of his workers. His predecessors had moved about Bethlehem like royalty, commanding police escorts to daily golf outings and setting off the panic of workers ordered to have the elevator waiting for them, but Trautlein was no longer even comfortable at the Saucon Valley Country Club, an institution created for The Steel's executives in the early 1920s.

In 1986, Trautlein and Bethlehem Steel's board decided it was time for a change. It was time to try to end an era of pain and begin a new one of healing. On the same unseasonably hot April day that Bethlehem Steel posted a quarterly loss of $91 million — a record 14th quarter of losses in four years — it announced that Trautlein would step down as chairman in May.

He had already turned over day-to-day control of the company to President Walter Williams, and this would complete the transition. Wall Street barely acknowledged the change as the company's stock remained level, but on the plant floors where 37,000 workers were trying to hang on to their jobs, there was widespread celebration.

Williams had dutifully worked closely with Trautlein, supported his moves and defended his cuts, but in the eyes of the workers he was the anti-Trautlein. Unlike his predecessor, Williams had arrived at Bethlehem Steel in 1951 as a member of its "Loop Course" for management trainees and spent more than three decades moving up in the company. Unlike Trautlein, the numbers man, Williams was a straight-talking, roll-up-your-sleeves engineer who spent virtually all his career in operations or shipbuilding. He'd helped design Burns Harbor, Bethlehem Steel's most profitable plant.

He knew steel, the workers rejoiced. He was the perfect medicine for a demoralized work force.

"When the surgery is over and the cancer has been removed, the patient usually goes back to their general physician," says Davis, the former company assistant vice president who went on to represent The Steel's Retired Employees Benefits Coalition. "The surgeon's work was done. It was time for Walt Williams to guide the patient through recovery."

That meant returning to its core product, Williams declared almost immediately. With the company cash-strapped and facing bankruptcy, he continued an asset sell-off started months earlier by Trautlein and expanded it by deeming everything that didn't involve making steel — even the vaunted Martin Tower — for sale.

Within months, the company raised $386 million with the sale of several Bethlehem Steel subsidiaries, including Georgia-based steel product distributor J.M. Tull Industries and plastics maker Kusan, which together netted $16 million in an otherwise dismal 1985.

Almost as if Bethlehem Steel's new chief executive had waved a magic wand, the red ink turned to black. The fourth quarter of 1986 brought net income of $34 million and was the first of what would be four consecutive years of profits. Williams, the guy who knew the sweat that goes into making a steel beam, was a hero to some workers.

By 1987, nearly a decade of payroll trimming, more efficient production and the end to extravagant spending, such as funding Suite 310 and lump-sum golden parachutes for executives, was starting to improve the bottom line. The continuous casters Trautlein built at Burns Harbor and Sparrows Point for $500 million were beginning to pump out profit-making steel. The state-of-the-art casters allowed workers to shape steel directly from its molten form, eliminating the need for large, expensive mills for rolling ingots into slabs and bringing Bethlehem out of the dark ages of steelmaking. Even the bankruptcy rumors that had dogged the company for nearly a year were starting to wane.

But Bethlehem Steel's fleeting resurgence also was the result of a strong national economy and the misfortunes of its competitors.

The nation's largest steel producer, U.S. Steel, wasn't producing steel during a six-month work stoppage. LTV, which acquired Republic Steel and Jones & Laughlin Steel and toppled Bethlehem as the second largest producer in 1984, was struggling to reorganize under Chapter 11 bankruptcy. Wheeling-Pittsburgh and Kaiser Steel companies were also mired in bankruptcy.

Meanwhile, the national economy was picking up. People were buying cars again, investors were building office complexes and demand for steel was rising after a sharp decline in the first half of the decade.

Most important, a weak dollar compared to foreign currency was making American steel a better buy internationally. What government trade quotas and tariffs couldn't do, a strong economy and a weak dollar did almost overnight. Imports that made up 26 percent of steel consumption through the mid-1980s plummeted to under 18 percent in the late 1980s and early '90s. Steel prices spiked by 10 percent, and Bethlehem was profitable once again. Between 1987 and 1990 the company recorded $830 million in profits, including a record $403 million in 1988.

Still, the 4,500 workers at the flagship plant in Bethlehem weren't buying it. Yes, the bottom line looked better, the company staved off bankruptcy and a stock that sank below $5 a share in 1986 was pushing $20 by the end of 1992. But there were ominous signs that trouble never really left.

Bethlehem Steel was shrinking fast. Pensioners outnumbered workers more than three to one, mini-mills Nucor and Chaparral Steel were selling beams that Bethlehem Steel executives thought could never be efficiently rolled from electric furnace steel. And most worrisome to workers, all the profits Bethlehem Steel intended for modernization were leaving Bethlehem. More than $80 million was about to be spent on a new electric furnace at the Steelton plant — something that workers desperately had wanted in Bethlehem. To employees, that was a clear message that the company had already given up on its flagship plant.

A $50 million upgrade of the Grey mill in 1988 was only a pitiful Band-Aid. It was spent to modernize the middle mill of a three-mill operation. The steel went into the same outdated blooming mill, where it was reduced to a dog-bone-shaped form, and still came out of the same obsolete finishing mill, where the beam was completed. The fact it was rolled into a beam by passing through a new, modern Grey mill in the middle didn't change the product. Without an additional $200 million to replace the two other mills, the money to replace the Grey mill was money burned, workers argued.

Management had given up on the flagship plant long ago, says Stephen "Hector" Nemes. He was a beam straightener and crane operator in the Bethlehem plant before he was elected to the union's grievance committee and worked his way up to staff representative for United Steelworkers International. With more than 16 years' experience in grievance arbitration and contract negotiations, he'd learned he was more likely to get what he wanted by checking the militant union talk at the door. He found respect and cordial words, even for the cutthroat company negotiators other union representatives treated with only scorn.

Nemes had been through the dark days of the 1980s and was convinced there was no turning things around in Bethlehem. The plant's fate was sealed; it was just a matter of time. He had believed this ever since the company spent a half-billion dollars to build continuous casters at Sparrows Point and Burns Harbor while delaying modernization at Bethlehem.

In 1986, the company threatened to close primary steelmaking in Bethlehem if the union didn't agree to trim 550 from the work force. Nemes recommended the cuts be accepted, angering some workers accustomed to a more hard-nosed stance from their negotiators. Big profits in some of the years since then hadn't changed his view of the company's future.

"Really, starting in 1986, I completely changed my strategy," Nemes says. "I decided that I would do whatever it took, give back whatever was necessary to keep those plants open a little longer. For me, it was all about getting more guys vested in the pension. Every year we stayed open meant thousands of more guys had pensions. That's what drove me, because I knew Bethlehem had no long-term future."

Nemes wasn't alone in that assessment, but in 1991, there was new reason for hope. On and

off for the previous two years, Bethlehem Steel's top brass secretly was negotiating with British Steel for a joint venture. As the deal came closer to fruition, the talks went public because concessions would be needed from the Bethlehem plant workers for the partnership to succeed. The deal was a double-edged sword for the 4,500 workers still making steel in Bethlehem. It would give the company that built the Golden Gate Bridge and much of Manhattan a chance to begin reshaping the skylines in Europe. But it also would mean concessions by the union and the loss of about 2,000 jobs at the Bethlehem plant.

Under the proposed deal, Bethlehem's last running blast furnace and its basic oxygen furnaces would be shut down. The Steelton plant would be modernized. Its electric furnaces would be used to make steel for structural beams for British Steel. Those beams would be sent to Bethlehem for finishing into beams by the 2,500 workers who survived the cut. Those remaining workers would have lower salaries and benefits.

British Steel would supply capital for modernization that Bethlehem Steel didn't have, a widened customer base and international marketing experience.

While analysts and executives billed it as the deal that could save Bethlehem from ruin, it was bitter medicine for union workers to swallow. How much more would they have to give up so that executives and stockholders could make more money, they asked. They were promised modernization that never came — modernization that could have allowed them to stand on their own rather than cater to a foreign company that wasn't even going to let them make the steel.

On Nov. 11, 1991, Bethlehem Steel announced that the deal was dead. Two years of negotiations had failed, and executives blamed the union for refusing to accept cuts in wages and benefits, among other concessions. One of the biggest sticking points was a provision that would have ended seniority and cut the Bethlehem workers out of the basic contract agreement, ending their right to transfer to other plants if they were laid off later.

O'Brien, by then assistant director of the United Steelworkers statewide, says the union was unfairly blamed for the deal's failure.

"If they thought we were going to let them throw up a wall at the Bethlehem plant, they were crazy," O'Brien says. "That deal wasn't happening anyway. British Steel didn't have the money to close it. The whole thing was smoke and mirrors."

After starting with such promise, 1991 ended with the company's fifth consecutive quarterly loss ($649 million), the demise of a deal that could have saved the company and a future more uncertain than ever.

The death of the British Steel deal, a venture that Williams fostered with countless trips overseas, prompted the six-year chief executive to begin planning his retirement. He had tried to steer Bethlehem's foundering ship and succeeded for a while, but he'd grown weary of frantically bailing water only to find there was a leak on the other side of the vessel. Since he had taken the helm, nearly 13,000 jobs had been cut, and the future of the money-losing Structural Products division, which made beams, angles and channels, and BethForge, which made steel rolls and parts for the Navy, was very much in doubt. And at 63, Williams was fast approaching the company's unwritten mandatory retirement age of 65.

As Williams launched a new two-year plan to lay off an additional 6,500 workers by closing or selling several plants, including the remaining ones in Johnstown and several in Lackawanna, he began making plans to turn the ship over to someone else.

It was only coincidence that the date was Halloween 1992, but that's the day Williams gave up what had turned into the scariest job in the Lehigh Valley. Curtis "Hank" Barnette, senior vice president, general counsel and longtime board secretary, took over the task of trying to revive one of the nation's most troubled companies.

Barnette was a different kind of chief executive officer than Bethlehem had seen. He was the only lawyer to be named CEO. He was not enamored of golf the way previous chiefs had been, and even sold the Weyhill Golf Course to Saucon Valley Country Club because it didn't fit the profile of Steel's "core product."

Barnette was a native of St. Albans, W.Va., and a former Army counterintelligence specialist who went to England on a Fulbright scholarship and played basketball for Queen Elizabeth as part of a traveling squad that filled 10 of its dozen spots with Americans.

After graduating from Yale Law School, he practiced law in New Haven, Conn., and tutored law students at Yale. But in 1967, he interrupted what he expected to be a stable, comfortable life in Connecticut to take a chance. In what he referred to as the "Tappan Zee Bridge Decision," he decided to interview at Bethlehem Steel.

On the bridge going back to Connecticut, Barnette told his wife, Joanne, that he thought The Steel people were terrific but he couldn't wait to get back to New Haven. Joanne asked him what he thought he would be doing in five years.

"Practicing law in New Haven and trying very important cases and, hopefully, be doing something at the law school," Hank replied.

"And that's very, very important," Joanne said. "Did you ever think what you'd be doing 10 years from now?"

"Yes, I'll be trying very important cases and ...."

Barnette realized that his life would be exactly the same in 10 years and that the Bethlehem offer was too good to pass up.

After 25 years in legal and executive offices, he took over a struggling $4 billion corporation. He pledged to carry on Williams' work and stop Bethlehem's free fall by following a simple credo: Improve, sell or restructure.

That wouldn't be easy. The year 1992 ended with $550 million in losses and there was no reason to be encouraged about 1993. Barnette decided that if he could get workers to take more cuts, he might be able to keep the Bethlehem plant running. This time, understanding how vulnerable the plant was, workers quickly accepted a new deal in May 1993. The 30-month agreement would freeze their wages through 1995 and break the Bethlehem plant into three separate operations responsible for their own success.

The struggling divisions of Centec, which made high-quality cast iron rolls for Bethlehem and other steel companies, and BethForge were spun off as isolated operations. The remaining Structural Products division was slated for modernization. The cuts were painful. Besides agreeing to a basic salary freeze, workers at BethForge and Centec had to agree to 30 percent cuts in incentive pay that sometimes made up half their paychecks and to eliminating 1,500 jobs over several years.

Somehow the feelings of mistrust that had long driven a wedge between labor and management seemed to have been left behind. Barnette announced the deal June 30, 1993, in the Hotel Bethlehem with 50 union leaders and company workers at his side. His pledge to consider investing $250 million into the Bethlehem plant made it easy to forget the past battles with management. Bethlehem finally was going to get its electric furnaces and a state-of-the-art continuous caster. Finally it was going to give the mini-mills a run for their money.

"This is history in the remaking," Lt. Gov. Mark Singel said triumphantly in a hotel banquet room. "By making this commitment to restructuring, Bethlehem Steel is saying, 'We're here for the long haul.' "

Don Trexler, president of United Steelworkers Local 2599, couldn't help but feel pride. "Getting a new caster was the greatest thing that could happen," he says. "It was a sign they believed in us a little bit."

Nemes, the union's staff representative who had thought Bethlehem's days were numbered, was excited. Maybe he was wrong — maybe Bethlehem does have a future, he thought. With the modernization, the last blast furnace and both basic oxygen furnaces would fade away. But electric furnaces and a continuous caster would give Bethlehem the weapons it needed to compete with Nucor and Chaparral for years to come.

By the mid-1990s, Nucor was selling almost as much steel as Bethlehem, its sales were growing every year and its stock was selling for three times as much as Bethlehem's. Its president, John Correnti, scoffed at Bethlehem's plan to add electric furnaces. "It's a joke," he said confidently during a visit to Lehigh University, founded by one of Bethlehem Steel's progenitors. "We'll kill them."

But Bethlehem's workers were primed for the challenge. When Barnette asked for concessions, Nemes, in early June 1993, gathered steelworkers at the 6,000-seat Stabler Arena to persuade them to accept a deal they never would have considered a few years earlier.

"This won't be easy. They want to cut benefits and freeze your pay," Nemes told three shifts of workers that day. "But we're going to save the plant. There will still be steelmaking in Bethlehem."

With the carrot of electric furnaces dangled before them, the workers overwhelmingly voted to accept the deal, and in no time, their leaders were standing at the Hotel Bethlehem with Barnette.

"Hank Barnette's on one side of me, the lieutenant governor [Singel] was on the other," Nemes says. "I couldn't believe what was happening. It was like a dream. The plant was going to be saved."

Seven months later, Nemes would wake from that dream.

In January 1994, Human Resources Director Gus Moffitt gathered Nemes and other union leaders in the fifth-floor conference room of The Steel's Third Street office building. The company decided against the modernization, they were told. The Structural Products division couldn't justify that kind of investment, and the company had decided to eliminate steelmaking and large-beam rolling and cut 2,000 more jobs by 1995.

At that moment, the battle-honed restraint that marked Nemes' negotiating character left him. As he jumped to his feet in disbelief, he kicked over a chair in the executive conference room and launched a vulgar indictment of the men he had trusted and the company he had respected. Other union leaders shared his disgust.

"You're all a bunch of fucking liars," Nemes said. "I'll never believe a fucking thing any one of you says ever again. We should have known you'd screw us."

All the good will Barnette had built with his labor force was gone in an instant. Barnette explained that low demand for heavy wide-flange structural beams and trends toward lighter construction didn't justify a three-phase modernization plan for the structural division. The total cost was estimated to be $250 million, but the first phase — the $105 million caster — was scheduled to be started in 1995. Barnette explained there was no point in doing Phase 1 if there'd be no money for Phases 2 and 3.

The company was trying to avoid the mistake it had made in blowing $50 million on Phase 1 of the Grey mill modernization. Instead of new equipment to melt and cast steel for beam-making, Bethlehem Steel would bring steel blooms from its continuous caster in Steelton and invest up to $50 million to modify its local combination mill, which would roll beams 6 to 24 inches wide. Barnette said the skyscraper market that used the wide-flange beam the new mill would have rolled was declining and the smaller beams were the future.

What Barnette didn't say was that the skyscraper market was no longer Bethlehem Steel's own. Weeks earlier, company President Roger Penny visited Nucor's new plant in Blytheville, Ark., and found that Nucor would soon be making the same beam.

Killing the modernization was a good business decision, Barnette explained. Wall Street agreed, as the company's stock shot up $1.63 that day to $23.25. But no explanation would satisfy a work force that felt betrayed.

"There was supposed to be some kind of trust between management and the union," said a somber Gary Ward, the local union leader.

Three months later, Barnette and four other executives split a $1.3 million bonus — their reward for turning a $266 million 1993 loss into an $80 million profit for the first quarter of 1994. Barnette also took a 30 percent raise, increasing his salary to $500,000 a year. The timing assured that relations with the work force would not be easily repaired.

"They're shutting us down and giving themselves a raise," Ward said in a conversation replete with four-letter-word descriptions for company bosses. "They took the money they were supposed to use for the modernization of our plant, and they stuck it in their pockets. ... We're back to the '70s, where all they do is line their pockets and don't give anything to the working people. And Hank was supposed to be our champion."

Barnette had fallen out of favor with his workers, but he was gaining respect in Washington. A year earlier, in 1994, he led the American steel industry's plea before the Commerce Department to stop foreign countries from selling steel cheaper in America than in their own country. Commerce officials agreed, finding that Japan and 19 other countries were selling their products for

an average of $150 a ton less in the United States.

Steel imports almost immediately dropped to an 18-year-low of 14 percent of the U.S. market, allowing The Steel to return to profitability in 1994. Barnette was also a key proponent of President Bill Clinton's effort to create universal health care. A true health care plan would stabilize skyrocketing prices and could have the government picking up the tab for some of Bethlehem Steel's out-of-control medical costs. While wages had increased 38 percent since 1980, the company's health care costs increased 285 percent. By 1994, medical costs made up 6 percent of the steelmaker's total costs, or about $26 per ton, Barnette said.

"Our nation's health care system is the most expensive in the world, and without change, it will cripple our ability to compete in the global market," Barnette said.

Clinton's health care plan failed, and Barnette continued beating the drum for more trade restrictions against foreign steel. But even the industry's trade victory in 1994 served as little more than a temporary painkiller for Bethlehem Steel's terminal illness.

More plants were closing, more layoffs were coming and the company's lopsided retiree-to-worker ratio had helped create a pension fund that was underfunded by $1 billion despite a $406 million payment that year by the company.

Two decades of decline had finally caught up to the plants that pioneered the Grey beam, defended America and turned a fledgling steel company into an industrial titan that once employed 283,765 people.

On Nov. 18, 1995, Bethlehem Steel stopped making steel in Bethlehem. For the first time in 122 years, the pounding, pressing, rolling and shaping ended.

The workers and the city had known it was coming, but still the end was painful.

Dean Lorrah wanted to go out with class that day. Nicknamed "Rambo" for his Vietnam War service and penchant for wearing camouflage hard hats with twigs attached, Lorrah wanted to do something different.

At 5:15 p.m., as the last ladle was poured at the basic oxygen furnace plant, Lorrah, wearing full combat gear, unfurled a 16-by-20-foot American flag and lowered it from his crane. On cue, his buddies in the chemical lab played a tape of Kate Smith's "God Bless America" over the loudspeaker as Lorrah threw an MIA-POW hat into the ladle as a tribute to fallen comrades. Employees who worked with Lorrah for 26 years wiped tears from their eyes with one hand and saluted him with the other.

Over at the blast furnaces, Herman Stangl, a 41-year employee who was known as "Casey," whistled "Amazing Grace" over a speaker. Some employees in other departments trashed their work stations and stole tools in protest. But Lorrah and Stangl didn't want to taint their last day.

Lorrah would close two more mills in the next three years as he moved from struggling mill to struggling mill, trying to keep his career in steel going.

Former employees still feel the pain of loss.

"The steel that built half of New York City was rolled in those mills and they just let it all die," says Tom Jones, business agent and former union president for the United Steelworkers local in Bethlehem. "That's just wrong. Have we completely forgotten where we came from?"

Stephen Donches hasn't. Donches grew up on Selfridge Street in the shadow of the mill, next door to the Check family, whose nine sons all worked at the plant. As he grew up, there was little question where he would work. Donches' father was a welder and union representative, and his grandfathers immigrated from Hungary and Slovakia to work at The Steel. They were proud that young Steve would be the first in the family to become a corporate executive.

He started in the accounting office in 1967 and soon moved into public affairs, where he focused on state government affairs. Other employees might have bad-mouthed the company, but Donches always preferred talking about its mystique and its impact on the community and the world. Bethlehem Steel or its forerunner, the Bethlehem Iron Co., had made steel since 1873, and he wanted everyone to know that.

As Bethlehem Steel was closing mills on the South Side, it was constructing a plan to reuse the vacated plant lands in a way that would carry the legacy of Bethlehem Steel into the next generation. Donches, the company's vice president of public affairs, was put in charge of that project.

"Steel made right here helped build America and defend it," Donches said. "If we don't do something to save this, it will be gone forever, and future generations will miss out on experiencing what happened here."

By 1996, most of the nearly 1,800 acres of Bethlehem Steel land that stretched along the Lehigh River for 4.5 miles was idle. The closing of the Structural Products division left only the coke works, the combination mill, the BethForge and Centec still operating. BethForge and Centec would be sold.

Brandenburg Industrial Services, a Chicago salvage company, had already begun the massive task of tearing down about half of the 4 million square feet of rusted and beaten plant buildings, but Bethlehem Steel had big ideas for the rest. In 1996, the company announced a $1 billion plan to turn the land and buildings into a bustling center for shopping, recreation and even heavy industry.

One hundred sixty acres would be the $450 million Bethlehem Works, a shopping, entertainment and cultural district that would include hotels, restaurants, trendy upscale bars, shops, an ice skating facility and a 14-screen cinema. The anchor of the project would be a $200 million National Museum of Industrial History set inside the cavernous No. 2 Machine Shop that Bethlehem Iron Superintendent John Fritz started building in 1887 to do work for the Navy. The museum would draw more than 1 million people a year to Bethlehem's struggling South Side and help the city replace the loss of the company that dominated and defined it for nearly a century.

The rest of the land would be the Bethlehem Commerce Center, a business, commercial and industrial district capable of drawing $1 billion worth of private investment. Office buildings, warehouses and light industrial companies would sprout from the scarred landscape. They would be funded by investors enticed by the built-in rail system, access to Interstate 78 and proximity to New York and other Northeast markets.

Standing in front of the empty, half-demolished structures that once brimmed with thousands of workers, Donches proudly proclaimed that Bethlehem Works and the Bethlehem Commerce Center would create 7,400 jobs, make south Bethlehem a tourist destination and draw millions of dollars a year in new tax revenues during the next two decades.

Bethlehem had long grown out of its dependence on The Steel. It had transformed its north side into a historic downtown that draws shoppers from across the region, and Lehigh University helped keep south Bethlehem vital as Bethlehem Steel withered.

Bethlehem had learned to survive without the company that once employed 31,523 people in the city. It parlayed its 18th century downtown and series of summer and holiday festivals into a business district that draws millions of cash-carrying shoppers a year. It learned how to live without Bethlehem Steel but not how to grow. Without The Steel's buying 8 million gallons of water a day and paying $1.2 million in real estate tax a year, city budgets were flat.

Mayor Don Cunningham, a steelworker's son who took office in 1998, deemed Bethlehem Works and the Bethlehem Commerce Center the future of the city.

"You'd expect gloom and doom, but actually there's an excitement about the future," Cunningham said soon after taking office. "There's a citywide enthusiasm that the city is about to bust out, that it is on the verge of a new exciting era of economic development."

The plan was Barnette's brainchild, but he wanted one thing clear: It didn't mean he had given up on the company. "Our core strength is steelmaking, not land development," he emphasized.

The 2,000 employees still working in Bethlehem weren't convinced. By October 1996, the company was on a roll, with 11 consecutive profitable quarters, but the Bethlehem plant was dragging it down. Barnette announced that the rest of the Bethlehem plant was for sale. The company's future was in Burns Harbor and Sparrows Point, where profits too often had drained into the money-losing Bethlehem operations. West Homestead Engineering and Machinery Co., based near Pittsburgh, was negotiating to buy the struggling BethForge and Centec operations and closed the deal in 1997. But while employees at those plants found hope in new management, the workers at Bethlehem's combination mill were told they would be out of work by March 1997.

Making matters worse was that Bethlehem Steel rejected a bid to buy the mill. The potential buyer was Noble Ventures, a group led by former Bethlehem plant manager Jack Roberts. Roberts said he'd keep the mill running, saving 430 of the 600 jobs, but Barnette explained that the deal was risky for Bethlehem because it required the company to guarantee continuous cast blooms from its Steelton plant. He added that he saw little hope that Noble Ventures could sustain a profit.

The rejection only inflamed an already angry work force.

"I think they were afraid it was going to work," Jones says. "If Noble Ventures steps in and makes money, [Steel executives] would have looked like idiots."

The coke works was the sole survivor. In a last-ditch effort to justify its existence, the department produced a video proclaiming the coke works the place "where steelmaking begins."

Like high school football players awarded stickers for their helmets as a reward for making a good play, the workers stuck coke oven labels on their hard hats in a show of pride. They had come to regard searing heat and the overwhelming odor of rotten eggs from the coking process as just another part of the job. They'd always been a resourceful department that functioned as a single unit. They could survive this, they told themselves.

But there would be no surviving the inevitable. Like the combination mills in 1997, the structural mill in 1995 and the seemingly endless string of mills that had gone dark over the past two decades, the coke works would meet the same fate.

On March 29, 1998, the last flame went out on The Steel's coke plant in Bethlehem. Plants at Burns Harbor and Sparrows Point still were supplying carmakers in the Midwest, rails still were being made in Steelton and steel products still were being galvanized in Lackawanna. But the flagship plant once so important to the country that it was thought to be targeted by wartime enemies was now a cold, lifeless monument to mismanagement, missed opportunity and lost dreams.

"You realize that the place was shutting down forever and there would never be an operation like this again," coke works supervisor Charlie Luthar says. "All of the friends that you have made over so many years were going to go all different ways. No longer were we going to have a single unit. That was really hard."

But the company's problem went beyond the money-losing Bethlehem plants. The year 1998 would be Bethlehem Steel's last profitable one.

Barnette continued to lobby Washington to stop other countries from dumping steel in America. He never gave up his mission to build a long-term future for Bethlehem Steel and its remaining 16,000 workers. He even bought Lukens Steel, the platemaker in Coatesville, Chester County, in the hope of making Bethlehem profitable. Lukens was the nation's premier maker of plates for heavy trucks and the construction industry, and Barnette hoped to seize that market for Bethlehem.

But by the time the 65-year-old Barnette was ready to turn the company over to Duane Dunham in April 2000, company stock that once sold for $58 a share was under $5, foreign imports had surged to 23 percent of the American purchases and The Steel was mired in a year in which it would lose $118 million.

Dunham streamlined Sparrows Point and won praise for guiding installation of a $325 million cold sheet mill that could roll sheets for cars, appliances and containers using half the labor. But he was being handed the captain's hat as the ship was sinking. Barnette said the big reason Dunham was chosen over Vice Chairmen Roger Penny, 63, and Gary Millenbruch, 61, was that at 58 he could hold the seat for more than seven years before he reached mandatory retirement age.

As it turned out, he would last just 16 months. Dunham continued Barnette's lobby against foreign dumping and helped the company secure $90 million in credit. He emphasized the need for the domestic steel industry to consolidate its profitable operations and eliminate its money-losing ones. By the time he completed his first year, losses were piling up as never before. That, of course, didn't stop the company from giving Dunham a $2.5 million severance package as he walked out the door.

"By midyear, my optimism began to wane, as steel imports flooded our markets at devastatingly low prices and energy costs began to sour," Dunham told shareholders. "Storm clouds were

gathering, and it was clear that changes in our business environment were accelerating."

The company posted a record $1.1 billion loss in the second quarter of 2001, and talk of bankruptcy was circulating through City Hall. In the previous two years alone, 15 domestic steel companies had filed for bankruptcy and Bethlehem appeared to be the next in line.

"From what we're hearing," then-Mayor Cunningham said in the summer of 2001, "it is not a matter of if, but when."

But Bethlehem Steel wasn't conceding anything yet. For months, Millenbruch had been meeting secretly with almost any steel company willing to hear his pitch. Quietly, Bethlehem Steel had constructed a long-term plan that not only would pull the company out of its financial grave but position it as one of the world's largest steelmakers. The plan called for a series of as many as five mergers or partnerships that would boost its production from 11.3 million tons a year to more than 40 million tons, a total rivaling that of the largest Russian, European and Chinese steelmakers. And the merger talks were not all within America's borders.

"If you go down the list of the top 20 steelmakers in the world," Millenbruch said, "we probably had talks, some of them very serious talks, with half of them."

Millenbruch would not give details of the negotiations, because The Steel signed confidentiality agreements in each. However, The Morning Call learned that the companies Bethlehem Steel negotiated with included top U.S. producer U.S. Steel, massive Japanese producer Nippon Steel Corp., NKK Steel of Tokyo and Paris-based Usinor, one of the world's largest steel companies. Smaller companies Bethlehem Steel talked with included the former Armco Steel of Middletown, Ohio; Dofasco Steel of Ontario, Canada; Wheeling-Pittsburgh Steel and National Steel of Mishawaka, Ind.

Some of the talks were little more than a search for isolated partnerships for specific products, but others went on for several months. The primary hurdle was always the same: Bethlehem Steel's labor contract, benefits and pension costs were overwhelming. Each potential merger candidate required deep cuts from a Bethlehem Steel labor force that didn't trust the company.

When Steel executives told union leaders that deep cuts were needed to complete a merger, the leaders said: Why should we ask 80-year-old widows to take cuts in their benefits just so your stockholders can make more money? File for bankruptcy and come back and see us.

Union members hadn't forgotten that in 1995 they were asked for cuts to pay for modernizing the Bethlehem plant, only to see the modernization plan killed after they agreed.

"Trust them, are you kidding me?" says O'Brien, who by 2001 had left his union position and was a Democratic candidate for Congress. "How can you trust someone who keeps lying to you?"

The reality was that no matter how much the union gave back, Bethlehem Steel's bankruptcy was inevitable.

Two weeks after Sept. 11, 2001, when the nation was devastated by terrorist-controlled planes crashing into the World Trade Center, the Pentagon and a field in Shanksville, Pa., Bethlehem Steel's board named Robert S. "Steve" Miller Jr. as its next chief executive. Miller had gained a reputation as a "fix it" specialist for failing corporations. He helped Chrysler Corp. get a $1.5 billion federal bailout and helped turn around trash disposal giant Waste Management Inc. and auto parts supplier Federal Mogul. This would be his eighth repair job in a decade.

Miller's ordination was unusual not only because it was the first time Bethlehem Steel looked outside the company for a leader — even Trautlein was in the executive offices for three years before he was named chairman — but for the speed with which it happened. Miller was a model railroad buff who, on Sept. 20, was attending a model train show in Salt Lake City when his wife called to relay a message to him. The next day he was meeting with Bethlehem Steel directors in New York City, and two days later he was appointed CEO.

"As much as I knew about Bethlehem was that in my earlier career as vice chairman of the Chrysler Corp., we bought a bunch of steel from them," Miller says. "But steel companies come a dime a dozen. I had never been to the Lehigh Valley."

Three weeks later, on Oct. 15, Bethlehem Steel filed for Chapter 11 bankruptcy. The decision was the board's, and in the haste of his appointment Miller was not told before he accepted the job, but he said there was no avoiding it. The company was on its way to losing a record $1.9 billion that year, and its shrunken work force of 13,000 was saddled with the impossible task of supporting 95,000 retirees collecting pensions and benefits. A faltering economy and a stock market crash after Sept. 11 left the pension fund underfunded by an estimated $3 billion.

In federal court, Bethlehem noted that its debt, at $4.5 billion, was $300 million more than the value of all its assets. Bankruptcy would give the company a chance to reorganize and provide new hope for a merger with another company. But the result, even in a merger, would bring more pain.

Bankruptcy meant that the government-run Pension Benefit Guaranty Corp. would take over Bethlehem Steel pensions and that retirees would lose the free health insurance they were promised.

"There is just no way that a single person doing an industrial job can generate the value to support 10 retiree families," Miller says. "If you add up all the people — active, retirees, and their dependents — and send us their medical bills, it's 130,000 total. Twelve thousand people can't pay that many doctor bills. That is the story. ... Can't be done."

Meanwhile, Wilbur Ross and Rodney Mott were watching. Ross was a self-proclaimed "vulture investor" who specialized in buying bankrupt companies, usually without the baggage that sank them. His company, Wilbur L. Ross & Co. of New York, swooped in to pick over the profitable pieces of companies such as clothingmaker Fruit of the Loom and fabricmaker Burlington Industries. His title as the "King of Bankruptcy" was well deserved.

Mott was a 30-year steel man with experience managing integrated and mini-mill operations. He had most recently risen to vice president and general manager of Nucor.

Together they watched as The Steel sank deeper into debt. They watched closely as Bethlehem Steel executives tried frantically to find a company with which to merge, and they watched excitedly when The Steel filed for bankruptcy protection. Unlike almost everyone else, they didn't see Bethlehem Steel in terms of what was going wrong but in terms of what was going right.

Sparrows Point was small enough to easily overhaul the management structure, and its location on the Chesapeake Bay made it the only remaining domestic steel mill with direct ocean access.

Steelton had built a great reputation for making rail products, and Mott saw its management team as survivors. Lackawanna was a lackluster sheet-finishing plant, but it was close to the Midwest automotive industry and fed the Burns Harbor plant.

But it was Burns Harbor that Ross and Mott coveted most. With its own coke works, continuous cast technology and direct access to the lucrative automotive market, it was the Cadillac of integrated mills. Best of all, it had been modernized but not expanded since it was built in 1964. Expansion at other Bethlehem mills made them inefficient because the company had refused to shut down during construction. To keep a furnace running, for example, the company would build a new furnace a quarter-mile away instead of next to the old one where it belonged.

Burns Harbor, however, was the nation's most modern and most efficient integrated mill.

"Burns Harbor was the target of anyone looking at Bethlehem Steel," Mott says. "It's just a fabulous plant."

Mott and Ross formed International Steel Group in April 2002 to take over the bankrupt LTV Corp.

On June 12, Bethlehem's stock, once considered blue chip, was removed from the New York Stock Exchange for trading below $1, banishing it to an over-the-counter bulletin board that is a netherworld of penny stocks and fledgling companies.

In November, Mott and Ross announced intentions to add Bethlehem Steel to their stable. Their bid came as no surprise to industry analysts, but it jolted The Steel's 12,000 workers and 95,000 retirees.

ISG would keep Bethlehem Steel's plants humming, but its work force would have to be trimmed to 8,000, the employees would have to

agree to new work rules and retirees would have to accept that ISG was only buying the plants, not taking on their pensions and health care cost.

Health care would be cut, pensions would be capped and the thousands of workers who were given a $400 monthly stipend for being put out of closed plants would lose that benefit. All retirees would lose their health care, but Miller emphasized that 88,000 would get their same pensions, simply signed by someone else.

That was small consolation to the 7,000 retirees whose pensions were reduced by the cap and the loss of the $400 stipend.

Richard Sterner, 61, was a 32-year veteran maintenance man in Bethlehem's beam yard when he was let go in May 1997. He had put his children through college, still had a mortgage to pay and wasn't ready to retire, but figured he had his more than $2,300-a-month pension to fall back on.

That was before the rug was yanked from under him in December 2002. When the government's Pension Benefit Guaranty Corp. took over the pensions, he lost his medical benefits and $600 was chopped from his monthly pension.

Today he is a bladder cancer survivor who in July 2004 lost what was his 13th job since he had been laid off — this one as a dump truck driver for $13 an hour. He has driven limousines, run a jackhammer, laid blacktop, worked as a flagman and is willing to do almost anything to keep from losing his Wind Gap home. But when he interviews for less-grueling work, he is considered too old or over-qualified. He thought he'd be retired by now but can't afford it. Where he sits seemed unthinkable only a few years ago.

"Hey, I was living the American dream," Sterner says. "I got a boat, we were talking about buying a camper or buying a cottage in Canada or something like that. I sent kids to school. It was great. But then the world drops out.

"I don't know how I'm going to get out of this financial mess," he says without a hint of self-pity. "I'm just going to keep fighting."

But 8,000 former Bethlehem Steel workers still have jobs, and they'll have them for a long time, Mott says. With help from a receptive work force, ISG has streamlined Bethlehem's old operations. Bethlehem's 32 job classifications are now just five, eliminating the specialization that forced Bethlehem to keep paying three or four men to do jobs being done by one man at Nucor.

Now that ISG operates pieces of Bethlehem Steel, LTV and Acme Steel, it has several basic oxygen furnaces and two electric furnaces. It will remain profitable by being flexible, Mott says. Unlike Bethlehem, it will not try to power through difficult stretches in the steel market. If market prices drop for one product, ISG will stop making it and focus on another. It will survive, Mott says.

"We're the fastest-growing steel company in the world," he says. "If we're going to keep growing, we're going to do it by flexing with the market."

ISG raised $463 million in November 2003 through an initial public stock offering — money it used to pay down some of the debt it took on from Bethlehem Steel. Despite a difficult first year, ISG lost a relatively small $23.5 million in 2003. It turned a profit in the first half of 2004 and bought West Virginia's Weirton Steel and a South Carolina mill from Georgetown Steel. Mott envisions that in five years, ISG will rival U.S. Steel in size.

Whether the company has a long future remains to be seen, but however it performs, it will be ISG's future.

Bethlehem Steel is no more.

Lewis Foy, 89, keeps going to the office he rents on Elizabeth Street in Bethlehem, refusing to let go of the days when he walked the streets like royalty and Bethlehem Steel dominated his every waking moment.

And Stephen Donches continues to dream that the blast furnaces — and maybe even a museum — will forever cast their reflection on the Lehigh River, towering over south Bethlehem as a monument to the company that defined and dominated the Lehigh Valley like no other.

Today on the South Side, workers outside The Steel's darkened mills build roads to carry motorists into south Bethlehem's blossoming business district.

But time stands still at the plant where men rolled iron rails during the Civil War.

The furnaces are cold, the forges silent. They lie in a graveyard of rusted, dreary mills inhabited by the ghosts of Bethlehem Steel's past.

In the No. 2 Machine Shop that once was a hive of workers crawling on newly machined battleship guns during World War I, moss creeps across the ground and fog rises around a 99-ton steel cylinder, never finished, now covered by a thin layer of rust and spray-painted with "Save BethForge."

Hundreds of tangled chains still hang from the ceiling of the welfare room, where generations of workers washed away the grime and soot of a day's work. The baskets suspended from the chains are filled not with a clean change of clothes, but with bird nests and a few pairs of weathered boots left behind.

Shards of sunlight poke through the beaten roof of a welding shop above a 60-foot gun, and rusted beams are strewn about the dusty floor below.

Trees and weeds grow from the cracked foundations of buildings that once hummed 24 hours a day, 365 days a year. Deer overrun the property at night.

So much is gone. Yet in the former headquarters across town, Cookie Burkhardt is still there.

Two years after being laid off on Black Friday in 1977, Burkhardt was called back to work at Bethlehem Steel. She spent the last quarter-century saying goodbye to friends and colleagues dismissed from their jobs and wondering when the ax would find her again.

It never did. She's still in Martin Tower, one of the last contract employees left to help transfer the remnants of The Steel into the hands of ISG.

There, in a lonely 10th-floor office, she counts the days until the end.

"Sometimes I wish I'd never been called back," Burkhardt says, her voice trailing off. "All of my friends who were laid off have moved on with their lives, gotten new jobs and built new lives. But here I sit waiting for the last gasp. Here I sit wondering where it all went."

EPILOGUE

A new era began at the old Bethlehem Steel site in 2009 with the opening of Sands Casino Resort Bethlehem, its sign mounted on a remnant of the plant.

As she did on Black Friday in 1977, Lorraine "Cookie" Burkhardt left her office one day in November 2008, carrying a box that held the remnants of her career with the steel company in Bethlehem.

But this time she wasn't being laid off. She was leaving on her own terms after 34 years, taking early retirement at age 62. And unlike that terrible Friday afternoon more than three decades ago, when she drank, cried and worried whether Bethlehem Steel would call her back and how she'd pay for a new house and car, now she felt at peace.

Never again would she have to fret over being laid off or say goodbye to colleagues losing their jobs. She'd never again have to worry that her company's new, international owners would close the Bethlehem office where the last three dozen workers — to this day — keep track of the remnants of the former Bethlehem Steel plants.

"I'm exercising, spending time with my 12 grandchildren," Burkhardt said 15 months into her retirement. "It's a shame we can't all retire when we're young because I'm loving this."

She'd finally moved on to life after Bethlehem Steel.

Ironically, after decades through which the proud company remained the world's No. 2 steelmaker — never quite reaching the pinnacle — by the time Burkhardt walked out the door for the last time, she was working for the world's No. 1 steelmaker. It just wasn't called Bethlehem Steel.

Much has changed since International Steel Group swooped in to buy the rotting carcass of Bethlehem Steel for $1.5 billion in 2003. By then, bankruptcy had helped the company shed its gargantuan pension plan, and ISG was able to persuade the steelworkers union to give up the lifetime medical benefits of 95,000 retirees, jettisoning another bottom line-bruising responsibility. The moves, combined with a worldwide spike in steel demand caused by building booms in China and India, helped ISG sell its assets to Netherlands-based Mittal Steel for $4.5 billion in 2005.

The deal vaulted ISG owner Wilbur L. Ross Jr. into an elite group of businessmen — billionaires.

ISG was one of many steel companies collected that year by what is now ArcelorMittal, helping to make its chief executive, Lakshmi Mittal, the world's fifth-richest man in 2010. The $18.8 billion he made in 2004 and 2005 alone helped him throw a wedding party for his daughter that reportedly cost $60 million. And it helped him buy a $127 million, 12-bedroom mansion in London that was the world's most expensive home.

But the workers left in the wake of Bethlehem Steel's demise face an uncertain future.

Richard Sterner, now 67, has been able to stay in his Wind Gap home and he's finally stopped working. But after years of taking whatever odd jobs he could find to make up for his reduced pension and the health care benefits he lost, his doctor told the former Steel maintenance crew chief his body could take no more. His bones riddled with arthritis aggravated by jobs such as his last one as a jackhammer operator, Sterner retired in 2006.

He's gone through a savings account it took him a lifetime to build, and he ignores the letters suggesting he may still have to pay back the $6,600 in pension money he was accidentally overpaid in 2003. He long ago gave up on his plans to spend his retirement traveling the country in an RV with his wife, Eileen.

For Sterner, retirement is very different from what he had planned.

"I play a little golf, I rest my weary bones and I thank God for what I do have. Honestly, I can't complain. Some of my friends from Steel have it a lot worse," he said. "We're making the best of it. We're surviving. That's what we do. We survive."

For now, steel is still being turned out for ArcelorMittal at the former Pennsylvania Bethlehem Steel plants in Coatesville, Conshohocken and Steelton, as well as at Burns Harbor, Ind. The rolled-steel finishing plant in Lackawanna, N.Y., was closed in 2009, and the Sparrows Point plant near Baltimore was sold in 2008 to Russian steelmaker Severstal because the U.S. Department of Justice argued that ArcelorMittal had cornered the tin-plate market.

Yet, the shells of a few of Bethlehem Steel's plants survive on its former flagship Bethlehem property, which once teemed with more than 31,500 workers. While many buildings have been demolished, the historic High House, for example, where 60-foot battleship gun barrels made in Bethlehem during two world wars were cooled and hardened, still juts above the passing cars on the Minsi Trail Bridge.

Even Martin Tower, the 21-story headquarters that serves as a monument to Steel's power and foolish extravagance, stands across town, empty and outdated — a victim of a global recession that has halted development projects worldwide.

But offsetting the quiet stillness of the massive No. 2 Machine Shop is the whirring of slot machines in the new building just a few paces away.

Somewhere, Bethlehem Steel founder Charlie Schwab is chuckling. More than a century after his flamboyant gambling excursions to Monte Carlo nearly derailed his career, the world's largest gambling company has built a $743 million casino in the same pit where Steel once stored as much as 2 million tons of iron ore to be fed into its blast furnaces.

And much the way Schwab gambled the prospects of his burgeoning steel company on an untested, innovative beam that went on to support some of the world's longest spans and tallest buildings, Bethlehem is wagering a good portion of its financial future on the Sands Casino Resort Bethlehem, which opened in May 2009.

Moravian Church leaders condemned the arrival of gambling to Bethlehem. It conflicts with the city's quaint, historic image, they said. Perhaps more importantly, the basis of gambling — the idea that someone can get something for nothing — defies the faith and work ethic Moravians brought when they founded the city in 1741.

Others, nostalgic for the idea that much of America was built on the site, argued a casino would be disrespectful to the legacy of Bethlehem Steel, like building a merry-go-round in a cemetery.

But religious belief and nostalgia can't balance budgets for a city that lost a company that employed thousands of city residents, paid millions of dollars a year in city taxes and dominated city finances, and politics, for more than a century.

Casino gambling is helping to fill the void left by Bethlehem Steel, argues Mayor John Callahan. In fact, there are few other industries with pockets deep enough to develop a site so scarred by almost 140 years of iron and steelmaking. Not only does Sands employ 1,000 people and pay the city more than $8 million in host fees a year, but the 4 million to 5 million visitors it attracts each year will be the catalyst for developing the entire 126 acres, Callahan contends.

"It was the easiest way to create the most jobs and the most investment on a very difficult site,"

Callahan says. "Bethlehem has taken a tremendous liability and turned it into opportunity."

The $26 million SteelStacks performing arts center broke ground in the fall of 2009 and will open in May 2011 to attract 750,000 people a year to concerts, theater shows, music festivals and outdoor fairs.

PBS39 broke ground in the spring of 2010 on a new broadcast studio, and the city is gathering grant money to build a visitors center in Steel's 1863 Stock House, at the foot of the massive blast furnaces that provide a majestic backdrop for the entire property.

Callahan adds that while most talk focuses on the casino, 1,600 acres of former Steel land just east of the slot-machine house — out of sight of passing motorists — is a growing business park that already has 11 warehouses, office buildings and manufacturing plants where 2,100 people work.

Still, former Steel executive Stephen Donches is determined to make certain no one will forget what went on at the site before. He's raised $17 million of the $26 million he needs to finish the National Museum of Industrial History he's building in the former Electric Repair Shop, and hopes to have the museum open by the end of 2011.

The casino itself, with its industrial architecture and giant mural of the blast furnaces at its entrance, will help remind people.

With time, the No. 2 Machine Shop can be developed into housing or new shops, and the old, 13-story Bethlehem Steel General Office building can become luxury apartments, Callahan says.

So, while people are losing $4 million to $6 million a week in Sands' 3,250 slot machines and rolling the dice on its gaming tables, others will be eating in south Bethlehem's newest restaurants. Or listening to music at SteelStacks. Or buying produce at the open-air market. Or watching a documentary about Bethlehem at the museum. Or taking walking tours of the site, conducted by former steelworkers. Or venturing out into other parts of the city.

It can never be the same. The piercing sound of the shift-change whistle will not echo through the South Side three times a day. Steelworkers won't flood into south Bethlehem bars after work, and the image of molten metal being poured from a giant ladle will probably never again be seen in Bethlehem.

But the site will honor Steel by once again becoming a hive of activity. Its legacy will forever be on display there — its might evident in the hulking blast furnaces, its demise apparent in the faces and stories of the former steelworkers giving the tours.

The city will not ever forget what happened there, Callahan says, but it cannot merely look back. In some ways, the city made internationally famous by the steel that was forged here is a lot like Burkhardt and Sterner.

It has moved on. It is surviving.

1840

Welsh immigrant David Thomas fires up first commercially successful anthracite-fueled iron furnace in America, producing 4 tons of iron on the Fourth of July at Lehigh Crane Iron Co. in Catasauqua. Ironmaking boom sweeps Lehigh Valley.

1846

On April 21, Delaware, Lehigh, Schuylkill & Susquehanna Railroad is organized, with former Mauch Chunk canal boatman Asa Packer among incorporators.

1852

Packer's choice, Robert H. Sayre, becomes chief engineer, and stockholders agree to let Packer build railroad himself in exchange for stocks and bonds.

1853

On Jan. 7, line is renamed Lehigh Valley Railroad.

1855

Railroad starts passenger service and on Sept. 15 carries first trainload of coal from Mauch Chunk (now Jim Thorpe) to Easton.

1857

Bethlehem merchant Augustus Wolle forms Bethlehem Steel Corp.'s earliest ancestor, Saucona Iron Co., on April 8 to create anthracite-fueled ironworks and use ore beds he owns in Saucon Valley. On July 29, ironmaster John Fritz's "three-high" rail mill begins operating at Cambria Iron Co. in Johnstown, revolutionizing production of iron rails.

1859

On March 31, Saucona Iron is reorganized as Bethlehem Rolling Mill & Iron Co. On Oct. 5, Fritz obtains patent for his three-high mill.

1860

Fritz becomes general manager and superintendent of Bethlehem Rolling Mill & Iron, arriving in Bethlehem on July 5. Eleven days later, ground is broken for new plant, which will make iron rails for Lehigh Valley Railroad.

1861

On April 12, Civil War begins. On May 1, Bethlehem Rolling Mill & Iron is reorganized as Bethlehem Iron Co.

1863

On Jan. 4, Bethlehem Iron plant's first blast furnace is "blown in." On July 27, puddling furnaces begin making wrought-iron blooms for rolling mill, which starts producing rails on Sept. 26. Bethlehem Iron becomes major rail supplier.

1864

Bethlehem Iron builds mill in Chattanooga, Tenn., to reroll rails torn up by Confederate guerrillas. On Sept. 6, first American steel plant using process developed in England by Henry Bessemer opens in Wyandotte, Mich.

1865

Packer founds Lehigh University with $500,000.

1868

Bethlehem directors vote to build Bessemer steel plant. Fritz goes to Europe to learn steelmaking process.

1873

Bessemer plant is completed. First "blow" is made Oct. 4, and first steel rails are made two weeks later. Panic of 1873 causes collapse in railroad building boom. Ironmakers across Valley start going out of business. St. Luke's Hospital is established in Fountain Hill.

1886

Bethlehem plant begins adding forging hammers, presses and large machine shops to produce ordnance and armor plate for Navy. Company becomes birthplace of modern American defense industry.

1887

On June 1, Bethlehem Iron signs $4 million contract with Navy to make armor plate and gun forgings.

1888

Bethlehem's first battery of open-hearth furnaces becomes operational in August.

1889

Spanish-American Iron Co. is formed by two Cleveland iron ore merchants to operate iron ore mines in Santiago, Cuba, known as Daiquiri Mines. Company becomes part of Bethlehem Steel Corp. in 1904.

1890

No. 2 Machine Shop, world's largest machine shop, begins operations. Robert P. Linderman, grandson of Packer and son-in-law of Sayre, becomes president of Bethlehem Iron.

1891

Bethlehem wins $4 million Army contract to make large-caliber guns. On June 3, company begins using giant steam hammer designed to forge guns and armor plate for warships. Bethlehem Iron is considered finest steel forging plant in world.

1892

Steelworkers in nation's largest craft union strike for better wages at Andrew Carnegie's Homestead Works near Pittsburgh. On July 6, in one of the most violent episodes in U.S. labor history, strikers battle 300 security agents sent to protect nonunion workers. Ten people die. Carnegie beats back union. In South Bethlehem, Fritz retires as general superintendent.

1893

Bethlehem forges a 45 1/2-foot-long axle for giant Ferris wheel set up at Columbian Exposition in Chicago. It is largest forged piece of steel created to date.

1896

Company decides to shut down Bessemer furnaces, betting its future on open-hearth steel.

1898

Spanish-American War brings first combat test of Bethlehem-built Navy. World's first efficiency expert, Frederick W. Taylor, applies time-and-motion studies at Bethlehem plant. Investment banker J. Pierpont Morgan takes over Lehigh Valley Railroad, Sayre is forced off board.

1899

On April 17, Bethlehem Steel Co. is created as holding company, with Bethlehem Iron as its only asset. Eugene G. Grace, who will later run Bethlehem Steel Corp., joins company as electric crane operator after graduating from Lehigh University.

1901

Former Carnegie Steel Co. President Charles M. Schwab becomes president of newly formed U.S. Steel Corp. on April 1, makes deal on May 30 to buy Bethlehem Steel for himself. Sale is completed on Aug. 15. Schwab pays $7.2 million, then sells company to J.P. Morgan & Co., U.S. Steel's underwriter, for same price.

1902

Schwab buys back Bethlehem Steel and sells it to U.S. Shipbuilding Co., a merger of seven shipyards and a manufacturing company, for $30 million in stocks and bonds. He holds large interest in new business. On June 17, U.S. Shipbuilding is incorporated. Bethlehem Steel thrives, but other subsidiaries do poorly. Schwab refuses to let Steel's profits prop up sinking parent company.

1903

U.S. Shipbuilding's other backers accuse Schwab of arranging its failure so he can grab assets. In June, U.S. Shipbuilding fails. Judge blames Schwab for "ruinous extortion." On Aug. 4, with scandal hanging over him and after repeated run-ins with U.S. Steel Executive Committee Chairman Elbert Gary, Schwab resigns as U.S. Steel president.

1904
In settlement of U.S. Shipbuilding debacle, Schwab keeps Bethlehem Steel. On Dec. 10, he forms Bethlehem Steel Corp., a holding company that includes South Bethlehem plant, iron ore mines in Cuba and shipyards on both coasts. During Russo-Japanese War, company supplies both Russia and Japan with naval guns and armor plate. Total sales for year: $10 million.

1905
Schwab tours Luxembourg mill that's first to make wide-flanged beam that can be rolled in one section. Inventor is Englishman Henry Grey.

1906
Schwab moves from New York to Bethlehem to direct company. Bethlehem starts making open-hearth steel rails, wins 600 percent increase in its share of European armor plate pool, giving it parity with big armament-makers Armstrong's, Vickers and Krupp.

1908
After getting exclusive rights to Grey's beam-making process, Schwab opens Grey mill at Bethlehem for production of wide-flanged steel beams. The beams make construction of skyscrapers possible, opening new market for company and transforming skylines. Schwab makes Grace his top executive.

1910

Bethlehem Steel has first major labor action as some of its 9,200 workers begin 108-day strike for shorter hours and higher pay. Schwab calls in state police, threatens to shut down plant permanently if local businesses support strikers. Trooper accidentally kills bystander. Men go back to work without pay increase. Also, Bethlehem gets largest single contract to date — $10 million to make armor plate, guns and shells for Argentine navy.

1913
Company buys Fore River Shipbuilding Co. in Quincy, Mass., near Boston, and becomes a major shipbuilder. Fritz dies.

1914
On Aug. 1, World War I breaks out in Europe. Rejecting $100 million purchase offer from Germany's Kaiser Wilhelm II, Schwab turns company into major supplier of ships, armor, ordnance, guns and munitions for the Allies — France, England, Russia and Italy.

1916
With sales of $230 million, Bethlehem becomes nation's No. 2 steelmaker, after U.S. Steel. Grace is named president; Schwab is chairman. Bethlehem doubles capacity with purchase of Pennsylvania Steel Co. at Steelton and its Maryland Steel Co. subsidiary at Sparrows Point, Md. It also buys American Iron & Steel Manufacturing Co. in Lebanon, an interest in the Cornwall iron mines in Lebanon County and coal mines in West Virginia.

1917
Bethlehem Steel is third-largest industrial company in America, after U.S. Steel and Standard Oil of New Jersey. On April 6, United States enters World War I. Schwab uses influence to get boroughs of Bethlehem and South Bethlehem to merge into city of Bethlehem, whose first mayor is Steel executive Archibald Johnston.

1918
In April, Schwab is "drafted" to run Emergency Fleet Corp., the U.S. war effort's shipbuilding program. Bethlehem plant employs 31,000, including significant number of women, for wartime production. National War Labor Board condemns Bethlehem's labor practices, cites Grace and colleagues for anti-union tactics. At end of year, Schwab and Grace organize company union, the Employee Representation Plan, to deflect government pressure on them to bargain collectively with workers.

1919
On Sept. 22, "Great Steel Strike" hits nation, centering on Pittsburgh and Chicago districts. Ultimately, 350,000 steelworkers walk off their jobs, demanding union recognition. About 2,000 of Bethlehem plant's 13,500 workers participate.

1920
American Federation of Labor's Iron and Steel Organizing Committee calls off strike on Jan. 8, its goals unmet.

1921
Bethlehem Steel's total employment in steel operations, mines, railroads and shipyards is 47,513.

1922
Company buys Lackawanna Steel Co. near Buffalo, N.Y., and iron ore mines in Great Lakes region.

1923
Bethlehem takes over Midvale Steel Co. of Philadelphia, except its armor and ordnance plant, and gains its subsidiary, Cambria Steel Co., which has steel operations and coal mines in Johnstown area. Bethlehem institutes pension plan and employee savings and stock ownership plan; eliminates 12-hour workday.

1925
Bethlehem's Fore River shipyard at Quincy, Mass., launches aircraft carrier USS Lexington, the "Queen of the Flattops."

1926
Schwab learns U.S. Steel is building a mill to make Grey beams without license from Bethlehem. He argues with U.S. Steel Chairman Elbert Gary, who denies it.

1927
Gary admits to Schwab that U.S. Steel intends to make Grey beams and apologizes. Gary dies; Schwab succeeds him as president of American Iron and Steel Institute, the industry trade group.

1929
Stock market crash brings on Great Depression. Bethlehem Steel is fifth-largest industrial company. Schwab loses fortune conservatively estimated at $25 million. U.S. Steel agrees to pay royalties for permission to make Grey beams after Bethlehem sues for infringement of patent rights. Grace gets $1.6 million in bonuses on top of his $12,000 salary.

1930
Bethlehem enters West Coast market, buying Pacific Coast Steel Co. and Southern California Iron & Steel Co., which have plants in Seattle, San Francisco and Los Angeles. It fails to get Youngstown Sheet & Tube Co.

1931

Bethlehem Steel buys McClintic-Marshall Corp., a major fabricator and builder of bridges and buildings. During decade, Bethlehem steel goes into Golden Gate Bridge, George Washington Bridge, Rockefeller Plaza, Waldorf-Astoria, Chicago Merchandise Mart and U.S. Supreme Court.

1934
Ailing Schwab quits as head of American Iron and Steel Institute, stays on as honorary chairman of Bethlehem Steel with $250,000 salary.

1935
National Labor Relations Act gives workers the right to collectively bargain, select their own unions, strike, boycott and picket, and sets up labor board. Social Security Act provides for a system of old-age insurance for workers at age 65 and survivor benefits for children or spouses of insured workers who die before 65.

1936
On June 12, Congress of Industrial Organizations sets up Steel Workers' Organizing Committee, or SWOC, to unionize all steelworkers.

1937
On March 2, U.S. Steel recognizes SWOC in so-called Big Steel agreement. Bethlehem and other Little Steel companies resist, keep their company unions. On May 26, SWOC calls strike against Republic Steel, Inland Steel and Youngstown Sheet & Tube. On May 30 in Chicago, police kill 10 demonstrators trying to march toward Republic mill in what became known as "Little Steel Massacre." On June 11, strike spreads to Bethlehem's Johnstown plant, but Grace breaks it. In August, SWOC complains to National Labor Relations Board that Bethlehem intimidates workers who want to join or help the union.

1938
In November, an NLRB trial examiner rules that Bethlehem engaged in unfair labor practices; Grace appeals. Fair Labor Standards Act sets maximum hours and mini-

mum wages, prohibits child labor in industries that produce goods for interstate commerce.

1939

On Aug. 14, labor board backs SWOC, orders Bethlehem to disband its company union; Grace takes appeal to federal court. On Sept. 1, World War II begins in Europe. Schwab dies. Company puts up new Star of Bethlehem for $5,000, lights it Dec. 15.

1941

Major and at times violent strike hits company's Bethlehem plant on March 24, as SWOC protests start of "illegal" Employee Representation Plan election of officers. Settlement, reached early March 28, defers further voting on company union officers until federal court case is resolved. About 4,000 people march in union victory parade. On May 12, U.S. District Court dismisses Bethlehem's appeal of NLRB ruling. In fall, workers choose SWOC as their exclusive bargaining agent. America enters the war.

1942

SWOC changes name to United Steelworkers of America, with Philip Murray as president. Bethlehem Steel becomes nation's top military contractor of World War II. Its 15 shipyards turn out 1,085 ships during the war, and repair, service or convert 37,778. On May 8 in Battle of the Coral Sea, Japanese sink Bethlehem-made USS Lexington. In September, Bethlehem's Fore River shipyard near Boston launches a bigger, more powerful USS Lexington.

1943

Bethlehem employs all-time high of 283,765 for wartime production. Of these, a record 31,523 people work at Bethlehem plant. Company's yards build 380 ships, surpassing Grace's goal of a ship a day.

1945

In December, Eugene Grace is elected chairman. Bethlehem Steel is seventh-largest industrial company in America.

1947

Taft-Hartley Act erodes protections in National Labor Relations Act by seeking to restrain union behavior that might restrict the "free flow of commerce."

1950-53

Bethlehem Steel provides much of the ordnance for U.S. armed forces fighting in Korean War.

1954

Company's second attempt to merge with Youngstown Sheet & Tube is blocked by Justice Department as an antitrust violation. Bethlehem fights ruling until 1957, to no avail.

1956

Industrywide three-year contract with USW grants first cost-of-living escalator clause. Separately, Bethlehem agrees to local union demand for Clause 2B, which says company can't change past labor practices.

1957

Bethlehem has 160,204 employees, a post-World War II high. Arthur B. Homer, who led Bethlehem's World War II shipbuilding program, runs company because Grace is ailing.

1958

Fortune magazine puts six Bethlehem Steel executives in the top 10 on the list of the nation's highest paid executives.

1959

On July 15, USW goes on strike against steelmakers. Strike lasts 116 days. At urging of Vice President Richard Nixon, industry settles and agrees to wage and pension demands affecting 540,000 union members. At 5 million tons, steel imports exceed exports for first time in 20th century. Also, Bethlehem Steel opens Homer Research Laboratories on South Mountain to develop more efficient ways

to make steel and search for new steels and steel products.

1960

Grace dies. Homer becomes chairman.

1962

President John F. Kennedy clashes with steel companies over steel price hikes they announced after his administration leaned on USW to accept modest package in new contract. Bethlehem Steel and other companies rescind increases. Bethlehem announces it will build major integrated steel plant in Burns Harbor, Ind., most ambitious single project in its history, to produce sheet and plate steel for fast-growing Midwest market.

1964

Burns Harbor plant begins production, and Steel's first basic oxygen furnaces begin steelmaking in Lackawanna. Company produces record 19.44 million tons of raw steel. Edmund F. Martin is elected chairman.

1966

Bethlehem fabricates steel for Madison Square Garden, Newport (R.I.) Bridge and second Delaware Memorial Bridge. It is 19th-largest industrial company.

1968

Basic oxygen furnaces are installed at Bethlehem plant.

1969

American steel production peaks at 141.2 million tons, but more-efficient steel plants with lower labor costs are being built abroad.

1970

Stewart S. Cort is elected Bethlehem Steel chairman.

1972

Company's Martin Tower, its 21-story, $35 million headquarters in Bethlehem, is completed.

1973

Big U.S. steelmakers, USW reach long-term no-strike agreement that includes 3 percent annual wage increase and makes automatic cost-of-living adjustments a non-negotiable provision. Pact is in effect until 1982. Bethlehem produces record 23.7 million tons of raw steel, ships record 16.3 million tons of finished steel. Bethlehem, U.S. Steel and eight other steelmakers agree to pay $56 million in back wages to 40,000 minority workers the federal government says were victims of discrimination.

1974

Lewis W. Foy becomes chairman. Bethlehem earns record $342 million, employs 115,720 companywide.

1975

Japanese steelmakers surpass Americans in productivity. Bethlehem's total employment is shaved to 106,685. Capital expenditures amount to record $674 million. Bethlehem's first continuous caster begins production at Burns Harbor.

1976

Company closes all six plants of Fabricated Steel Construction division, successor to McClintic-Marshall Corp. On April 1, government-sponsored Consolidated Rail Corp. takes over bankrupt Lehigh Valley Railroad.

1977

Bethlehem Steel lays off 3,800 at Johnstown plant and 3,500 at Lackawanna. Steelmaking capacity is cut back at both plants. On Sept. 30, "Black Friday," company lays off 2,500 white-collar workers, including 800 at headquarters. Total employment drops to 99,930. Now the 28th-largest industrial company, it reports $448 million loss.

1979

Bethlehem plant employs 11,795.

1980

Former Price Waterhouse accountant Donald H. Trautlein becomes first Steel chairman who wasn't prepped in company's management training system. A thousand white-collar workers are laid off. On July 24 in federal court, Bethlehem Steel pleads guilty to conspiring to defraud foreign ship owners by billing them for illegal commissions on ship-repair work. Judge fines Bethlehem $325,000.

1981

Bethlehem Steel's sales reach record $7.3 billion.

1982

Company reports record loss of $1.5 billion, the first of five years of losses. It ends steelmaking at Lackawanna, closes or sells other plants, mills, mines and shipyards, and cuts work force by more than half over next four years. Total Steel employment stands at 66,869.

1983

On Feb. 27, for first time in industry's history, USW approves contract granting concessions — a 9 percent cut in wages and benefits over three years.

1984

On Jan. 24, Bethlehem Steel launches industry's campaign to persuade U.S. government to curb steel imports, which reach record 26 million tons. President Ronald Reagan responds by setting five-year voluntary trade quotas. Bethlehem's total employment is 51,360. LTV Corp. absorbs Republic Steel and Jones & Laughlin Steel to form LTV Steel, toppling Bethlehem as nation's No. 2 steelmaker.

1985

Employment at Bethlehem plant plummets to 5,661.

1986

Walter F. Williams is elected chairman. Company concentrates on making its steel operations competitive, restructuring businesses, rebuilding financial strength. New continuous casters begin production at Sparrows Point and Burns Harbor.

1988

Bethlehem reports record net income of $403 million.

1989

Company announces it will build hot-dip galvanizing lines at Burns Harbor and Sparrows Point. Work proceeds on modernization of Sparrows Point hot-strip mill.

1990

Bethlehem revamps structural and rail operations. Total employment: 29,574. Bethlehem plant: 4,340.

1991

Joint venture with British Steel that might have modernized Bethlehem plant and ensured its long-term survival falls through because companies and USW can't agree on concessionary labor contract. On Nov. 11, Bethlehem announces deal is dead.

1992

Company exits bar, rod and wire business. Its plants are established as individual business units responsible for production, marketing and financial performance. Curtis "Hank" Barnette becomes chairman.

1993

New galvanizing lines begin production at Burns Harbor and Sparrows Point. Bethlehem and USW negotiate a six-year agreement.

1994

Major capital improvements include new coke oven battery and coal injection facility at Burns Harbor, and new electric furnace and rail line at Pennsylvania Steel Technologies division in Steelton. But in December, company announces Bethlehem blast furnaces will be shut down and half the plant's work force cut.

1995

On Nov. 18, company ends steelmaking in Bethlehem. For first time since 1873, steel is not being made in Lehigh Valley.

1996

Company announces that Structural Products, BethForge and Centec divisions in Bethlehem and BethShip shipyard at Sparrows Point will be sold or closed. Coke ovens in Bethlehem will be written off as "impaired asset." Company forms Bethlehem Works, a subsidiary to preserve, interpret and redevelop portions of plant.

1997

On Feb. 26, Bethlehem Steel and Smithsonian Institution announce plans for industrial museum on Steel's south Bethlehem property. BethForge and Centec divisions are sold to West Homestead Engineering and Manufacturing Co. Company also sells BethShip and coal-mining interests, ends production of structural shapes, announces investment in new cold rolling mill at Sparrows Point. Company is dropped as one of 30 stocks in Dow Jones Industrial Average.

1998

On March 28, Bethlehem Steel shuts down coke works at Bethlehem plant. Company establishes Bethlehem Lukens Plate as a division after merger with Lukens Inc., America's oldest continuously operating steelmaker, and becomes top plate producer in North America. Steel has 15,900 employees.

1999

On Jan. 13, Barnette announces plans for $600 million Bethlehem Commerce Center for Norfolk Southern Corp. truck-to-rail terminal and other businesses on 1,600 acres of Steel land near Bethlehem Works site. Bethlehem reports losses of $183.2 million due to "unfairly traded steel imports."

2000

Company reports losses of $118.4 million, is dropped from Standard & Poor's 500 index. Duane R. Dunham becomes chairman. New $325 million cold-sheet mill opens at Sparrows Point.

2001

Robert S. "Steve" Miller Jr. takes charge. With net worth of negative $153.8 million, Bethlehem Steel files for Chapter 11 bankruptcy protection on Oct. 15. Companywide employment totals 13,100.

2002

Bethlehem enters talks in November with a recently formed steel company, International Steel Group of Cleveland, to sell all or parts of its operation. Bethlehem is dropped from New York Stock Exchange. On Dec. 18, U.S. Pension Benefit Guaranty Corp. says it will take over Steel's pensions.

2003

International Steel Group buys Bethlehem Steel's assets for $1.5 billion, closing its purchase May 7. Steel employs about 11,000 nationwide, fewer than 300 in Lehigh Valley. Through purchase of assets of LTV Steel, Acme Steel and Bethlehem, ISG becomes nation's second-largest integrated steel producer, after U.S. Steel.

2004

On July 5, Pennsylvania Gov. Ed Rendell signs a controversial law legalizing slot machine gambling in Pennsylvania. It allows up to 61,000 slot machines to be placed at up to 14 race tracks, casinos and resort hotels, and imposes a slot-machine tax to raise an estimated $1 billion a year for property tax relief.

2005

In April, shareholders of ISG and Netherlands-based Mittal Steel approve Mittal's acquisition of ISG for $4.5 billion, making the new company the largest steel producer in the world.

2006

In a Dec. 20 vote, the Pennsylvania Gaming Control Board chooses the former Bethlehem Steel plant lands as one of 14 sites to get a slot-machine license. Las Vegas Sands Corp. has promised to spend $600 million to build a casino, shopping mall, hotel and events center on the 126-acre site that would also include the SteelStacks performing arts center and the National Museum of Industrial History. The Bethlehem site was chosen over one in east Allentown.

2008

Saddled by a global recession, Las Vegas Sands halts construction on the hotel, mall and events center in November, until the economy and credit markets improve. Casino construction moves ahead on schedule.

2009

The $743 million Sands Casino Resort Bethlehem opens on May 22. It's the most lucrative opening day of any casino in Pennsylvania. The hotel, mall and events center remain incomplete and idle.

2010

Pennsylvania lawmakers on Jan. 6 approve a bill legalizing table games such as poker, blackjack and roulette at the state's slot-machine casinos. Sands table games start July 18. Work on hotel resumes.

BIBLIOGRAPHY

BOOKS

Antonsen, Peter J., *A History of the Puerto Rican Community in Bethlehem, Pa., 1944-1993,* Council of Spanish-Speaking Organizations of the Lehigh Valley Inc., 1997.

Archer, Robert F., *A History of the Lehigh Valley Railroad: The Route of the Black Diamond,* Heimburger House Publishing Co., Forest Park, Ill., 1977.

Bailey, Ronald H., *The Home Front: U.S.A. — World War II,* Time-Life Books, Alexandria, Va., 1977.

Bartholomew, Craig L. and Lance E. Metz, *The Anthracite Iron Industry of the Lehigh Valley,* Center for Canal History and Technology, Hugh Moore Historical Park and Museums Inc., Easton, Pa., 1988.

Brenckman, Fred, *History of Carbon County, Pennsylvania,* James J. Nungesser, Harrisburg, Pa., 1913.

Camp, J.M. and C.B. Francis, *The Making, Shaping and Treating of Steel,* second edition, Carnegie Steel Co., Pittsburgh, 1920.

Cotter, Arundel, *The Story of Bethlehem Steel,* The Moody Magazine and Book Co., New York, 1916.

Dewing, Arthur S., *Corporate Promotions and Reorganizations,* Harvard University Press, Cambridge, Mass., 1924.

Eisenhower, Dwight David, *Waging Peace: The White House Years 1956-1961,* Doubleday & Co. Inc., New York, 1965.

Federal Writers' Project, Work Projects Administration, Commonwealth of Pennsylvania, *Northampton County Guide,* sponsored by Northampton County Historical and Genealogical Society, Times Publishing Co., Bethlehem, Pa., 1939.

Fritz, John, *Autobiography of John Fritz,* American Society of Mechanical Engineers, New York, 1912.

Garn, Andrew, *Bethlehem Steel,* Princeton Architectural Press, New York, 1999.

Gipson, Lawrence H. and Robert C. Cole, *Asa Packer,* Asa Packer Society, Lehigh University, n.d.

Halberstam, David, *The Fifties,* Villard Books, New York, 1993.

Henry, M.S., *History of the Lehigh Valley,* Bixler & Corwin, Easton, Pa., 1860.

Hessen, Robert, *Steel Titan: The Life of Charles M. Schwab,* Oxford University Press, New York, 1975.

Hogan, William T., *Economic History of the Iron and Steel Industry in the United States: Volume 1,* Lexington Books, D.C. Heath and Co., Lexington, Mass., Toronto, London, 1971.

Kuchta, David, *Memoirs of a Steelworker,* Canal History and Technology Press, National Canal Museum, Hugh Moore Historical Park and Museums Inc., Easton, Pa., 1995.

Kulp, Randolph L., *History of Lehigh Valley Transit Co.,* Lehigh Valley Chapter, National Railway Historical Society Inc., Bethlehem, Pa., 1966.

Levering, Joseph Mortimer, *A History of Bethlehem, Pennsylvania: 1741-1882,* issued as a memorial volume by the sesquicentennial committee of the Moravian congregation of Bethlehem, Times Publishing Co., Bethlehem, Pa., 1903.

Martin, Edmund F. with David J. Morrison, *Bethlehem Steelmaker: My 90 Years in Life's Loop,* BMS Press, Bethlehem, Pa., 1992.

Matthews, Alfred and Austin N. Hungerford, *History of the Counties of Lehigh and Carbon, in the Commonwealth of Pennsylvania,* Everts & Richards, Philadelphia, 1884.

McCullough, David, *Truman,* Simon & Schuster, New York, 1993.

Misa, Thomas J., *A Nation of Steel,* Johns Hopkins University Press, Baltimore, 1995.

Myers, Richmond E., *Lehigh Valley the Unsuspected,* Bethlehem Globe-Times and Allentown Sunday Call-Chronicle from 1955-72. Vol. 5 in the publications of the Northampton County Historical and Genealogical Society, Easton, Pa., 1972.

Porter, Penny, *Eugene Gifford Grace — 1876-1960: As We Remember Him,* privately printed for the Grace family, 1994.

Reutter, Mark, *Sparrows Point: Making Steel — The Rise and Ruin of American Industrial Might,* Summit Books, New York, 1988.

Roberts, Charles Rhoads and Rev. John Baer Stoudt, Rev. Thomas H. Krick and William J. Dietrich, *History of Lehigh County, Pennsylvania,* Lehigh Valley Publishing Co. Ltd., Allentown, Pa., 1914.

Schlesinger, Arthur M. Jr., *A Thousand Days: John F. Kennedy in the White House,* Houghton Mifflin Co., Boston, The Riverside Press, Cambridge, 1965.

Strohmeyer, John, *Crisis in Bethlehem: Big Steel's Struggle to Survive,* Adler & Adler, Bethesda, Md., 1986.

Strouse, Jean, *Morgan: American Financier,* Random House, New York, 1999.

Swank, James W., *Iron in All Ages,* second edition, Allen, Lane & Scott, Philadelphia, 1891.

Taylor, Paul S., *Mexican Labor in the United States: Bethlehem, Pennsylvania,* University of California Press, Berkeley, Calif., 1931.

Van der Zee, John, *The Gate: The True Story of the Design and Construction of the Golden Gate Bridge,* Simon & Schuster, New York, 1987.

Wall, Joseph Frazier, *Andrew Carnegie,* Oxford University Press, New York, 1970.

Walton, Francis, *Miracle of World War II: How American Industry Made Victory Possible,* MacMillan Co., New York, 1956.

Warren, Kenneth, *Big Steel,* University of Pittsburgh Press, Pittsburgh, 2001.

Wertime, Theodore A., *The*

BIBLIOGRAPHY

Coming of the Age of Steel, University of Chicago Press, Chicago, 1962.

West, Stanley A. and June Macklin, editors, *The Chicano Experience,* Westview Press, Boulder, Colo., 1979.

Whelan, Frank and Lance E. Metz, *The Diaries of Robert Heysham Sayre,* Lehigh University, Bethlehem, Pa., 1990.

Yates, W. Ross, *Joseph Wharton: Quaker Industrial Pioneer,* Lehigh University Press, Bethlehem, Pa.; Associated University Presses, London and Toronto, 1987.

Yates, W. Ross, *Bethlehem of Pennsylvania: The Golden Years 1841-1920,* Lehigh Litho Inc., Bethlehem, Pa., 1976.

Yates, W. Ross, *Asa Packer: A Perspective,* privately printed for members of the Asa Packer Society, Lehigh University, Bethlehem, Pa., 1983.

Yates, W. Ross, *History of the Lehigh Valley Region,* Joint Planning Commission of Lehigh and Northampton Counties, 1963.

PAMPHLETS

A Brief History of Bethlehem Steel Corporation, Bethlehem Steel Corp., Bethlehem, Pa., 1990.

Charles M. Schwab: Man of Industry and Culture — 1862-1939, exhibit guide, Hugh Moore Historical Park and Museums, Easton, Pa., 1986.

John Fritz — 1822-1913: His Role in the Development of the American Iron and Steel Industry and His Legacy to the Bethlehem Community, Lance E. Metz, historian, Canal Museum and Hugh Moore Park. Hugh Moore Historical Park and Museums Inc., Easton, Pa., and Annie S. Kemerer Museum, Bethlehem, Pa., 1987.

Historical Sketch of the Development of Bethlehem Steel Company and Bethlehem Steel Corporation, Bethlehem Steel Corp., Bethlehem, Pa., June 1, 1914.

Making Iron & Steel — The Historic Processes: 1700-1900, Jack Chard, Roebling Chapter, Society for Industrial Archaeology, Bogota,

N.J., 1986.

Saturday Night on the South Side, Joan Campion, South Bethlehem Historical Society, Bethlehem, Pa., 1988.

Souvenir History Book of the Borough of South Bethlehem, Pennsylvania, issued in connection with the semicentennial celebration Oct. 3-9, 1915.

SPEECHES

Foy, Lewis W., chairman, at Bethlehem Steel Corp.'s 75th anniversary dinner, Homer Research Laboratories, Bethlehem, Pa., Dec. 10, 1979.

Grace, Eugene G., *Charles M. Schwab,* first address in Charles M. Schwab Memorial Lectureship of American Iron and Steel Institute, New York, 1947.

Stuart, Milton C., *Asa Packer — 1805-1879: A Connecticut Yankee in King Coal's Court,* address given at fourth annual meeting of the John Packer Association at the Packer homestead in West Mystic, Conn., July 20, 1940.

DIARIES

Robert H. Sayre diaries, 1851-1905, courtesy of the National Canal Museum, Easton, Pa.

NEWSPAPER ARTICLES

Ecenbarger, William, *The Year Babe Ruth Was a Dodger,* The Philadelphia Inquirer, April 5, 1987.

Loftus, Joseph A., *Bethlehem Puzzled by Dismissal of Steel Aide Over Racial Stand,* The New York Times, March 22, 1964.

Charles M. Schwab Tells the Story of Bethlehem, The New York Herald, Sept. 26, 1915.

MAGAZINE ARTICLES

Bethlehem Steel, Fortune, June 1941.

Jackson, David, *Pennsylvania Steel: 1867-1916,* The Keystone, quarterly magazine of the Pennsylvania Railroad Technical and Historical Society, Vol. 31, No. 4, Winter 1998.

Kallman, Diane, *Steel on the Susquehanna,* Pennsylvania Heritage magazine, Summer 1990.

Marek, Angie C., *The Laborer's Lot,* U.S. News & World Report, Sept. 22, 2003.

Mockler, E.L., *Lesson of Bethlehem's Victory,* Spalding's Soccer Guide, New York, 1916.

Sixty Years of Corporate Ups, Downs and Outs, Forbes, 60th anniversary issue of Sept. 15, 1977.

Thomas, Samuel, *Reminiscences of the Early Anthracite-Iron Industry,* Vol. 29, Transactions of the American Institute of Mining Engineers, 1900; courtesy of the Lehigh County Historical Society, Allentown, Pa.

ACADEMIA

Vadasz, Thomas Patrick, *The History of an Industrial Community: Bethlehem, Pennsylvania, 1741-1920,* dissertation for doctor of philosophy degree, history department, College of William and Mary; University Microfilms International, Ann Arbor, Mich., 1985.

West, Stanley A., *The Mexican Aztec Society: A Mexican-American Voluntary Association in Diachronic Perspective,* dissertation for doctor of philosophy in anthropology degree, Syracuse University; Arno Press Inc., 1976.

DOCUMENTS

Minutes of the board of directors, Bethlehem Iron Co., March 1898 to August 1901; courtesy of the Hagley Museum and Library, Wilmington, Del.

INDEX

INDEX

INDEX

INDEX

INDEX

INDEX

INDEX

CPSIA information can be obtained at www.ICGtesting.com

264818BV00003B/1-186/P